INFORMATION PROCESSING

Applications in the Social and Behavioral Sciences

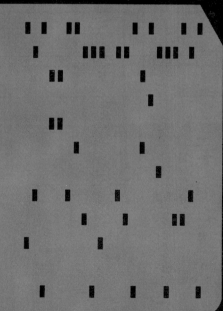

WILLIAM I. DAVISSON

INFORMATION
PROCESSING

INFORMATION
PROCESSING
applications in the social
and behavioral sciences

William I. Davisson
University of Notre Dame

APPLETON-CENTURY-CROFTS
EDUCATIONAL DIVISION
New York MEREDITH CORPORATION

PREFACE

This book is designed for the social and behavioral scientist. Specifically, it is for those who desire to utilize the computer in their work. The book assumes no mathematical prerequisite.

I wish to thank Dr. Harry E. Pople, Jr., of the University of Pittsburgh, for his constructive advice in developing a user oriented book. Dr. Leon Winslow of the University of Notre Dame has spent considerable time reviewing the work and helping to develop the idea of the computer application approach used. The staff of the Social Science Training and Research Laboratory of the University of Notre Dame have contributed generously of their time and aid in developing the manuscript. Individual contributers are indicated at the chapter or section contributed.

CONTENTS

Introduction

This book has been written as a guide for social science and behavioral science scholars who desire to utilize the computer in analyzing and evaluating data. The book is not designed as a FORTRAN language book; although a FORTRAN review for social science readers is included as an appendix. However, it is strongly suggested that persons using this book supplement it with the manual of FORTRAN for the computer available to the individual.

FORTRAN is not an end in itself; it is only a means to an end. It is a language that allows instructions to be written to direct computer operations. The end result is the analysis and evaluation of data. FORTRAN is only useful to the scholar or researcher who has a problem which may be efficiently solved by using the computer.

The book is divided into three parts. Part I is a statement of a generalized social science methodology, or model analysis. The second chapter of the part relates the model analysis to computer analysis or computer simulation.

Part II of the book (Chapters 3–9) considers the dual problems of data and computer utilization of data files. Each data file represents a unique set that presents its own problems for the researcher. This section sets the stage for the application of computer methodology and technology to research problems in the social and behavioral sciences. Part II concludes with a discussion of standardized program procedures (canned programs), and the ways in which they may be useful to the researcher in evaluating data (Chapter 9).

Part III of the study considers computer technology together with social and behavioral science methodology in solving research problems in the social and behavioral sciences. In short, Part III considers the application of the computer to the social and behavioral sciences.

This section employs a "case study" approach. Chapters 10–15 are composed of separate problems that the researcher or scholar is likely to encounter. Each of these chapters poses a typical computer problem for a discipline; indicates the data set, the methodology to be used in developing a solution, and the nature of the solution. In instances where it will increase the understanding of the process and the solution, the actual programs are shown and explained.

1

one

INFORMATION PROCESSING
AND COMPUTER USE

Social Science Computer Use

What is analysis?

Analysis of any problem or issue precedes any possible computer or other information processing or statistical analysis. In a broad sense, social science analysis consists of two steps and involves the use of two kinds of tools: *logic* and *statistics* (statistical inference).

Evaluation of social science problems usually focuses on the policy implications thereof. The state legislature will require the evaluation of the effect of a particular program in order to decide whether to increase the spending on the program or to eliminate the program. The federal government may desire an evaluation of the expenditures on the Poverty Program in the United States, or on the Peace Corps, in order to decide whether to increase or decrease the expenditures thereon. Somebody has to make a decision whether to give federal and state monies to a given city in the United States to help with the cost of an urban redevelopment or sewage control project. The unique aspects of social science analysis are that the results of the analysis almost always point (in one way or another) at immediate policy decisions by someone, and the social scientist never works with a test-tube situation. The social scientist deals with a situation in which he himself is a *part* of the decisions or questions that he is testing. Rarely is the physical scientist part of the experiment that he is undertaking — e.g., he is not part of the atom *being exploded*. In a very real sense, for anyone familiar with government, business, or social science decisions, the person doing the evaluating may be the same person or thing being evaluated.

One of the more difficult elements of social science analysis is to formulate a specific question (policy) that may be analyzed. Rarely does one ever find a nice, precise, social or economic question standing around all by itself in a form that is immediately susceptible to testing.

A primary problem of social science analysis, therefore, is to break up the overall issue into questions that may be answered. In short, the big problem in the social sciences is to formulate these questions. The second problem of the analysis is to be able to give statistical or quantifiable answers to the questions.

The first step of the problem is usually termed "developing or formulating the hypothesis — i.e., the question — to be answered." The second step involves testing the hypothesis. Thus, there are two broad sets of tools in the social scientist's kit: logic and statistics. Let us summarize the question of analysis and determine where logic and statistics fit into this overall picture. We may use the schematic outline below to illustrate the point:

I. *Logic:*
   A. Statement of the overall policy or issue.
   B. Delineation of assumptions: What component elements of the problem will not be discussed?
      These elements are considered to be the things that will be taken for granted, or at least will be omitted from the discussion. Assumptions are so-called negative elements — things that will not be considered.
   C. Focus of the overall issue into its component parts with the eventual definition into a specific question. The answer to this question will measure the overall policy or objective. *This is the hypothesis.*

II. *Statistics* (Methodology):
   A. Methodology.
      1. The Information Source: What statistical or arithmetic information is available to be used in answering the question?
      2. The Selection of the Sample: Shall all the available information be used in answering the question, or shall less than all the available information be used?
      3. The Calculations: The process of converting the raw statistical (arithmetic) information into a specific numeric answer to the hypothesis.
   B. Verification of Information, Sample, Methodology: Is the analysis proceeding in a manner to actually do what it is supposed to do?
   C. Conclusions: Let us take this schematic outline into the real world of social science analysis and see exactly how it is applied.

Urban renewal

Urban renewal[1] was one of the more widely discussed and argued domestic issues of the 1950's and early 1960's, and still is today. Urban renewal primarily involves removal of defined substandard (slum) housing and replacement with newly constructed housing sponsored by federal aid. Aside from the groups directly affected, many different groups get into the act: realtors, contractors, political scientists, sociologists, city planners, architects, local housing authorities, and several federal agencies. The critics of the so-called urban renewal are almost as numerous as the number of persons involved.

Civil rights groups have protested that urban renewal is "Negro removal." Social workers suggest that relocating families from areas to be renewed means simply moving the slums from one part of the city to another. Economists have noted that urban renewal programs substitute high- or middle-income (priced) rental units for low-income (priced) rental units, and that the basic problem is poverty, not housing renewal. The federal agencies and the cities hope that urban renewal will halt the continual decline in property values in the central city.

At this point, no specific problem of urban renewal has been brought into focus. Before a problem can be analyzed, that problem — or the relevant segment of the

[1]See Chapter 10.

problem — must be sharply defined. When the problem is defined, then it may be analyzed to determine the nature of the problem, and how an answer may be developed. The first point in analyzing the "problem" of urban renewal, therefore, is to define precisely what the problem is. This in itself is often a real problem. The Urban Renewal Program, as with many other programs, was a matter first of federal policy supplemented by local government policy. In order to appropriately criticize urban renewal, one must turn to the instruments of public policy (statutes) that established the program to determine what the major objective or objectives of the program were.

The main goal of public policy here appears to have been the decrease in the stock of substandard and overcrowded housing in a city. If we accept for the moment that the major purpose of the Urban Renewal Program was to decrease the stock of substandard and overcrowded housing, we have defined our problem. We then intend to analyze the efficacy of a major federal expenditure policy program. Were the expenditures justified as measured by the impact of the expenditures on the housing supply? In short, what were the actual results of major urban renewal efforts on the changes in the population and housing characteristics of cities?

Without reference to a computer, to data processing, or to programming, how would you, as a social science student, *analyze* that problem? What would you have to do, and how would you go about developing an answer to the question posed? We do not contend that this is the only–or even the most important question surrounding urban renewal. We only ask, if you as a social scientist were faced with answering the problem posed, how would you do it? If you had only a pencil and piece of paper, could you answer that problem? If so, how?

In considering our question, let us start at the beginning and determine how we arrived at it. It is important to understand that from the viewpoint of social science analysis, once one has been able to pose the question, one has already progressed in the analysis.

The basic policy involved is the federal policy of providing aid funds to local governments for various kinds of "urban redevelopment." In other words, the federal government gives money to cities for a given purpose. The logical question is then: Has the policy (urban redevelopment) been successful? The question posed above indicated that the success (or failure) of the policy was to be measured in terms of population and housing characteristics of cities. Our problem here is to determine just how the problem was defined to this point. In order to do this step by step, let us again take the broadest possible question: Has urban redevelopment (expenditures by the federal government) been successful?

Immediately one is faced with the problem of definition: What is success? In order to answer this question, it is necessary to determine what was the major intent of the policy. The urban redevelopment expenditures are made according to federal law. The first step, therefore, is to examine the law itself to see what it says concerning the avowed purpose of federal expenditures. If the law itself says something concerning the purpose of the expenditures, this may be a help. However, in a democratic society, a law is nearly always a compromise — a compromise among those who wanted the law in a stronger form, those who wanted the law in a weaker form, those who wanted no law on the subject at all, those who wanted a different law but took this one, and so forth.

Thus, in order to determine of what the existing law was a compromise, it is necessary to determine who the interested parties to the issue were. In order to do this, it is necessary to go to the Committees (House and Senate) bills, speeches, hearings, and presentations of other interested groups (lobbyists). In this way, the social scientist may gather some idea concerning the various groups who were interested in and working toward or against some kind of urban redevelopment bill. In this way, one may gain an impression of the manner in which the existing federal enabling statute (as signed by the President into law) was and is a compromise. This kind of preliminary analysis is essential in order that the researcher may be able to have some understanding of the nature of the policy issue involved, and therefore, some understanding for the type of yardstick by which to measure the success or failure of the law.

Success of the federal policy of urban redevelopment, therefore, in some elemental sense is really a measure of what the various contending groups would measure as success:

A. Success to the city might involve improvement of housing conditions, taxable property values, and overall city beautification. Sucess to the elected city officials might involve being reelected.

B. Success to realtors and property owners might be improvements in property values.

C. Success to businessmen might be an improvement in general business and sales in the center of the city occasioned by the results of redevelopment expenditures.

D. Success to civil rights groups might include improved (and/or subsidized) housing for the ethnic groups.

E. Success for the so-called relatively uninterested but esthetically inclined city planners might be a more ordered and beautiful city.

F. Success for the so-called preservation societies might be defeat of the program because it would tear down some old existing landmark that is in some way identified with the history of the city.

G. Success for the contractor and the federal politician might be the full employment attendant on the federal expenditures.

Thus, the question of the success of a federal policy such as expenditures on urban redevelopment involves a host of questions, and in one way or another means that the researcher must concern himself with the parties contending the issue.

A clue, however, to the nature of the problem is found in the fact that the federal policy of urban renewal was implemented by means of federal monetary expenditures to cities for a given purpose. Another clue to the nature of the issue is that in most of the presentations of the parties involved, the question of *slum clearance* was involved — i.e., overcrowded and substandard housing.

Since the major aim of the urban renewal expenditures has been in the direction of slum clearance, including primary emphasis on removal of substandard and overcrowded housing, it may be quite logical to determine the success or failure of the policy in terms of the degree to which the federal expenditures alleviated conditions of overcrowded and substandard housing. Thus, this quite theoretical analysis has brought us through a maze of political and other obstacles to a clear statement of the aim of this study in measuring the success or failure of urban renewal: *What were the actual results of major urban renewal efforts on the changes in the population and housing characteristics of cities?*

At this point, the analysis (breakdown of the problem or issue into manageable component parts) has proceeded to the formulation of the question and the development of a hypothesis. The testing of the hypothesis with the resultant answer will, accurately or not, then answer the question asked. Three things still need to be done:

first, the social scientist must develop a methodology that will allow him to answer the question posed; *second*, he must determine whether the approach will in fact provide the desired answer; *third*, the social scientist must finally evaluate how adequately the question posed and answer developed bears upon the original and basic question. In other words, just how precisely does an answer to the question of housing and population bear upon the question of the success of the federal policy of urban renewal? Thus, in broad scale, the social scientist's analysis of the problem of urban renewal has been divided into two parts: (1) the definition of the basic issue of expenditures on urban renewal to a manageable policy issue; (2) the development of a methodology to answer the issue defined.

In order to answer the question posed, it is necessary for the social scientist to have data that will permit an answer. The question posed concerned housing and population. Immediately, then, there are three consistent and reliable sources of information that bear directly on housing and population. The decade population census figures show for each city, and for each census district in each city, detailed figures on population, ethnic groups, housing, and related matters. The second basic source of information that the researcher might utilize would be building permits — although in some cities these would not be available because of the nature of the record keeping (or non-keeping) or for other reasons. The final source of information that would bear on the question of housing, and to a certain extent on population or housing residents, would be the city or county property tax rolls. Of all these sources only the census figures may be relied on as being relatively consistent over a period of time and among various cities. Thus, without detailed personal research in the cities or urban areas involved, only the census data may be reliably used.

The determination of the cities to be used in the examination will undoubtedly turn on two factors: the size of the cities and the comparability of the cities as to geographic area, industrial-economic characteristic, general income level, and ethnic patterns in the city. In evaluating the significance or success of urban renewal, it will be most appropriate to choose cities of about the same size measured by population, with a similarity in the other factors noted.

Having selected the cities, then, two questions must be answered using the data available. The condition of the cities, measured by population characteristics and substandard and crowded housing, before the urban renewal program was initiated, must be determined. The condition of the cities, measured by population characteristics and substandard and crowded housing, must be determined after some time period has elapsed. Normally, the city selection should involve one or more cities that did not utilize urban renewal funds, and one or more cities that did utilize these funds. By statistically evaluating the changes in the population and housing condition, these data utilized will permit some kind of quantitative evaluation of the impact of urban renewal programs on population and housing conditions, *both for cities utilizing the program and for those cities not utilizing the program.* Evaluation of the data will permit some kind of conclusion on the success or failure of urban renewal insofar as population and crowded and substandard housing are concerned. It should also be clear that the definitions used of population characteristics and of *crowded* and *substandard* housing are those provided by the census data itself (another caveat.)

For the social scientist, the conclusion that one derives depends upon the accurate definition of the problem, the nature of the data used, and the limiting definitions within which the research must be undertaken. Careless analysis, or inappropriate methodology (approach to solving the problem) will not provide accurate answers. In summary, the steps (analysis) involved:

A. Statement of the overall policy and objective: the success of urban renewal.
B. Analysis (breakdown) of this into its component parts and the eventual derivation of a specific question, the answer to which will measure the success or failure of the overall policy.
C. The methodology:
   1) The information sources.
   2) The selection of the sample (cities).
   3) Statistical information desired:
      a) Before urban renewal.
      b) After urban renewal.
      c) Impact or urban renewal (or of not using the program).
D. Verification: Will the methodology answer the specific question?
E. Conclusions.

Where the computer fits

The point made above is that the primary function of the computer is to manipulate information with the intent of drawing conclusions from it. The computer may be used to handle arithmetic or alphabetic information. The computer may be used as a giant calculator to perform arithmetic manipulation of the information. It may be used as a combination clerk and file cabinet for data storage and retrieval. The computer may be used as a statistical tool in developing a predetermined and defined sample from a mass of information.

Actually, the method used to solve or evaluate the problem depends on the equipment used. If one used a desk calculator, a good deal more time is spent in insuring that you have a valid sample to work with. Without automatic data-processing equipment, it is simply not possible to handle all the information available on a subject, nor even a major portion of the information. It is necessary to extract from the data a relatively small sample — random, stratified, or otherwise. The *sample* is then evaluated by hand, and the characteristics of the whole are inferred from the sample.

Once it is decided to bring a computer into the picture, one simply uses the *entire* population — i.e., all the information — or a very large sample of the data. It is then possible to evaluate the information using statistical techniques and the computer. Once the decision is made to use the computer, less time is devoted to insuring a representative small sample, and more time is devoted to evaluating a very large sample or the entire population.

Let us review our outline indicating the steps taken in analyzing the problem to see where the computer fits.

A. Statement of the overall policy and objectives.
B. Analysis of the overall policy or issue into its component parts and the eventual breakdown and definition into a specific question. The answer given to this question or *hypothesis* shall measure the success or failure of the overall policy or issue.
C. Methodology (Statistics)
   1) The Information Source.
   2) The Selection of the Sample
      COMPUTER   INFORMATION PROCESSING
   3) The Information Calculation.

D. Verification of Information, Sample, and Methodology.
E. Conclusions.

STATISTICAL INFERENCE AND COMPUTER USE

We noted in the preceding section that statistics were of significance in social science work primarily in the area of testing hypotheses, or providing quantifiable answers to specific questions. It is necessary, therefore, to comment at this point about information processing and about statistics.

Statistics and the social sciences

For the past fifty years, it has become increasingly important in each person's daily life to be able to use numerical information in order to express information in a quantifiable way. Fifty years ago a person was a name only. Today, a person can hardly be considered to be real unless he can identify himself with several numbers — social security number, a driver's license number, a bank account number, an income tax number, an employment number, etc. People today interpret nearly every aspect of their lives, from their income and expenses to federal government policy, in terms of numbers. This general increase in the use of numeric data and the decrease in the use of quantitative alphabetic information has led to certain recent and perhaps ill-defined statistical concepts.

The most important element of statistics is the analysis of numeric data using so-called statistical techniques.[2] This use of statistical techniques to evaluate and analyze numeric data is often called statistical inference. Statistical inference may be defined as generalizing for the whole from data representing only a part of the whole. Our specific concern here is with the ability to use statistics and statistical techniques in evaluating numerical data in order to develop answers to specific questions which we call *hypotheses*.

There are certain uses of statistics that are quite important in evaluating numerical data. These may be illustrated as follows:

1. We may desire to know something about a very large group: the attitudes of voters on a given issue; the preferences of consumers with respect to a prospective new product; the effect of a given government expenditure policy in creating the desired effect; or the popularity of a new TV program or of a president. What is normally done here is to *sample* the large group; that is, we take a few people of the large group and attempt to obtain their opinion on the subject. We generalize from the sample to the group: for instance, if 18 percent of the sample are in favor of the given thing, we *infer* that 18 percent of the whole group would also be in favor of the thing — i.e., statistical inference.

2. We may desire to determine whether or not two things or two variables are related. We may wish also to know how closely they are related. We may wish

---

[2]Statistical techniques are sometimes divided into two categories:

A. Descriptive statistics—methods of organizing, summarizing, and otherwise manipulating masses of data.
B. Statistical inference—inferring or generalizing from a sample to a population. The characteristics of the population are described *from* the characteristics of the sample.

to know whether the average number of cavities per person in the United States is related to the growth of the American economy. A correlation study could tell us whether these two variables — the average number of cavities per person *and* the growth of the American economy — are related, and how closely they are related.

3. We may have theorized that two variables are causally related — that the amount of money spent on personal and household goods varies directly with the level of a person's income. We may, however, not know what the expenditures are for some desired income level. In order to accomplish this maneuver, it is necessary to predict what the consumption would be for the given income level, by generalizing from the known income-consumption levels. This technique of "fitting" the consumption trend line from the known observations to the unknown prediction is called *regression analysis*.

There are other ways of using statistical techniques to evaluate numeric data in testing hypotheses in the social sciences. The important point to remember is that the computer is important in accomplishing the statistical manipulations required of the given numeric data in providing the required answers (testing) for the hypothesis. Whether one likes it or not, the social sciences today are constantly confronted with increasing quantities of numeric data which must be analyzed and evaluated. To this end, the social scientist can no longer afford to ignore either statistical techniques or computers.

Information processing

Information processing refers to the way in which data transactions are handled. Technically, we may divide this idea of "information processing" into four categories as follows:

1. *Data Specification* — laying out the data, coding the data, detailed description of the data required for the problem, memory allocation, and input/output.
2. *Calculation* — statistics, etc.
3. *Input and Output* — What data is to be input and how is it to be laid out? What data is to be output, and how is it to be laid out?
4. *Control* — Sequence of operations.

As may be obvious to the reader, this particular categorization of the information processing is oriented to the computer.[3] Analysis, therefore, is the process of breaking down information into its component parts for more precise definition. In a similar way, we were able to analyze any transaction by breaking the transaction into its separate functions.

---

[3]The following example may be helpful to those who have been information processors all their lives but who have not recognized this fact. Say that one's wife goes to the store and purchases a small $150.00 trinket. Subject to certain domestic disruptions that might accompany such action, we may say that this is a fact: a transaction has occurred. Historically speaking, something has happened. Certain things will occur in the future, one of which is that someone will become an *information processor:*

1. The transaction will be *coded* as an account payable.
2. A series of *computations* will be engaged in to determine whether there is money to pay the bill, whether the bill is correct, etc.
3. The bill will be *sorted*—i.e., organized—into a file labeled "account payable."
4. At the end of the month, the accounts payable will be *summarized*—i.e., added up.
5. The accounts payable will be *recorded* on pieces of paper called checks.
6. Someone will *communicate* with the creditors by sending them the checks.

Thus, we return to the point at which the computer may be of aid. The steps involved in the processing of numerical data may be more effectively accomplished using the computer. The statistical tests that must be performed on the data, or the actual performing of the necessary calculations on the data, may be most usefully performed by using a computer. In a somewhat more liberal definition, information processing may be defined as the total manipulation of the data, whether done by a computer or mentally.

In a very real sense, the problem for the social scientist is just the opposite of that confronting the physical scientist. The physical scientist most often works from generalization to detail. The social scientist is more often confronted with a situation where he must synthesize a generalization from a mass of data. Prior to the advent of the use of the high-speed digital computer, the social scientist tended either to specialize on narrow segments of a problem, or to engage extensively in sampling that may or may not have been statistically valid. The real world, with its overwhelming mass of data on nearly every conceivable subject, tended to force social science research into ever narrowing channels. The computer may prove to be the most powerful tool developed to aid the social scientist in his confrontation with the real world. The computer provides this aid, strangely enough, by giving the social scientist increased ability to be able to theorize — that is, to abstract desired segments of reality from the totality of the real world.

Data are what?

Information

Social scientists are fond of talking about information or data processing — sometimes with little consideration of what constitutes data. Let us assume a more or less realistic situation and attempt to determine just what kinds of data are present. An entry found in the *Philadelphia Gazette* of March 15, 1733, might read as follows:

The Brigantine Peggy with one G. Davy as Master with a cargo of 0.5 tons of provisions and 30M barrel staves and 15M hoops has just docked at Philadelphia from Jamaica.

This newspaper entry is information which we would call *a (complete) transaction*.

Data

First we note that the *Brigantine* named *Peggy* just entered *Philadelphia* from *Jamaica*. This we would call alphabetic data. The alphabetic data essentially consists of various kinds of *nouns* or name words. The alphabetic information tells *what*, *where*, and *who*. Peggy is the name of a ship. The word Brigantine tells what kind of vessel it is — the type of rigging and sails. The other alphabetic information tells who the master of the vessel was, what port the vessel entered, where the vessel came from, and where it was headed (*from* or *to* a given port).

There is another kind of data that may be determined — the date. The date of the vessel entry into Philadelphia was March 15, 1733. This is a combination of alphabetic and numeric data. For convenience, many users convert the data to numbers. By giving the *month* a number value (01-12), March 15, 1733 becomes 03/15/1733 (or 15/03/1733 depending on personal preference). The first two digits refer to the month. The second two digits refer to the day, and the last four digits to the year.

There are two kinds of numbers that must be considered. The first is a number where a fraction is not important. The second is a number where a fraction is *or* may be important.

In the instance of the numbers shown above, fractional units — i.e., less than 1.0 — are not important. One does not normally say 1735.5 in referring to June, 1735. The dates shown above are examples of the kind of number where fractions are not important. Numbers of this kind we shall call *integers*.[4]

We also noted that the vessel carried:

> one-half ton (0.5 ton) provisions,
> thirty-thousand (30M) barrel staves,
> fifteen-thousand (15M) hoops.

One must use *real* numbers to record the above transactions. Since the integer number form *drops* all values less than *one whole number*, all fractional values of the cargo and in the calculation of averages would be omitted, if integer numbers were used.

There are, then, three kinds of data that the social scientist is concerned with: *alphabet, integer numbers,* and *real numbers.* Since it was normal in the eighteenth century to use the symbol "M" to mean "1,000," we find in the various records, for instance, the term "15M hoops" to mean 15,000 hoops, or 10.8M lumber to mean 10,800 (board feet) of lumber.

Furthermore, in certain trade routes, ships would carry provisions measured in tons and *fractions* of tons. If we desired to know what the *average* cargo of provisions was (by weight) on a ship operating between Philadelphia and Barbados we might have to take an average of:

	0.5 tons provisions
Real	30.0 tons provisions
Number	10.8 tons provisions
Form	5.6 tons provisions
	46.9
	11.7 tons average.

There are four defined terms the reader should be aware of that are used when referring to the data types shown above. A record is used here to mean all the data available that is relative to some particular business or other action. The information noted, concerning the entry of the Brigantine Peggy into Philadelphia in 1733, is a record.

Summary

A *character* refers to any one alphabet letter or number digit (including certain other special characters such as a period, decimal point, comma, etc.). A *field* refers to a series of characters comprising a discreet or unique unit such as a *brigantine*. The characters comprising the rig type would fit into a defined field. As shown in the above entry, as many fields could be defined as it was desired to have words of information. A *record* consists of all the pertinent fields necessary to contain all the data information on any single transaction. A *file* consists of all the records relating to a common or defined source. A file would consist of all the records showing ships entering or leaving Philadelphia for any defined period.

---

[4]A mathematician would term as *integers*, whole numbers.

We have noted certain terms that may not be significant in manual use, but become of critical importance when using a computer. It is essential to distinguish the three common kinds of data encountered in the social sciences:

1. Alphabetic.
2. Integer numbers.
3. Real numbers.

Furthermore, it is necessary to distinguish certain terms which define primarily a given *amount* of data.

1. Character — a digit of alphabetic or numeric data.
2. Field — a series of digits comprising a discrete name or a discrete piece of numeric data.
3. Record — all the data pertaining to a given transaction.
4. File — all the records pertaining to some defined topic.

QUESTIONS FOR DISCUSSION

1. What does the social scientist mean when he refers to analysis?
2. Logic might be defined as breaking a problem into two aspects:
   a. The assumptions: things we will not examine.
   b. The focus on the problem: the things that we will examine. Discuss.
3. A *model* is a limited version of the real world which contains its own assumptions. Discuss.
4. Statistics might be termed the "quantitative methodology" of the social sciences. Discuss.
5. There is a tendency to consider that *statistics* is the only approach used by the social sciences. A little consideration will indicate that there are many problems of the social sciences that involve counting, matching, and comparing that have no necessary statistical basis. Discuss.
6. Discuss the steps that together comprise *information* or *data processing*.
7. The things that primarily concern the social sciences are: What, Where, Who, When, How Much?
   What are the kinds of data available to answer these questions?
8. Define: a. Character
   b. Field
   c. Record (unit record)
   d. File
9. Describe each of the following processes (manual):
   a. Coding
   b. Computing
   c. Organizing
   d. Summarizing

Models and Computer Simulation

COMPUTERS
AND SIMULATION

We are interested here in the specific application of computing science to the problem of simulation. Let us take two relatively common types of computer use as examples:

1. Accounting: computers may be programmed to make out payrolls, keep accounts, send out bills, etc. The programmer does not need to know the magnitude of the checks made out, the number of accounts, or any of the details. The programmer may simply work out a complete algorithm — i.e., a complete symbolic representation — of all the steps needed to do the particular job. When data are fed into the computer system as input, the program will sufficiently manipulate the data—to allow for payroll deductions, converting time to money, etc.—that the final results repeat the hand process.

2. The computer may be used to solve problems. Programs may be devised to handle inventory problems, to predict sales, to control output. These kinds of problems are *facilitating* in carrying out business operations but are not the accounting or payroll operations.

There is, then, the computer use that provides insight into many types of problems. This is the area of simulation. One of the most familiar areas of computer simulation is that of business game theory or election prediction. The whole problem of simulation begins with the real world. The problem is that the real world is a very big and a very complex and unwieldy place.

The social science researcher or behavioral research scientist who looks at the real world finds it usually too complicated to handle. What the researcher needs is a limited version of the real world. This version of the real world is a model. What must happen in constructing a model is that all portions of the real world are eliminated (as assumptions) leaving only the segments of reality that are directly relevant for the specific purpose. The result for the social sciences is usually a type of operating model.[1]

A model is a systematic consideration of a particular problem. Basically, it is a problem-solving technique. That is, most models represent limited and controlled

---

[1]c.f. Richard A. Brody, *Some Systematic Effects of the Spread of Nuclear Weapons Technology: Study Through Simulation of a Multi-Nuclear Future* (Evanston, Ill.: Northwestern University, 1963).

considerations of specific situations. Models are essentially problem-solving devices.

Basically, a model simply eliminates from consideration all elements of the real world except those concepts directly related to the focus of the study. Any model, therefore, has its own assumptions, or in other words, its own institutional framework. Whether or not the assumed conditions or the institutional framework of the model reflect the real world is said to test the validity or the truth of the model. The extent to which the model reflects the real world is the (presumed) test of the usefulness of the model.

One might add that the social researcher has not always regarded the real world as the test of the model. Adam Smith, Plato, Thomas Hobbes, and Karl Marx illustrate four social science researchers who regarded the model as a test of the world. These four would argue that if the world were unlike the model, the world ought to change to become like the model.

The first type of model is the picture model. Nearly everyone is familiar with the chronological diagram of the presidents of the United States that purports to explain, in model form, American history as Presidential history (the Great Man Theory of History). Most students are also familiar with the diagram showing how a bill becomes law. The movement through committees and passage by both legislative houses seems quite clear when shown in schematic forms with lines, blocks, and arrows. Of course, what is left out is all of the lobbying, pressure, and arm-twisting that might influence a bill. This is omitted because the focus is on the *legislative* mechanics of passing a bill. In any event, the graphic *model focusing on some specific problem* is undoubtedly familiar to all readers.

The prose, or verbal, model is another device often used to permit focus on some particular problem. Chapter 1 of this book (combined with Chapter 10) constitutes a good illustration of such a model. Chapter 1 is a prose model of the problem of urban redevelopment. The problem posed in Chapter 1 was simply to consider whether urban redevelopment was successful. In order to do this, it was necessary to:

a. Define urban redevelopment.

b. Define what constituted success for urban redevelopment.

The process of defining these two parts of the problem in fact permits focus on the problem *as envisaged* by the researcher. This allows the researcher to focus his efforts on what he considers to be the problem. The reader may wish to review Chapter 1, keeping in mind that this constitutes a *prose model* of a specific problem.

One of the more universal models of the real world insofar as political and cultural matters are concerned is Plato's *Republic*. One of the obvious assumptions of this model is that of the existence of a slave class to do the work. One of the more obvious policy implications of this model is that the world should be like the model.

Chapter 10 represents a kind of statistical model of urban redevelopment. This permits a conclusion about the success of urban redevelopment according to the assumptions laid down for considering this statistical version. The model shown, like other models, does not purport to examine or to explain the totality of any problem. The model simply attempts to examine the problem according to certain well-defined and quite limited guidelines (the assumptions). The reader may wish to look ahead at Chapter 10, remembering that it is a very simplified statistical model.

The operations research model is a model in the same sense that all models are abstractions of reality. However, operations research models attempt to represent *processes*. We may have a model of multi-country nuclear weapons relations, a model of the production process of a firm, a model of the sales processes of a firm, or a model of ambulance and medical needs in various types of military situations. All of these kinds of models attempt to *simulate* an ongoing process found in the real world. Simulation is an attempt to identify and/or reproduce the behavior of an individual or a system (business or government).[2]

Simulation will necessarily involve two separate and distinct operations. The first is description and the second is evaluation. The model must describe what the process is. The model must also be able to examine alternative courses of action in order to evaluate which course of action is the best according to specified criteria. Models will rarely attempt to examine all phases of even a particular process. For instance, a model will attempt to examine the impact of inventory policy on a firm's sales costs. *If it were desired to examine a firm's inventory on the firm's distribution efficiency, a separate model would probably be required.*

The term "simulation model" or "operations research model," often or usually implies that computers will be used in effecting the model. In models such as business game theory, humans are usually involved primarily as experimenters. The person's decisions are given to the computer as input, and the computer carries out the calculations necessary to indicate the impact of the decisions made on the process being examined. Since most operations research (simulation) models involve a *behavior over time* (dynamic model), the calculations become quite complex. The computer becomes a convenient device for facilitating the model operations. Social scientists have long used static models (involving only a single time period). The advent of computers has made the dynamic-process model feasible.

Properly, the term computer simulation applies to model analysis of behavior patterns. Specifically, the model analysis will usually involve alternative behavior patterns over time, with the necessity to choose one pattern according to particular criteria. In short, then, computer simulation or computer operations research involves the analysis of system (business, government, human relations, etc.) behavioral patterns — i.e., what will happen, *if* . . . .

The purpose of the simulation is to answer certain questions — i.e., problem solving — concerning the system. This is generally known as the problem. The model, then, is the limited version of the real world. The model developed is a model of the system, whether it is a country, a government unit, or a business. As examples, one might construct a model of a business production unit, a model of inventory processes and sales cost, a model of behavior of countries where multiple countries have atomic weapons, a model of individual action under certain conditions.

The third aspect of the computer simulation involves the assumptions to be made that limit the model and the system. For instance, the three normal steps here would be:

1. Definition of the problem so that the behavioral process may be described.
2. Limitation of the scope of the problem, or the range of the alternative patterns to be considered. No model includes *all* variables about either the system or the range of behavior alternatives. Only the variables directly relevant to the specific problems are included.
3. Criteria for evaluation of the range of alternative behavior patterns.

The assumptions define the system, define the problem, and define the range of choices to be considered in the simulation model.

The overall simulation or operations research procedure must include the methodology to solve the problem and the development of the solution. The computer science version of *methodology* would be *algorithm* or flow chart. The algorithm

---

[2]See the bibliography at the end of this section for citation of published simulation models and discussion thereof.

would normally include the general methodology, the computer algorithm, the data source, and the necessary statistical, mathematical, or other procedures to arrive at a solution to the problem.

TYPES OF SIMULATION MODELS

We might generally divide computer simulation into general categories.[3] The discussion by Professor Richard M. Cyert in the *IBM Proceedings* indicates a very useful insight into computer simulation. Professor Cyert notes that the essence of a simulation is that the study involves examination of a *process over time* and the reduction of that process to a series of logical steps. Professor Cyert also notes that in general simulation, models tend to be deterministic because the behavior of individuals in the (types of) processes simulated is reducible to a logical structure. There appear to be four major classes of simulation models according to the purposes for which the models were developed:[4]

1. Descriptive simulation of existing systems.
2. Simulations of quasi-realistic systems (we might be tempted to call these intellectual or quasi-academic studies).
3. There are normative simulation studies useful for determining which of various types of alternatives are most suitable to particular goals and criteria.
4. Man-machine simulations that are intended to train people to function better in particular organizational settings.

Let us take a moment here and examine these four different types of simulation models. The first type of simulation model involved the descriptive simulation of existing systems. Two studies, or computer simulation models, illustrative of this type of operation would be the descriptive simulation of a department store buyer.[5] The department store buyer makes relatively independent price and output decisions. The department store pursues two general objectives: sales objective and markup objective (or profit). The buyer formulates sales estimates that are consistent with its sales goals and develops a routine ordering plan for advance orders. As sales are recorded, if all goes according to plan, orders are entered according to the standardized routine.

What happens, however, when sales are not achieved? There are certain actions that can be taken:

1. The buyer can attempt to renegotiate the purchase price.
2. The buyer can initiate a markdown to stimulate sales.
3. The buyer can search for new goods at lower prices but that have standardized markups — for instance, foreign market goods.

The buyer's reaction to the failure to achieve the standardized or determined markup is similar. If the markup is not being achieved, he can search for ways to achieve it. Basically, this would have to involve alteration of the product mix to achieve the markup on the goods. (This model, for instance, may not consider within its own limits the impact of *advertising* in changing the consumer demand for the

---

[3]*Proceedings, IBM Scientific Computing Symposium: Simulation Models and Gaming,* (White Plains, N.Y.: *IBM Data Processing Division,* 1966), p. 4.
[4]*Ibid,* p. 4.
[5]*Ibid,* pp. 5–6.

products *available*.) If the buyer has control of promotion and advertising, these may be utilized, because the added cost of promotion in selling available goods would lower the realized margin or markup on the standard-priced goods.

The formula for these decisions has been accomplished in a computer model where it was possible to simulate the decisions of the buyer over a very wide range of alternative circumstances. It was also possible to present the simulation model with actual facts of real decisions from a department store. In this way, the simulated decisions could be compared with the real decisions. The simulation model was able to predict about 95 percent of the buyer's decisions to the penny. The authors of the model indicate that by modifying the program to take cognizance of rare situations, the program could operate at 100 percent accuracy.[6]

The second type of simulation model is the experimental (or quasi-realistic system) model. This type of simulation model differs from the first or descriptive model in that it is not intended to describe an actual process. The model is intended to explore certain relations under a given situation but not to represent any specific organization or system. For instance, the department store buyer simulation was intended to represent an actual situation and to test the various decisions that were made and could be made under various situations. The second type of model is intended to explore various relations that are not necessarily related to particular situations.

The example of the type of simulation model used here is one done by Balderston and Hoggatt.[7] This is a model designed to explore behavior over time (dynamic) of firms in a two-stage market. In this model, suppliers sell to wholesalers, who in turn sell to customer firms. There are flows of *information*, *materials*, and *money* among the various levels, *but no horizontal communication among firms at the same level*.

In order to give the model a bit more realism, rather than to make up a completely arbitrary situation, a quasi-realistic model was developed based on the West Coast lumber industry. The basic approach of the model was not primarily to study the lumber industry, but to study firm behavior in a two-stage market situation, over time. T hus, the general approach of the experimental model is to focus on the behaviorpatterns in a given or prescribed situation, rather than on an actual situation.

The third type of computer simulation would be described as a *normative model* simulation. This can be best explained as a simulation model which examines the impact of changes in information, organization, and environment on the performance and operation of the system. The student may wish to refer to a study by C. P. Bonini.[8] This is a model of a single firm that is divided into three major areas: manufacturing, sales, and an executive committee. The structure used was based on rough empirical evidence. The firm plans by making forecasts; operates by setting price and output, incurring costs and administrative expenses, and making sales. The firm controls its operations by using standards and quotas. A full discussion of

[6]These citations are not exhaustive, but are illustrative of the various types of department store and individual firm simulations that have been done and are possible:

1. R. M. Cyert and J. G. March, *A Behavioral Theory of the Firm* (Englewood Cliffs, N.J.: Prentice Hall, 1963).

2. Harold Borko, *Computer Applications in the Behavioral Sciences* (Englewood Cliffs, N.J.: Prentice Hall, 1962), Chaps. 22, 23, 24.

See also G. P. E. Clarkson, *Portfolio Selection: A Simulation of Trust Investment* (Englewood Cliffs, N.J.: Prentice Hall, 1962).

[7]F. E. Balderston and A. C. Hoggatt, *Simulation of Market Processes* (Berkeley, Calif.: University of California, Institute of Business and Economic Research, 1962), cited in *IBM Proceedings*, p. 8.

[8]C. P. Bonini, *Simulation of Information and Decision Systems in the Firm*. (Englewood Cliffs, N.J.: Prentice Hall, 1963).

the methods of forecasting and control may be obtained with reference to the cited work.

The basic implications of this model concern the nature of how an efficiently operating firm may be designed and implemented. Bonini chose to examine the effects on the firm's performance of different variables: external (economic conditions), world variability, market growth, industrial standards (engineering), sensitivity to (outside) pressure, contagious pressure, average cost versus LIFO[9] in inventory control, use of present versus past information, and sales force knowledge of inventory. Each of these represents parameters that may be quantified and inserted into the model in a way to determine the impact of the change in the parameter on the firm operations.

This type of model simulation represents the step most distantly related to the descriptive simulation. This model is interested not in *what is*, but in *what ought to be*.

The final type of simulation model would be the so-called simulation gaming. This is basically the use of a computer model to simulate an environment within which humans are performing. A feedback system is used wherein a model is presented (business model, etc.) and the participants in the game make a decision. The model result is affected by the decision, and the results of the impact are related back to the participants. One of the models of this type is the *Carnegie Tech Management Game* which is a rough, but not exact, simulation within the framework of the detergent industry.[10]

The simulation models tend to assume linearity in reducing the models and their relationships to linear situations.[11] Thus, there is a considerable use of the multiple regression formulae in developing the models. We have no basis for assuming that the linear relationship is the proper one. We can, by using computer studies, develop much more complex models, which the computer may handle. Models that are too complex defeat the purpose of the model. The second problem is that the output is dynamic — i.e., a series over time — hence, is provided as a time series for each variable. Thus, a difficulty arises in testing which time series of which variable is relevant for the given problem.

Despite the problems involved (see the previously cited *IBM Proceedings* for discussions of the limitations and possibilities of model-simulation techniques), the use of simulation models and gaming has the potential of providing great contributions to business and social science education and research. We suggest that the student consult the other materials cited below for a further introduction to the ideas of and the use of computer simulation in social sciences and business research.

Suggested reading

The following references would be helpful to those interested in following this subject further. The bibliographies in each are also quite helpful.

a. Evans, George W., and others, *Simulation Using Digital Computers* (Englewood Cliffs, N.J.: Prentice Hall, 1967).

Chap. 3 would be what we have defined as a *normative simulation model* in that it was developed by Stanford Research Institute in 1960 to aid the Department of

[9]Last-In-First-Out method of inventory control.
[10]K. J. Cohen and others, "The Carnegie Tech Management Game," *Journal of Business*, **33**, pp. 303–327. Also: K. J. Cohen and others, *The Carnegie Tech Management Game: An Experiment in Business Education* (Homewood, Ill.: Irwin Press, 1964).
[11]Models assuming linear relations assume predictive capability for the variables.

the Army in designing a field experiment. Title: "Computer Simulation of Armed Combat."

Chapter 4 was designed as a simplified model for evaluation of problems affecting the conduct of battles. It would fit into the normative simulation model classification. Title: "Computer Simulation of Armed Combat."

This volume has additional chapters on other simulation models as well as necessary background materials on computer systems, programming, statistical, and mathematical background used in computer manipulation of the simulation models.

b. *Proceedings, IBM Scientific Computing Symposium: Simulation Models and Gaming* (White Plains, N.Y.: IBM Data Processing Division, 1966).

The various individual papers and discussions will be most helpful to students interested in computer simulation.

c. Harold Borko, *Computer Applications in the Behavioral Sciences*, (Englewood Cliffs, N.J.: Prentice Hall, 1962).

This volume is a series of essays edited by Mr. Borko ranging from basic considerations of what a computer is, and how it works, to various applications in the behavioral sciences. The essays and discussions vary from consideration of statistical techniques — what they are and how they are used — to actual considerations of simulation models. The bibliography at the end of each essay is useful to the student.

d. Richard A. Brody, *Some Systematic Effects of the Spread of Nuclear Weapons Technology: A Study Through Simulation of a Multi-Nuclear Future* (Evanston, Ill.: Northwestern University, 1963).

This is the discussion of a socio-political process involving consideration of nuclear weapon proliferation. As noted on p. 155 of the study, a high level of prediction was accomplished. Changes in simulated international system (after the spread of the nuclear capability), conformed to a high degree to the predicted results from the model. The bibliography provided by Professor Brody is excellent, especially for one interested in the political, military, international relations simulation models (pp. 176–182).

two

COMPUTERS AND DATA

3

Preparation of Data for Processing and Storage

We have already noted that there are three types of data that the social scientist primarily encounters: alphabet information, integer numbers, and real numbers. In order for this information to be entered (input) into a computer, it must be prepared in a way that the computer may utilize it. Just as an individual has to key information (via the keyboard) into an adding machine, information must be keypunched before it can be utilized by a computer. Information is presented to the adding machine by depressing certain keys in a given sequence on the keyboard. Information can be prepared for the computer by keypunching a Hollerith Card.

Morse code

CODING INFORMATION

People talk to each other, providing that both understand the same language. When a machine is involved, however, some sort of coding is necessary. Let us take a moment and discuss this problem of coding. One of the most familiar ways of coding information for transmission of data is the Morse Code. In the Morse Code the familiar letters of the alphabet and numbers are coded so that each letter of the alphabet and each number is represented by a unique or singular combination of dots and dashes. We are all familiar enough with the somewhat romantic history of the Western Union Company to be aware of the significance of this coding device for transmitting messages. Since a person was not able to shout from Washington, D.C., to Fort Kearny in the Old West to tell the cavalry to go get the "bad guys," some alternative had to be devised. A machine was necessary. However, man had to be able to communicate (with) through a machine in order to send the message.

With the invention of electricity, there are two ways of sending a message — by sending a constant electrical impulse and varying the intensity of the signal; or by sending an interruptable electrical signal. It has always been easier to handle interruptable electrical impulses, hence the Morse Code was devised to send electrical impulses of various lengths. In a somewhat similar manner, it is easier for the computer, an electrical machine, to handle an interruptable current than to handle a constant electrical impulse.

People are not bothered by the fact that information must be *coded* for transmission over a wire. Ask any boy scout about the coding necessary for Morse Code telegraph transmission, and the result will be something as follows (International Morse Code):

Letter, Number, or Other	How Coded
A	· —
B	— · · ·
C	— · — ·
D	— · ·
0	—
1	· — — — —
2	· · — — —
3	· · · — —
,	— — · · — —

Hollerith code: external to the computer

We have noted that it is possible to develop a number of types of codes: the Morse Code, secret codes, and others. In keypunching information onto a Hollerith Card, it is common to use a series of punch locations to represent each digit or letter. The card shown in Figure 3-1 is a Hollerith card.

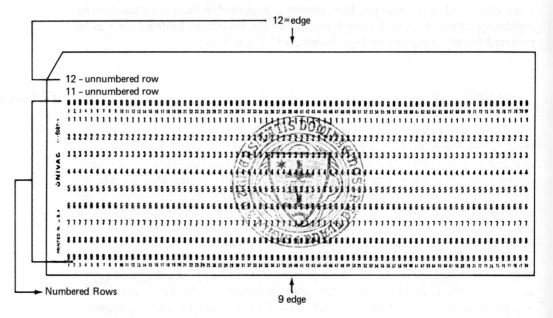

FIGURE 3-1. Hollerith card.

On the illustration shown, the face of the card is covered with a series of numbers. Some of the cards are so-called "blank stock" with no numbers or printing on either the face or on the back of the card. The card is divided into twelve rows as shown. There are ten identified or numbered rows shown on the illustration as 0–9.

There are two unnumbered rows, identified as the "11" row and as the "12" row. Thus, the "9-edge" of the card is the bottom edge (as shown) and the "12-edge" is the top edge of the Hollerith card.

There are 80 columns on the card from left to right. The column number is indicated by a small number (from 1–80) that appears immediately below the "0" row and the "9" row. The only function of these small numbers is to facilitate visual identification of columns on the card.

Number information is punched into the card with a single punch representing that number. Alphabet information is punched into the card by punching two punches in the same column. One point must be kept in mind at all times. When one is reading *only* numbers into the machine, the 1–9 rows act *only* as 1–9.

In summary, then, there are 80 columns on each Hollerith card. Information may be punched into each column. One may utilize conventional punctuation (commas, periods, etc.) in the data presented, or one may leave it out. If the information being fed into the machine is numeric only, one punch is necessary for each number digit. A "1" punch in any column is read or understood as a 1. A "2" punch in any column is read or understood as a 2. Alphabet letters represent combinations of punches.

On any one Hollerith card, there are a total of 960 locations where a punch may appear (80 columns x 12 punches per column). As the card enters the input device, it passes across a *read area*. The read area is a space exactly the same size as the card. The bottom of the read area contains 960 electrical contact points, exactly corresponding to the possible number of punches in the card.[1] The top of the card passes under 960 brass brushes, each brush corresponding exactly to the number of punch possibilities in the card. If a given location — e.g., a 2 in Column 20 — is punched out, then the brush on the top of the card makes contact with the plate on the bottom of the card, resulting in an electrical contact. This contact *being made in a given location of the read area* is the way in which the computer input device *reads* the data on the Hollerith card, and subsequently transmits that data either to the computer storage (memory) or to a peripheral storage device — tape, drum, disk, etc. The important point to remember is that the information is coded onto the Hollerith card by use of the *location of the punch in the card itself*.

Thus, coding of information on a Hollerith Card for use by a computer or a data-processing machine is nothing more nor less than punching holes in the card in certain locations. The card code, then, is the location in the card where the hole is punched. The location of the hole or holes in each column designates what the data character is. The computer translates this Hollerith code into an internal computer code as the card is read by the card reader.

Table 3-1 is a list of the numbers, letters, and special characters that most computers will accept. Some computers will accept more special characters, and some fewer, but the list shown indicates the group of data characters that most computers will accept, and the punch designation on the Hollerith card representing that data digit. A data character, in this use, is simply a single data character such as a letter (A), a number (3), or a special character (comma).

Whenever the Hollerith card is in the CARD READ position of an input device for a computer (a card reader) and the brush for *any one* of the 80 columns makes contact with the plate beneath the card for an 11-4, the computer "reads" this as a data alphanumeric M. Conversely, the letter M is read by the computer as a 11-4 in the same column. The computer *reads* the character in the given column because the

---

[1]No known card reader works this way, but this facilitates the explanation.

TABLE 3-1. FORTRAN (computer) alphanumeric* characters Hollerith card representation (FORTRAN Alphabet).

FORTRAN Alphabet	Card Code		FORTRAN Alphabet	Card Code
A	12–1		0	10
B	12–2		1	1
C	12–3		2	2
D	12–4		3	3
E	12–5	Numbers	4	4
F	12–6		5	5
G	12–7		6	6
H	12–8		7	7
I	12–9		8	8
			9	9
J	11–1			
K	11–2			
L	11–3			
M	11–4			
Letters N	11–5			
O	11–6		. (period)	12–3–8
P	11–7		)	12–4–8
Q	11–8	Special	+ (add to)	12
R	11–9	Characters	$	11–3–8
			* (multiply)	11–4–8
			— (subtract)	11
			/ (divide by)	10–1
S	10–2		, (comma)	10–3–8
T	10–3		(	10–4–8
U	10–4		=	3–8
V	10–5			
W	10–6			
X	10–7			
Y	10–8			
Z	10–9			

*An alphanumeric character is any letter of the alphabet, any number, or any special character that is acceptable to FORTRAN. The 46 alphanumeric characters shown are standard characters acceptable to almost any computer using FORTRAN. Additional characters are used by some computers and FORTRAN SYSTEMS.

card has been punched; hence, an electrical contact can be made in specific locations on the card. Figure 3-2 shows the punched card representing the 46 alphanumeric characters shown on Table 3-1.

In short, each column represents a single alphanumeric character. The Hollerith card represents essentially a sentence that may be 80 characters long. Each column of the 80 is punched with one or more punches necessary to code the proper alphanumeric character in the column. The number and location of the holes in each column of the card is the way of coding the information into that column. The information is punched into the Hollerith card for computer use. The printed data on the top of the card is only used when people are handling the cards.

In summary, the data punched into the Hollerith card is completely up to the wishes of the person working with the data. It makes little difference to the programmer and none to the computer whether one uses full names and words, or whether one abbreviates. If all the data will not fit onto a single card, then two or more cards may be used to contain the information. In the event that two or more cards are to be used to contain information on the same item, then one must devise a method of controlling the cards so that they do not get out of order. This might be done in a number of ways.

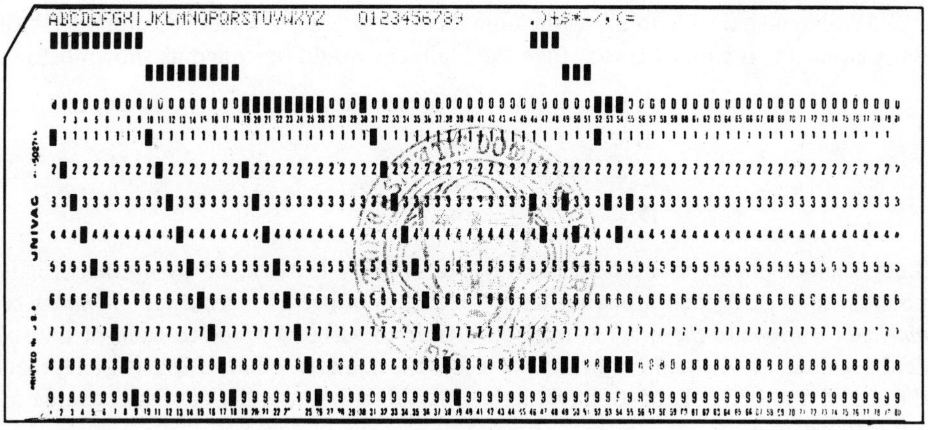

FIGURE 3-2.   Hollerith card — FORTRAN character set.

Computer code: internal to the computer

Once the Hollerith card passes under the read area of a card reader, the Hollerith code is translated into a type of number code for storage in the computer. Rather than try to show an actual internal code of some *one* computer, let us simply indicate here, generally, what an internal computer code is in theory.

Let us imagine for a moment a computer code of our own. Let us suppose that we have a code based on the location of a mark in any one of six positions. The mark can be illustrated as a line that is divided into six sections. The line might look as shown below:

The line is shown as being divided into six different compartments or units. Each unit may be designated as having a mark or not having a mark. For convenience let us give a value to each of the six sections as follows:

$$32 \quad 16 \quad 8 \quad 4 \quad 2 \quad 1$$

We can develop a code, then, based on a series of numbers. For instance, if we regard our line as being divided into six compartments with a number value for each compartment, we would indicate the number 1 by placing a mark in the first position as follows: The mark in the first position represents a number "1." A number 2 would be indicated by placing a mark in position No. 2, as follows:

A number 3 would be indicated as follows:
The number 36 would be indicated as follows:

With our six-position field, we can handle any number up to and including 63.

Since we can indicate up to number 63 for each digit, we can now put our code together. We shall let 0 be indicated by blanks, and the numbers 1–9 be numbers 1–9 on the field as follows:

0 =	5 =
1 =	6 =
2 =	7 =
3 =	8 =
4 =	9 =

We can also decide to allow the alphabet to represent a series of numbers. If we let A equal 11, B equal 12, etc., then the alphabet would be coded as shown below:

$$A = \underline{\ |\ \ ||\ } = 11 \text{ (numeric value)}$$
$$B = \underline{\ ||\ \ \ } = 12$$
$$C = \underline{\ ||\ |\ } = 13$$
$$D = \underline{\ |||\ } = 14$$

Since each segment of the field is indicated only by a mark, or by *no mark*, it is possible to regard each alphabet letter or each number as a *sequence of marks or marked locations in the field*. It is also possible to assign a value to each of the six field segments, and to allow the marks to have a numeric value. If this is done, then the arabic numbers, or the alphabet letters would have a number equivalent value or a location value.

In some instances, it might be worthwhile to indicate whether a number is a positive or a negative number. It might also be worthwhile to use a decimal point in some numbers. To do this we could change the basis of the code from a six- to an eight-position code as shown below:

sign	decimal point		number code	

The number 50 would be coded:

$$\underline{\ ||\ \ |\ }$$

The number 50. would be coded:

$$\underline{\ |||\ \ |\ }$$

The number −50. would be coded:

$$\underline{\ ||||\ \ |\ }$$

While we could go further, this is perhaps sufficient to indicate the basis for the so-called internal computer code.

THE INDEX CARD

The basic social science research technique has tended to center on the 3 × 5 index card. Each card was duly noted, indexed, and made the basic unit of storage. In a real sense, each index card contained an observation or a series of observations. When the index file became large, it became a real problem to remember and to find what was written on the cards. The problem became particularly difficult when more than one item was written on each index card. When the index file became too large, progress bogged down (even when indexed) and the social scientist tended to spend much of his time looking for a card that had some dimly remembered fact or citation written thereon.

The Hollerith card is the basic device for preparing data for storage or for input to a computer. The card itself is exactly three and one-quarter inches by seven and three-eighths inches. Normally each card may contain up to 80 alphabetic characters, numbers, or spaces — or groups of characters, numbers, and spaces in sequence.

Just as a 3 × 5 index card could be utilized to store or contain data, Hollerith cards may also be utilized to store or contain data. A 3 × 5 index card could contain several written sentences plus certain codes or index information so that the information could be found. In this way the 3 × 5 card corresponds to a paragraph, as the Hollerith card may be said to correspond to a sentence. As many Hollerith cards may be used in sequence as is necessary to incorporate all the data desired concerning any given subject. The example below may illustrate the point.

III A 1

Federalists — Anti-Federalists

According to Main were commercial vs. noncommercial yet many of the anti-Federalists were of the commercial element or very respectful to commercial element — opposed Constitution at ratifying conventions but later supported it. Hard to say why they were anti-Federalist — hints that anti-Federalism was ambiguous and even superficial among rank and file who opposed the Constitution. No serious inquiry into this question.

William Miller, Review, Main, THE ANTI-FEDERALISTS, *Mississippi Valley Historical Review*, **49**, 119–120.

FIGURE 3-3. Index card data file. (The cards are maintained in 3 × 5 card boxes with major divisions according to the first Roman numeral designation. Subdivisions are maintained within each major division.)

An historian has set up a 3 × 5 card index file for American history. Each card contains factual information, or opinion, or other, as noted. Below the information he has noted the source. His overall card file consists of some twenty major parts. The 3 × 5 card shown in Figure 3-3 has a coding on it of III, A, 1. The subtitle of Code III, A, 1 is *Federalists and Anti-Federalists*. The Roman numeral "III" refers to the period of colonial history pertaining to the period from the American Revolution to the adoption of the federal Constitution — approximately 1770–1790. "A" refers to political facts, and "1" refers to the notation for biography. The actual set-up of the code itself is not important except to indicate that some sort of code is necessary. The content of the card is reproduced exactly as in the file, in Figure 3-3. Figure 3-4 shows the series of Hollerith cards necessary to contain the same information.

The difference between the two ways of recording information should be immediately apparent. The 3 × 5 card contains all the information pertaining to a given transaction. The Hollerith cards are such that each card contains only a part of the overall record. The cards and the coding sequence necessary to handle the cards as a unit are explained in Figure 3-4. This example indicates how information can be placed on a Hollerith card for automatic electronic storage and retrieval.

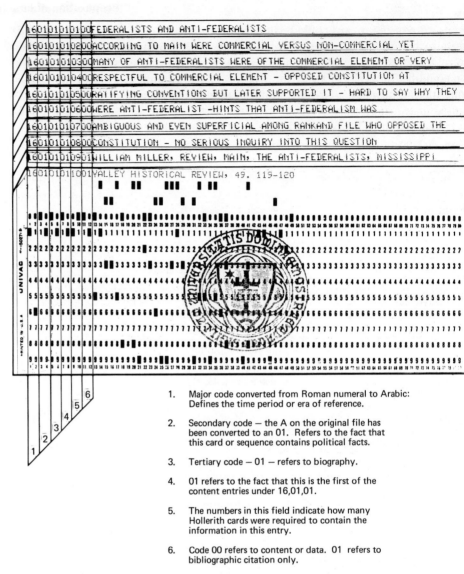

1. Major code converted from Roman numeral to Arabic: Defines the time period or era of reference.

2. Secondary code — the A on the original file has been converted to an 01. Refers to the fact that this card or sequence contains political facts.

3. Tertiary code — 01 — refers to biography.

4. 01 refers to the fact that this is the first of the content entries under 16,01,01.

5. The numbers in this field indicate how many Hollerith cards were required to contain the information in this entry.

6. Code 00 refers to content or data. 01 refers to bibliographic citation only.

FIGURE 3-4. Hollerith data card file, Federalist — anti-Federalist.

appendix 3-1

New York Naval Office Records

The Hollerith card is the basic device for getting information, either a program or data, into a computer system. The Hollerith card is a type of storage device that in itself constitutes a record. That is, each Hollerith card is complete in itself. Each Hollerith card may or may not contain a complete transaction. Data are coded onto the Hollerith card by a series of punches. The Hollerith card is divided into eighty columns, where each column may contain one or more punches. Each field may consist of one or more columns and each field contains a discrete piece of information.

One of the more fascinating studies for economists and historians has been the study of the Navigation Acts of the English Crown as applied to the American Colonies. In 1696 the British Parliament made provision for the development of certain statistical data for all of England's colonies. The data were to determine, primarily, ship and cargo movements. The significance of these data was in the fact that the major source of the Crown revenues was from the taxation of the trade of the Colonies and England. For instance, on a shipment of tobacco from Virginia worth 490/00/00, approximately 358/00/00 was paid to the English Crown in the form of tax duties.

In the 1930's a research project under the Federal Writers Project, headed by Professors John H. Cox and Lawrence A. Harper, University of California, obtained microfilm copies of these records for New York and had them copied. The professors had the information copied onto 3 × 5 cards as shown in Figure 3-5.

a. Industry
b. Jonathan Pearson
c. Brig 040 00 07
d. New York, 1727
e. New York, April 21, 1740
f. From Dover
g. November 8, 1741
h. Peter Rutgers, N.Y.
   David Provoost, N.Y.
   Christopher Banker, N.Y.

i. European Goods 76 cases, 22 casks, 1 bale, 8 packs; 32 iron pots and backs; 40 iron bars; 230 bottles; 259 corn fans; 9,000 tiles; 6,000 bricks; 20 marble stones.

FIGURE 3-5. New York trade record.

From Figure 3-5, the alphabetic letters at the beginning of each entry constituted the key to the data contained on the cards or paper used. The letters indicate the following:

1) Name of vessel.
2) Master of vessel.
3) Rig type, number of tons displacement, guns, men.
4) Place and date of construction.
5) Place of and date of registration.
6) From (to), port of origin of cargo or destination.
7) Date of entry into or clearance from New York Port.
8) Names of owner(s) and residence, if different from registration.
9) Detail of cargo.

The problem that arose, almost from the beginning of the project, was that the study of New York (which was completed on cards as shown) contained approximately

14,000 cards representing some 3,000 ships — one ship might make several round trips in and out of New York — and there was simply too much data to handle manually in any reasonable sense. The manual tabulation that was attempted was quite superficial, so that the answer to the problem clearly lay with the automatic data-processing applications. The first step involved keypunching the data on to cards.

At the outset there was too much information about each ship entry (one transaction) or clearance (another transaction) to get all the data on a single Hollerith card. Since each ship entry or clearance represents a transaction, multiple Hollerith unit records would be required for each transaction. The decision was made to use a four-card layout — that is, four types of cards were required to get all of the information punched for computer use. The four types of cards were:

A-card: ship card (one card only)
B-card: voyage card (one card only)
C-card: owner card (multiple cards, one card for each owner)
D-card: cargo card (multiple cards, one card for each cargo item)

It was necessary to provide a number code to relate the transactions and it was necessary to be able to use the card series either separately or together; that is, one had to be able to use only the D-cards in some instances, or to use the A-, B-, C-, and D-cards together if one desired to correlate products, ports of origin, and ship cargos.

To solve one problem, each of the 14,000 cards was numbered. This number was designated the *ship control number* which appeared in the first five columns

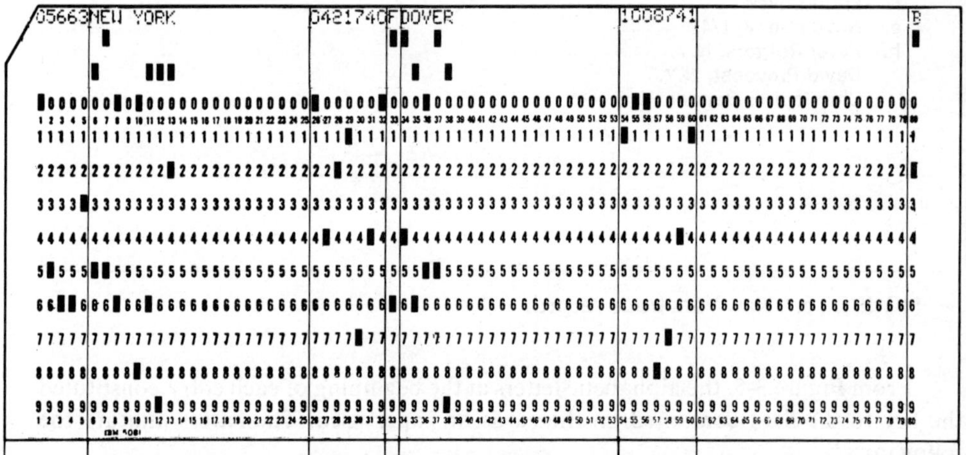

CARD COLUMNS	1-5	6-25	26-32	33	34-53	54-60	61-79	80
CARD DATA	Ship Control No.	Place of Registry	Date of Registry	*	Port of Exit or Entry	Date of Exit or Entry	Blank Columns	Control B

*F or T: From or to what port

FIGURE 3-6. B-card — voyage card.

of each card (A-, B-, C-, and D-card). Column 80 of each card contained the A-, B-, C-, or D-card designation. For the sample entry shown in Figure 3-5, there were a total of 17 separate cards:

1 A-card
1 B-card
3 C-cards
12 D-cards

Design a card layout for the A-card (layouts are shown for the B-, C-, and D-cards in Figures 3-6, 3-7, and 3-8 respectively). Be sure that the ship control number appears in the first five columns, and the card-type designation (A, B, C, D) appears in the 80th column. Identify each of the types of data which appears on the card. Identify each field on the card. Identify the blank columns on each card. Remember, in designing your card layout, you must be sure to be able to:

1) utilize all the data in answering any conceivable question relative to that data;
2) use each card type separately if desired;
3) use two or more types of the cards together — e.g., relate the A- and C-cards to determine whether multiple ownership was more common on smaller or larger vessels, and to determine how often the master was the owner. Use the A- and B-cards to determine the round-trip-time of a vessel, etc.
4) leave as much room as possible in fields where names appear, since the names may be larger than the sample shown.

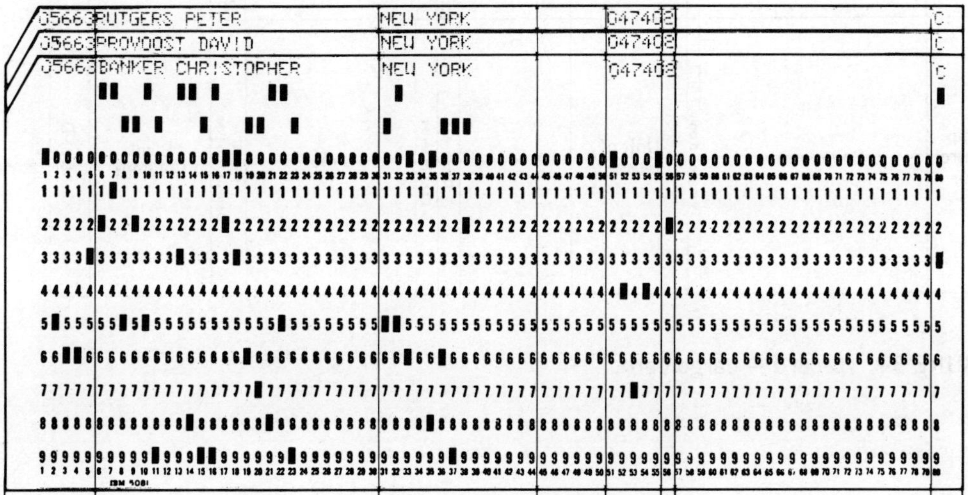

1–5	6–30	31–44	45–50	51–55	56	57–79	80
Ship Control No.	Name of Owner	Residence or Place of Registry	Blank Column	Date of Reg.	*	Blank Columns	Control C

*1) executor
2) by endorsement
3) per registry
4) on photo

FIGURE 3-7. C-card — owner card.

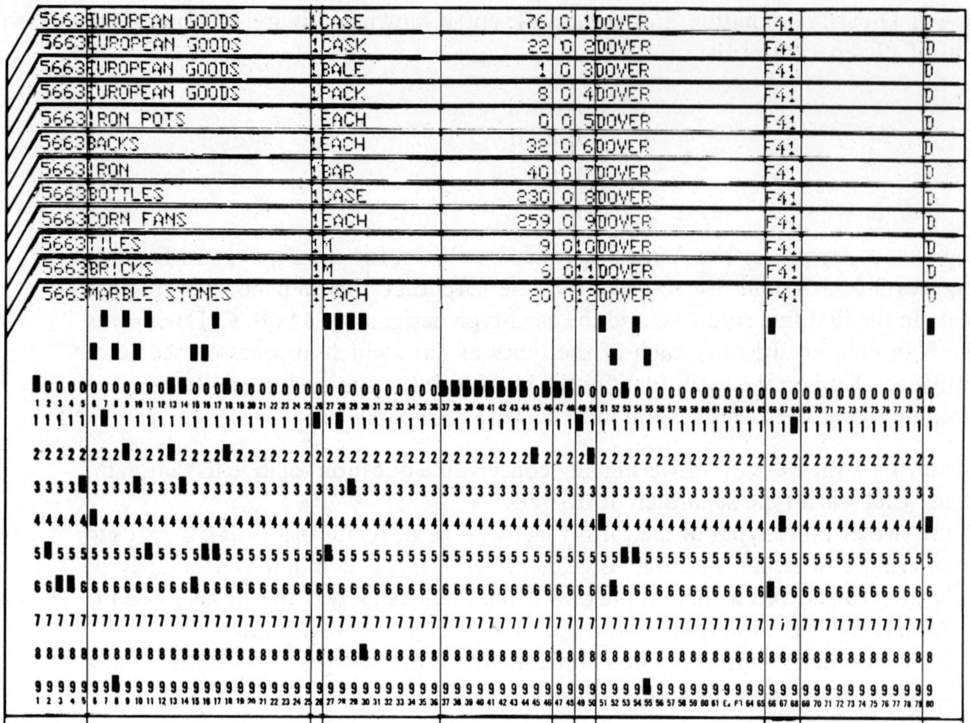

CARD COLUMNS	1–5	6–25	26	27–36	37–46	47 48	49 50	51–65	66 67 68	69–79	80
CARD DATA	Ship Control No.	Commodity	Final card only	Unit of Measure	Amount	Decimal	Card in series	Port	F or T Date of trip (year)	Blank Columns	Control D

FIGURE 3-8.   D-card — cargo card.

4

Peripheral Storage of Data

Many different types of devices are currently used to prepare information for processing by a computer, to enter information into the computer, to temporarily store information while the computer storage unit contains other information, and to output results. The devices performing these services are called *peripheral-storage devices*. The actual devices used for any computer problem application depend upon the devices available on the computer being used, the amount of data to be processed, the type of processing to be performed, and the "mobility" required of the data.

Peripheral-storage devices may be classified as input only, output only, or both input and output. In addition, devices may be either *serial access* or *random access*. The computer storage unit is an example of a random-access device — the time taken to gain access to the contents of any location of storage is the same, regardless of the actual position of the location in relation to the *previously* accessed location. In a serial-access device, the next sequential unit record of information must be accessed. Referencing any other unit record of information necessitates accessing all intervening unit records of information. Thus, the access time depends upon the relative positions of the current unit record and the next desired unit record of information.

Today's "second or third generation" computers operate at such fast internal speeds that, in most applications, the limiting factor to full and efficient utilization of the computer is the speed of getting information into and out of the computer. A wide variety of input and output devices have been developed and utilized. Some of the more generally available devices are described in this section.

A peripheral-storage device is an electronic unit that is tied (on line) to the computer. Most peripheral units or devices, such as card readers or magnetic tape reader-printers, have no useful function that is independent of the computer.

The use of any peripheral-storage device involves two ideas:

1. Getting data into (and out of) the computer memory.

2. Making data available to the computer memory when the data will not all fit at once into the memory. (In this instance, the data are stored or held on the peripheral-storage device and made available to the computer core storage as successive amounts of the data are required by the program.)

37

PERIPHERAL-STORAGE DEVICES

Serial-access devices

Cards

The punched Hollerith card is probably the most commonly used input medium at the present time. The Hollerith card can contain up to eighty characters of information. In a sense, the card is the storage device as well as the vehicle for getting information into (and out of) the computer. Computer "readable" information is placed in a Hollerith card by a device called a keypunch machine. This keypunch machine operates like an electric typewriter except that the information is transferred to the punched cards as punched holes in appropriate positions in each column of the card. Most models of keypunch machines also print the character at the top of the card column. The printed character is *not* read by the computer — it is placed there to facilitate checking and arranging the punched cards.

The various characters are shown in Figure 4-1. Data are entered into the computer from Hollerith cards by an input device called a card reader. Card readers can "read" from 60 to 2,000 cards per minute. Some of the reasons Hollerith cards are so universally used for input are:

1. They are inexpensive and can be prepared by inexpensive devices.
2. They are easily prepared.
3. They are sturdy and thus can be processed over and over before wearing out.
4. Since most models of keypunch units also print the character punched in each column of the card at the top of the card, checking and ordering decks of cards is straightforward.
5. Each card is a unit record; thus, the correction of errors involves the replacing of just the mispunched cards.
6. Many supplementary devices, such as card sorters and collators are available.

Cards, however, have some serious disadvantages. Most notably, these are:

1. They are susceptible to variations in temperature and humidity — that is, they have a tendency to warp and stick together when exposed to variations in temperature and humidity. This tendency can be overcome, however, by storing the cards under pressure; thus minimizing the exposed card area.
2. Cards lack data density. The limit of eighty characters of information per card presents a serious problem in the storing and transporting of vast amounts of information. For example: the number of cards needed to store the contents of an average-size novel (assuming 425,000 characters) is approximately 5,300 cards, or a stack of cards two and one-half feet high.
3. It is easy to shuffle cards out of order. When dealing with hundreds or even thousands of cards, the possibility of accidentally disordering the cards must be taken into account. This is usually handled by numbering the cards. The numbering process, of course, further reduces the amount of useful information contained on the card.
4. They have a low transfer rate. The transfer rate is normally defined as the number of characters of information read by the computer per second. Most computers are equipped with card readers capable of reading up to 1,000 cards per minute. This is equivalent to 1,333 characters per second. To "read" the average novel mentioned above takes 5.3 minutes. Although this may appear to be extremely rapid, it is, in actuality, much too slow for most large-scale computers.

Hollerith Card

Upper right
Corner cut

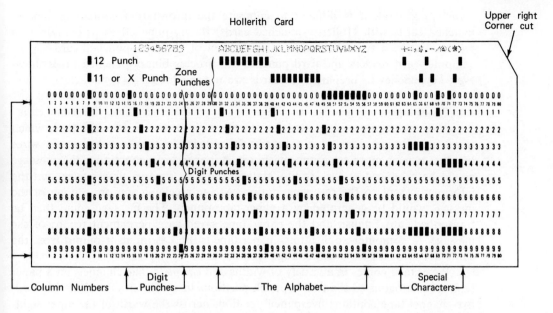

Paper Tape

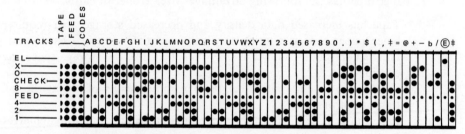

FIGURE 4-1. Illustration of Hollerith card and 8-channel paper.

SOURCE: IBM Systems Reference Library, *IBM 1620 Input/Output Units*, IBM
Products Publications Division (San Jose, California, 1962), pp. 5,15.
(File No. 1620/1710-3).

Card punch

In addition to card readers, most computers are equipped with card punches —
that is, output devices which punch information into cards. These cards may then
be saved and used as input to some other computer program. The cards are punched
in the Hollerith format; however, the content of each card column is not printed
at the top of the column. Card punches are usually considerably slower than card
readers, punching at the rate of 60 to 400 cards per minute. Obviously, the same
advantages and disadvantages apply to Hollerith-card output as to Hollerith-card
input.

Examination of the punched card shown in Figure 4-1 shows that, although
there are twelve possible punch positions in each card column, only single punches
or some combinations of two and three punches are allowed. It is possible to increase the data density of punched cards by allowing more combinations of punches
in each column. Cards punched in this manner are frequently called *binary-punched*

cards. In general, it is difficult to compare the information content of binary-punched cards with Hollerith-punched cards. Binary-punched cards contain *at a minimum* at least twice the information content of Hollerith-punched cards. Most computer-card readers and card punches can process binary-punched cards; however, keypunches to prepare such cards are not available.

Paper tape

A second medium often used for storage of information is paper tape, which was originally developed for transmitting coded telegraph messages over wires between two or more telegraph machines. A paper tape containing the message would be produced at the sending station, fed into a paper-tape reader, and the information sent to the receiving station. At the receiving station, a copy of the message would be generated by a paper-tape punch. The message could then be transcribed into English and the paper tape saved as a permanent record of the message. In computer applications, paper tape is used as input or output from the computer or as a permanent storage record.

Paper tape comes in a variety of widths and *channels.* The channels on a paper tape are analogous to the twelve-punch positions in a column of a Hollerith card; five-channel tape contains five punch positions across the width of the tape; eight-channel tape contains eight punch positions, etc. Like Hollerith cards, various punch combinations are used to represent each character. Figure 4-1 compares a seven-channel paper tape and a (twelve-channel) Hollerith card as storage medium.

Paper tape has the following advantages over Hollerith cards:

1. Tape has increased data density and decreased storage area requirements. Since paper tape is considerably narrower than punched cards and paper tape is continuous (and thus may be rolled up), the storage space saving is considerable.
2. Since paper tape is continuous, there is no possibility of getting the information out of order.
3. Paper tape is less susceptible to temperature and humidity changes than punched cards.

There are, however, disadvantages in using paper tape; most notably, the difficulty in correcting data. Once a tape is punched it is difficult to correct a portion of the tape. Tape correction normally involves duplication of the tape up to the point of the error, repunching the erroneous information and duplicating the remainder of the tape. Also, because paper tape is continuous, data cannot be rearranged.

Magnetic tape

A relatively recent development, magnetic tape is at the present time the cheapest, and perhaps the most efficient, input-output device for computers. Like paper tape, magnetic tape has a various number of channels ranging from six-channel tape to ten- or twelve-channel tape. Magnetic computer tape is similar to the recording tape used in home tape recorders. Magnetic tape is one-half inch wide, plastic, and is coated on one side with a metallic oxide. Data are recorded as magnetized spots on the various tracks or channels of the tape. Each company puts out its own brand of tape with a different number of channels and a different code configuration for the tape. The tapes are usually about 2,400 (or 1,200) feet long.

Let us take a little closer look at magnetic tape and examine a hypothetical example. We shall look at a six-*channel or track tape.* There are six separate channels

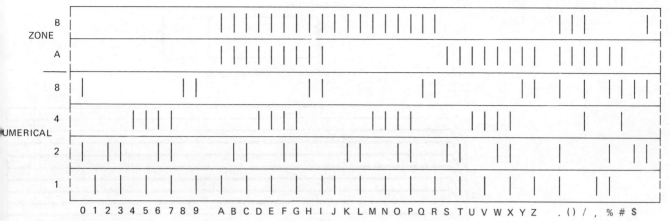

FIGURE 4-2. Six-channel magnetized tape. (Hypothetical magnetic-tape symbol configuration.)

or tracks on the tape, as shown in Figure 4-2. A character is represented by the presence or absence of one or more magnetized spots for each column in any one of the channels or tracks. As shown in the illustration, numbers are represented by a series of magnetized spots (called bits) in the so-called numeric channels. The zone channels shown are used for indicating alphabet characters and special characters.

There are two major advantages and two disadvantages of magnetic tape. The first advantage is the amount of data that may be coded onto a tape. Up to approximately 1600 characters may be stored on each inch of magnetic tape. One of the obvious advantages of magnetic tape is the relatively small size of the storage unit. While it would take a cabinet 3 feet $\times$ 3 feet $\times$ 4 feet to store 60,000 Hollerith cards, the same data could be stored on a magnetic-tape reel that was about ten inches in diameter and one-half inch wide. The storage capacity of magnetic tape is illustrated in Figure 4-3.

When reading paper tape or Hollerith cards into the computer, the process of getting the data into the computer is limited to the speed of the card reader or the paper-tape reader. For instance, a relatively fast card reader will read 600 cards per minute. A paper-tape reader will read perhaps the equivalent of 225 cards per minute. Obviously, then, if a considerable amount of data is involved in a particular computing project, the speed of getting the data into the machine is a limiting factor. If the data are found on 60,000 cards, it would take at least one hour and thirty minutes to get the data into the computer. If this were on magnetic tape, the data could be read into the computer in approximately five minutes.

Random-access storage

All the devices that we have discussed up to this point have one characteristic in common. If one is going to try to find some specific datum that is somewhere in the file, one must go all the way from one end of the file to another, reading each successive unit record at a time. A tape search, or a card file search, involves having the computer scan each card or each record on the tape until it finds the correct or designated record. The next step can then be taken in the program. In short,

On this much tape:

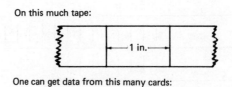

One can get data from this many cards:

FIGURE 4-3. Magnetic-tape storage/card storage.

cards and tape are not *random-access* storage devices. The tape is wound on a reel, and in order to search the tape (or the card file) one must read each entry from one end of the tape toward the other until one finds the desired data.

In order to speed up the process of getting information from the middle of a tape, or from anywhere on the tape, or from the cards, a kind of hybrid was developed. We shall, for convenience, simply call this *random access*. The process of providing random access to data anywhere on a storage device involves two basic principles:

1. Each entry anywhere on the storage device must have a specific address.
2. It must be possible to access that address at any time.

Magnetic drum

The first random-access device is a "drum." Conceptually, we could take some magnetic tape, and wrap it around a large metal cylinder. This gives us the capability of storing the data, as magnetic bits, not on a reel of tape, but on the open surface of a drum. Then we attach a motor to the drum and cause it to spin around. Next we divide the drum surface into channels and provide an address for each unit record in each channel. Then we attach a drum read-write arm that would automatically position itself to the required address location of a specified channel in response to a command. All this would give us a random (data) access storage

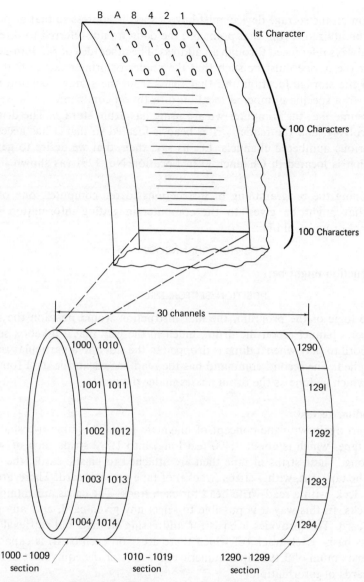

FIGURE 4-4. Drum storage.

device. Of course, the actual technical description of a drum operation would vary considerably from the above.

Drum-storage devices vary from company to company, but Figure 4-4 illustrates a typical drum-storage device. As suggested, the drum is capable of maintaining a magnetic-field charge whether the current is on or off. Thus the drum, like the tape, is a permanent record-storage device. Each drum has a specific number of storage locations, and each location has a specific address. There are thirty so-called channels on the drum as shown in Figure 4-4, and each channel contains six tracks for writing. Therefore, the coding configuration for data on a drum channel could be like the configuration for data on a six-channel tape. Each addressable location on each channel contains one or more character spaces.

The drum depicted here is a hypothetical one, but it does illustrate the basic principle of random access. The basic idea of random-access storage is that each storage location on the storage device must have a specific address so that a specific location may be utilized. From that point on, the data are not referred to directly. The data are always referenced through an address. The other idea of random-access storage is that the device must be such that the reader or printer device that puts the data onto the storage location and that reads from the storage location must be able to get to a specific numbered location directly on command.

Let us assume that the computer we are using has drum storage. The drum is constantly revolving, and the reader-writer head is located so that it has access to any of the various numbered channels. Let us say, then, that we desire to get the information that is located in Channel 30 in Location No. 1291 (as shown in the illustration).

In developing the programming of instructions to the computer, one of the instructions that might be given to the computer in getting information from the hypothetical drum would be:

POSITION/CHANNEL/30

The next instruction might be:

POSITION/SECTOR/1291

Following the logic of the program, the first instruction would position the read-write head over Channel 30 on the drum, much in the way that a jukebox selects the proper record to play when a dime is dropped in the slot and a particular record button is punched. The second command has the read head scan the data found in Sector 1291, which is done as the drum passes under the head.

Card random access[1]

Let us start again with the concept of magnetic tape. This time, we shall cut the magnetic tape (which is about 2,400 feet long) into 1,792 strips each of which is 14 inches long. These strips of tape then are attached to plastic cards, the magnetic side of the tape out, with 7 strips (tracks) of tape on each card. There are 256 cards in each deck, with a read-write head for each track. The cards are numbered, as are the tracks. In this way it is possible to select any given card, and any given track of any card. This provides a basis for addressing storage and retrieval on a random-access basis. Each track (of which there are 7 on each card) is capable of containing a maximum of 3,100 alphanumeric characters or the equivalent of about 38 punched cards of information.

Using this kind of system, which operates at a speed compatible with computer speed operations, a random-access system is possible.

Disk random access

A third type is the random-access disk-storage package. In a certain sense the disks storage device looks a great deal like a half-size jukebox with a number of records in position ready to be played. The major difference is that in the disk pack there is a read-write head for each side of the pack, as shown in Figure 4-5.

The disk package rotates at a speed of about 1,500 rpm. Each recording location on the disk storage package has a designated numbered location — an address. There are, in essence, 10 tracks on each of the 10 sides of the disk package. There are thus 100 tracks on which data may be stored. Each disk track is divided into 20 sectors, and each sector will contain 100 alphanumeric characters. There are 2,000 alphanumeric characters per track; hence, there is a total storage capability of

[1]Based on a random-access device marketed by National Cash Register, Computer Division.

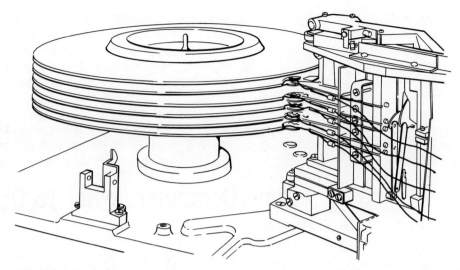

FIGURE 4-5.   Disk storage unit.

SOURCE: IBM Systems Reference Library, *IBM 401 System Summary*, IBM
Product Publications, Endicott, New York, Fig. 33, p. 28. (File No.
1401-00; A24-1401-1).

2,000,000 characters. Each sector will contain somewhat more than the contents
of one 80-column Hollerith card. Each sector has a given address associated with
it, and the programmer need only provide the appropriate sector number (address
location) in order to read data from, or write data onto a given sector.

The point that should be noted for all types of random-access storage devices
discussed is their similarity in that the data are coded onto the device by using a
code similar to that for the computer itself. Each storage location on a particular
storage device is numbered so that the data in that numbered storage location may
be referenced at any time. Most computers can utilize one or more of these storage
devices. Thus, the computer system may have immediate access to relatively large
amounts of stored data. The data are coded onto the peripheral-storage device in a
way that makes it immediately available to the core memory.

QUESTIONS
FOR DISCUSSION

1.   Discuss: a) serial access, versus b) random access.
2.   Why are *drum*, *disk*, and *card random-access* devices considered random-
access storage devices? Discuss.
3.   Why are *paper tape*, *magnetic tape*, and *Hollerith cards* considered as serial-
access devices? Discuss.
4.   Why are so-called *peripheral-storage devices* (other than Hollerith cards)
needed in computer use?

5

Telling Computers What To Do[1]

INTRODUCTION

Using a computer to "solve" a problem implies that: 1) the problem is suitable for solution by a computer; 2) a recipe or procedure for solving the problem is available or can be developed; 3) the recipe can be translated into a form understandable by the computer; and 4) the problem can be solved in a finite (given) number of steps.

Determining whether a given problem is suitable for solution by a computer is a difficult problem in itself. A discussion of what constitutes a "computer solvable" problem will be deferred until the reader has a better grasp of what a computer is and how it is used as a tool. For the present, problems meeting conditions 2 through 4 will be considered suitable for computer solution.

A computer can only do what it is instructed to do — therefore, developing a method to solve the posed problem is a necessary step in using a computer. The process of instructing a computer, called programming the computer, requires that the programmer know at least one procedure to be followed to solve the problem. Developing a procedure to be followed in solving a problem is called constructing an *algorithm*. The remainder of this chapter is devoted to developing and expressing algorithms in a concise symbolic notation; the remaining chapters are devoted to translating algorithms into a form or language understandable by computers.

ALGORITHMS — WHAT ARE THEY?

For our purpose, it is sufficient to define an algorithm as a procedure or a set of instructions for solving a problem. Algorithms are encountered many times during our daily lives; for example, assembling a do-it-yourself television table by following the algorithm with the kit, or preparing a quick lunch by following the algorithm on the back of a can of soup.

Algorithms can be divided into three sections: 1) A statement of the area of applicability of the algorithm (the domain); 2) A statement of the sequence of steps

[1]This chapter was developed with Dr. Nicholas DiCianni, UNIVAC Corporation, Philadelphia, Pennsylvania.

(or operations) that must be followed to perform the algorithm; and 3) The possible result or output values (the range).

The statement of the area of applicability of the algorithm involves specifying the acceptable values for each input quantity (datum) used in the algorithm (termed the *domain*), and the acceptable values for each output quantity (result) produced by the algorithm (termed the *range*). For example, in the algorithm for the assembly of the television table, the list of parts preceding the assembly instructions can be considered as the specification of the *domain*, and the picture of the completed assembly can be considered as the specification of the *range*.

Three characteristics of all good algorithms are definition, completeness, and precision. Often, the initial statement of the problem contains ambiguities or omits one or more necessary conditions. Before an algorithm can be constructed, all necessary considerations must be known and any inherent ambiguities resolved. Completeness in an algorithm means that every conceivable contingency has been anticipated and provided for. Finally, the algorithms must be precise — a single error in a single statement invalidates the algorithm.

ALGORITHMS — HOW DO WE EXPRESS THEM?

Consider the problem of constructing an algorithm for determining the smallest of three numbers. Since the numbers may have any value, the domain for the problem is any three real numbers; likewise, the range is any single real number. A statement of the algorithm might be:

1. Pick up the first number.
2. Compare it to the second number.
3. If the first number is smaller or equal to the second number save it.
4. If the second number is smaller than the first number save it.
5. Compare whichever number was saved to the third number.
6. If the saved number is smaller or equal to the third number save it.
7. If the third number is smaller than the saved number save it.
8. Whichever number was saved is the smallest.

Notice that at the time the algorithm is constructed, it is not necessary to know the actual numbers that will be used. The algorithm will work for any three numbers — as is specified in the statement of the domain and range of applicability.

For a complicated problem, a verbal statement of the steps of the algorithm would be impractical. To express large algorithms concisely, certain symbolic conventions are used, as shown in Figure 5-1.

For example, let the *symbols (or names)* A_1, A_2, and A_3 represent the three *values (or numbers)* to be compared. The algorithm may be expressed as:

1. Let $S \leftarrow A_1$.
2. If $S \leq A_2$ go to Step 4; otherwise go to Step 3.
3. Let $S \leftarrow A_2$.
4. If $S \leq A_3$ go to Step 6; otherwise go to Step 5.
5. Let $S \leftarrow A_3$.
6. The value currently associated with S is the smallest.

In this statement of the algorithm, many phrases have been replaced by a single symbol. The symbols (names) normally used in expressing algorithms include:

Symbol	Description

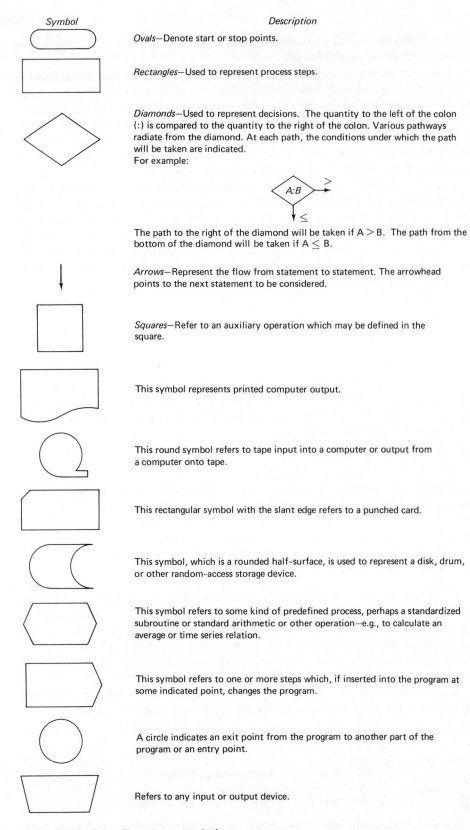

Ovals—Denote start or stop points.

Rectangles—Used to represent process steps.

Diamonds—Used to represent decisions. The quantity to the left of the colon (:) is compared to the quantity to the right of the colon. Various pathways radiate from the diamond. At each path, the conditions under which the path will be taken are indicated.
For example:

The path to the right of the diamond will be taken if A > B. The path from the bottom of the diamond will be taken if A ≤ B.

Arrows—Represent the flow from statement to statement. The arrowhead points to the next statement to be considered.

Squares—Refer to an auxiliary operation which may be defined in the square.

This symbol represents printed computer output.

This round symbol refers to tape input into a computer or output from a computer onto tape.

This rectangular symbol with the slant edge refers to a punched card.

This symbol, which is a rounded half-surface, is used to represent a disk, drum, or other random-access storage device.

This symbol refers to some kind of predefined process, perhaps a standardized subroutine or standard arithmetic or other operation—e.g., to calculate an average or time series relation.

This symbol refers to one or more steps which, if inserted into the program at some indicated point, changes the program.

A circle indicates an exit point from the program to another part of the program or an entry point.

Refers to any input or output device.

FIGURE 5-1. Flowchart symbols.

←	REPLACE: **A** ←- **B** means replace the current value associated with the name **A** with the value associated with the name **B**.
=	EQUALITY: **A** = **B** means the quantity associated with the name **A** is identical to the quantity associated with the name **B**.
≠	NONEQUALITY: **A** ≠ **B** means that the quantity associated with the name **A** is not identical to the quantity associated with the name **B**.
>	GREATER THAN: **A** > **B** means the quantity associated with the name **A** is greater than the quantity associated with the name **B**.
≥	GREATER THAN OR EQUAL: **A** ≥ **B** means the quantity associated with the name **A** is greater than or equal to the quantity associated with the name **B**.
<	LESS THAN: **A** < **B** means the quantity associated with the name **A** is less than the quantity associated with the name **B**.
≤	LESS THAN OR EQUAL: **A** ≤ **B** means the quantity associated with the name **A** is less than or equal to the quantity associated with the name **B**.
+	ADDITION: **A** + **B** means the quantity resulting from the addition of the quantities represented by the names **A** and **B**.
−	SUBTRACTIONS: **A** − **B** means the quantity resulting from subtracting the quantity represented by **B** from the quantity represented by **A**.
*	MULTIPLICATION: **A** * **B** means the quantity resulting from multiplying the quantity represented by **A** by that represented by **B**.
/	DIVISION: **A** / **B** means the quantity resulting from the division of the quantity represented by **A** by that represented by **B**.

The symbolic approach to algorithm representation shown above can still be improved. For describing algorithms involving many decisions (IF conditions) which include almost any problem, a pictorial approach has been developed. This technique known as *flowcharting* or *flow diagramming* uses different geometric figures connected together with flow lines or arrows to represent the various operations required by the algorithm. For example, the algorithm to determine the smallest of three values could be expressed as shown in Figure 5-2.

The problem used to illustrate the construction and expression of an algorithm is not representative of most real problems. Real problems usually involve the repetition of one or more steps of the algorithm until a certain condition is met. The repetition of a step or series of steps in an algorithm is called *looping*. A single execution of the repeated steps is called a *pass*.

As an example, let us increase the domain of the algorithm we have been using by generalizing it to find the smallest of an arbitrary number of values. Once the various options applicable to the comparison of any two values has been specified, the sequence could be repeated for all the values by comparing the result of a comparison with the next value and so forth. Such an algorithm is shown in Figure 5-3.

Notice in the algorithm given above that neither the range nor the domain has been specified. The common assumption would be to specify the domain as any number of real values. Examination of the algorithm shows that this is not an accurate specification of the domain.

Assume the number of values to be considered is one (1). The algorithm would function correctly until READ B was reached. At this time, the attempt to read

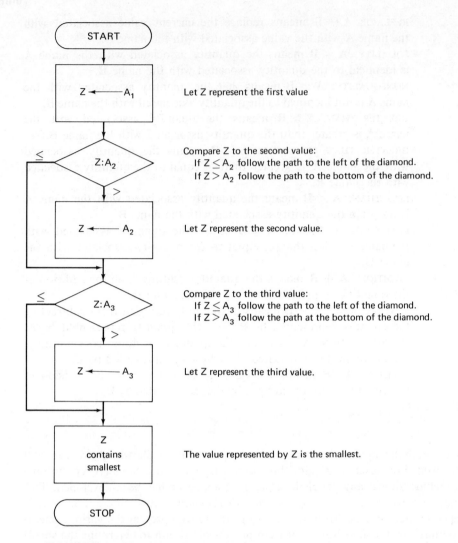

FIGURE 5-2. Flowcharting the algorithm.

the next value would fail since there is no next value. Thus, the actual domain of the algorithm is "two or more real values."

Close examination of flowcharts has often helped programmers eliminate redundancies and unnecessary steps or detect steps that would be better performed in some other section of the algorithm. To illustrate this point, consider constructing an algorithm for determining the range of an arbitrary number of values. Since the range of a series of values is obtained by subtracting the smallest value from the largest, the solution of the problem requires a search through all the values to first determine the largest and smallest. In this respect, the algorithm for determining the range is just an extension of the algorithm previously considered.

For convenience, assume the numbers are in the form of a table. The table will be referred to by the generic name A. The value contained in an individual position in the table will be specified by subscripting the generic name. For example, A_2 refers to the value located in the second position of the table; A_8 refers to the value located in the eighth position of the table, and so forth. Generalizing one step further, if the current value associated with the name I is 3, then A_I refers to

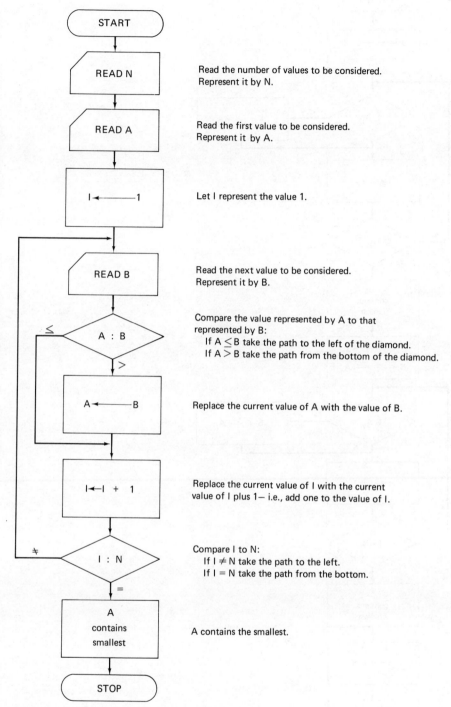

FIGURE 5-3. Flowcharting an algorithm.

the value located in the third position of the table. If the actual number of values in the table is represented by the name N, the individual elements in the table are referred to as A_1, A_2, up to A_N. Thus, a flow chart outlining a method to determine the range of a table of values would resemble the one shown in Figure 5-4.

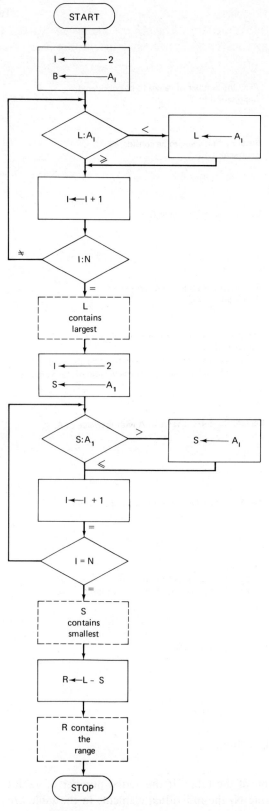

FIGURE 5-4.   Flowcharting an algorithm to determine the range of a table of
numbers.

A study of the flowchart shows that the loop to determine the largest value is similar to that used to determine the smallest value. As a matter of fact, only the decision statement and the transfer process statement associated with it differ. It should be possible to combine these operations into one loop and thus eliminate the loop control statements for one loop, considerably reducing the operations involved (see Figure 5-5).

Initially, the student may find the process of constructing and expressing algorithms difficult. This is to be expected because a good algorithm must be constructed and expressed in suitable detail for its intended audience. Algorithms for solution of problems with computers must meet two demands:

1. They must be detailed enough to allow easy translation into the computer's language.

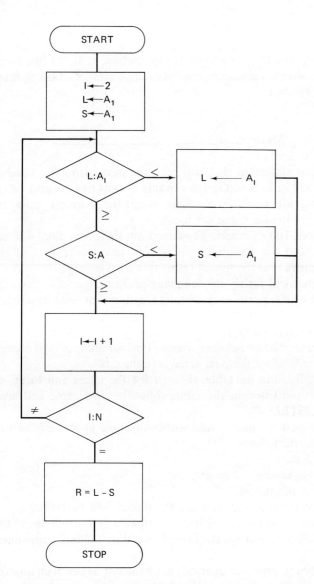

FIGURE 5-5. Flowcharting an algorithm to determine the range of a table of numbers.

2. They must be detailed enough to satisfy anyone interested in using the resulting program (including the programmer) that the algorithm is suitable for his application.

The first of these requirements obviously cannot be satisfied until the student has had some experience programming computers. But, programming computers requires that the programmer be able to express in detail the required operations. We chose to break into this vicious circle by first discussing algorithms and flowcharting because a flowchart lacking detail still provides some insight into the logic of the problem and tends to keep the overall problem in sight. Programming a computer without a flowchart is akin to writing without an outline — the student is quickly submerged in details which often obscure the overall problem that is to be considered.

QUESTIONS FOR DISCUSSION

1. What is an algorithm? Try to give a general explanation in about five lines.
2. Explain, in your own words, the conventional flowchart symbols. Give a short explanation for each symbol.
   For example:

       Y   Means _____.

   This refers to an input statement that will read the next card. The number punched in this card will be assigned to the variable Y as its new current value.
3. Draw a flowchart that will read 100 numbers, count the numbers, calculate the mean, and print out the total and the mean.
4. Suppose that you have 100 numbers. Flowchart an algorithm that will describe the maximum and the minimum value. You also desire to find the mean of the 100 numbers and the modal (most frequent) number.
5. Write an algorithm that will satisfy the following problem:
   A. You have a list of 100 ports, each with its location expressed in latitude and longitude.
   B. Set these into a reference table.
   C. Make provision to read an *unknown number* (any number) of port names, and check to see whether the port name is in the table.
      1. If the port is listed in the table, show or list the name and location;
      2. If the port is not listed in the table, show the port name and label NOT LISTED.
6. A person wishes to invest his money and wishes to know how much he can earn by doing so. He will tell you:
      1) initial investment,
      2) the month and year he will invest,
      3) the annual rate of interest,
      4) the number of months and/or years the money will be invested.
   Assume the investment is compounded daily, beginning on the first day of the investment and added to the account quarterly in March, June, September, and December.
   Flowchart an algorithm to print out quarterly after the last day of each quarter the new balance and earnings that quarter. Make any assumptions needed to complete the algorithm.

The following algorithms have reference to the data set forth in Appendix 3-1 concerning the New York Naval Office Records. The reader may wish to refer to this appendix before trying any of the following algorithms.

7. In algorithmic form, tell how one would find the average size of all different ships (vessels) engaged in traffic in New York harbor.

8. Do an algorithm that would ascertain the largest ship and the smallest ship (measured by displacement, *and* measured by crew size) engaged in the New York trade.

9. Flowchart (diagram) to determine the average size of all ships engaged in the New York trade.

10. Write a flowchart that will convert the time lag represented by two different dates (date for ship into New York and date for ship out of New York) into a statement of the *average* port time of each ship in New York.

11. Write a flowchart to determine how many ships carried guns.

12. Write a flowchart to determine how many vessels had the owner (C-card) as the master (A-card).

13. Write a flowchart to determine which port was most frequently visited by ships engaged in trading out of New York.

14. Write a flowchart that could determine which commodity was most frequently IMPORTED, and the commodity most frequently EXPORTED from New York harbor.

6

General-Purpose Digital Computer[1]

COMPUTER: FUNCTIONAL PARTS

In a very general sense, a digital computer is a machine that consists of five separate parts or separate machines. When the five parts or five separate units are combined, the result is a computer. The five functional parts or units that comprise a computer are defined below.

Input Units transfer information into the computer.

Output Units transfer information out of the computer.

Arithmetic/Logical Unit performs the basic arithmetic operations of addition, subtraction, multiplication, and division, and also performs comparisons.

Storage Unit (*Computer Memory*) contains the information pertinent to the problem currently being solved.

Control Unit serves in a supervisory capacity. This controls the movement of information between the various other units and interprets and directs the sequence of operations provided to solve the problem.

The functional units of the computer are often compared to the various components of an adding machine or desk calculator. The operator makes information available to the adding machine by depressing various keys on the keyboard. The keyboard might well be referred to as the input unit of the adding machine. From the keyboard, the information is transmitted by a series of levers and gears to the actual counting wheels. These gears, levers, and wheels can be considered the arithmetic section of the adding machine. In a sense, the counting wheels also serve as a storage unit of the adding machine since these wheels store the current information. Once information is in the machine, instructions are provided to operate on the information (add, subtract, total, etc.). This is accomplished by depressing the appropriate button. These buttons serve as control devices of the adding machine. Finally, the printing mechanism whereby results are made available to the operator can be considered the output unit. In this analogy the machine operator would be the control unit.

There is, however, a significant difference between an adding machine and a computer. In the adding machine, the sequence in which the various operations are

[1]This chapter was developed together with Dr. Nicholas DiCianni, UNIVAC Corporation, Philadelphia, Pennsylvania.

performed is controlled by the operator — in a computer the sequence of operations is performed automatically by the control unit, which is based upon coded information contained within the storage unit. Computers which store both the instructions to be performed and the information upon which to perform them are called *stored-program* computers. The almost unbelievable speed of the modern digital computer can be attributed to the stored-program concept, together with the electric circuitry of the computer.

FUNCTIONAL UNITS AND OPERATION

The storage unit, or memory, of any computer is composed of a number of locations. Each storage location has a unique numeric address associated with it. Normally addresses are sequential (0, 1, 2, etc.) up to the *capacity* of the unit. Most computer systems differ both in the capacity of the storage unit and in the amount of information that can be stored in each location.

A computer system is either a *fixed word-length* computer or a *variable word-length* computer. A word computer is one that can store a given number of characters in each core location. For instance, one well-known computer will store in each numbered core location:

> *either*
> 6 alphabet characters (maximum)
> *or*
> 9 real number digits (maximum)
> *or*
> 11 integer number digits (maximum).

Variable word-length computers (now obsolete) operated on a different principle. In either case, the information contained in a location is called its *contents*.

The computer storage unit is often compared to a series of safe deposit boxes, as is illustrated in Figure 6-1. Like the computer storage unit, the safe deposit unit is divided into individual boxes. *Each box, although identical in appearance to any other box, can be distinguished by the address associated with it.* The analogy fails, however, when the mechanism for storing and retrieving information in the storage unit is examined. A safe deposit box can conceivably hold many stock certificates at the same time; the storage location can hold only one word of information at a time. As soon as a new word of information is stored in the location, the original information is destroyed. The retrieval of information is also different. Removing the certificates from the safe deposit box leaves the box empty, while in the computer storage unit, only a copy of the information is removed. The original information is still retained in the location. These two features are termed:

1. *Nondestructive Read:* referencing the contents of any location does not destroy the information contained therein.
2. *Destructive Write:* placing the information into a storage unit location destroys the previous information contained in that location.

The contents of any storage location can be either an instruction or a datum. Since the information contained in a storage location is in numeric form, the various instructions must be in the form of numeric codes. These codes must contain at least the following information: 1) what operation is to be performed (operating code),

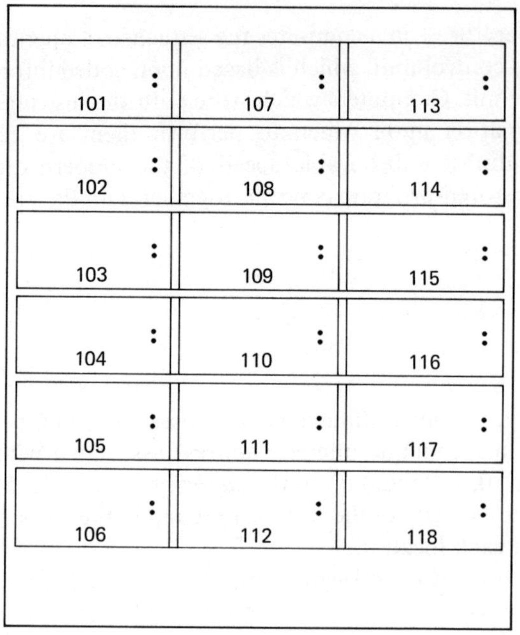

FIGURE 6-1. Storage units: safe deposit boxes.

2) what data is to be used in performing the operation (operand). Thus the instruction must contain an operating code and one or more operands. Computers may be classified as one-address, two-address, or three-address computers, depending upon the number of operands specified in the instruction. In a three-address computer, instructions have the form:

OP AD1 AD2 AD3.

OP stands for or specifies the operation to be performed; and AD1, AD2, and AD3 the various operands. If the operation code specified addition, the contents of AD1 would be added to the contents of AD2 and the result would replace the contents of AD3.

In a two-address computer, the instruction would have the form:

OP AD1 AD2.

In this case, for addition, the contents of AD1 would be added to the contents of AD2, and the result would be stored in AD2.

Most computers have a one-address instruction of the following type:

OP AD1.

In such computers a special storage location, called an accumulator, is used to hold one of the operands. Addition, in a one-address computer, would be described as: add the contents of AD1 to the current contents of the accumulator and place the result in the accumulator. For these computers, instructions must be provided for moving information from the various instructions. These comprise the instruction set of the computer.

For any computer the instruction set is comprised of various classes of operations. These include:

Data Transfer Operations — specifying the movement of information between the various components of the computer. For example, the movement of data between storage and the accumulator.

Arithmetic Operations — such as addition, subtraction, multiplication, and division.

Control Transfer Operations — operations which modify the sequence in which the instructions are executed.

Input/Output Operations — used to transfer information into the computer and to transfer results out of the computer.

All computer operations are performed under the direction of the control unit. The operations performed by the control unit are the transfer of information between the various other components (such as the transfers from storage to the accumulator), and the fetching, analyzing, and performing of the instructions provided to solve a problem. As was mentioned previously, these instructions are stored in the storage unit along with the required data.

Two registers located in the control unit are of special interest: the *instruction register*, and the *location register*. The instruction register holds the instruction currently being analyzed. The location register contains the address of the storage location containing the next instruction to be analyzed. In most computers, instructions must be stored in consecutive storage locations; thus, the operation of the control unit can be described as:

1. Fetch the contents of the storage location address specified in the location register and place it in the instruction register.
2. Add 1 to the address specified in the location register.
3. Analyze and perform the instruction currently contained in the instruction register.
4. Go back to Step 1.

If a computer only operated in this sequential manner, it would not be possible to program algorithms involving the repetition of a sequence of instructions. The flexibility of the computer would be extremely limited. Fortunately, this is not the case. Various instructions in the computer's instruction set allow the control unit to alter the contents of the location register and, thus, modify the execution sequence of the instructions. Instructions of this type are called *transfer of control* operations. Two types exist: *unconditional* and *conditional*.

The execution of an unconditional transfer of control instruction *always* modifies the sequence in which the instructions are executed. The execution of a conditional transfer of control instruction alters the sequence in which the instructions are executed if and only if a specified condition is met. Such conditions might depend upon whether the current contents of a storage location are positive, negative, or zero value.

A HYPOTHETICAL COMPUTER

The discussion of the previous section will be made more understandable by considering the operation of a hypothetical computer. This hypothetical computer, hereafter called HYPO, contains most of the features associated with real computers, but in a considerably less complicated manner. HYPO is a one-address computer with a special accumulator register to develop and to hold the result of the various arithmetic operations.

The storage unit of HYPO contains 1,000 locations of storage. The locations are addressed sequentially from Address 000 to Address 999. Each storage location can contain a 6-digit decimal number and a sign (+ or −). The word size of HYPO is thus 6 digits and a sign, as shown on Figure 6-2.

The contents of any storage location can be either an instruction or a datum. When the contents of the storage location are considered as an instruction, the interpretation of the various digit positions is different than if the information were considered as a datum. Figure 6-2 illustrates the two distinct ways that the information contained in a HYPO storage location may be interpreted. For convenience, the digit positions have been numbered from right to left, from 0 through 5.

When considered as datum, the content of Digit Position 0 is taken as the number of *units* in the number; the contents of Digit Position 1 is taken as the number of *tens* in the number; the contents of Digit Position 2 as the number of *hundreds* in the number, and so forth. For example, if the contents of the location referenced were:

$$+\ 0\ 1\ 0\ 3\ 5\ 2$$

the information would be interpreted as:

$$
\begin{array}{llr}
0 \text{ hundred thousands} & = & 0 \\
1 \text{ ten thousands} & = & 10{,}000 \\
0 \text{ thousands} & = & 0 \\
3 \text{ hundreds} & = & 300 \\
5 \text{ tens} & = & 50 \\
2 \text{ units} & = & \underline{2} \\
& & 10{,}352
\end{array}
$$

When considered as an instruction, the information is divided into three sections: the contents of Digit Positions 4 and 5 specify the operation to be performed; the contents of Digit Position 3 specify whether or not the index register feature is to be used; and the contents of Digit Positions 0, 1, and 2 specify the operand or storage-location address associated with the operation.

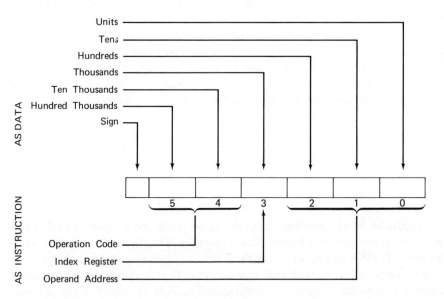

FIGURE 6-2. Computer storage word.

For example, assuming that the contents of the location referenced as an instruction contained the value,

$$+ \ 0 \ 1 \ 0 \ 3 \ 5 \ 2$$

this information would be interpreted as:

01 specifies the operation to be performed.
0 specifies that the use of the index register is inhibited.
352 specifies the operand address.

The instruction set of HYPO is extremely limited compared to that of most real computers. However, the variety of operations is sufficient to acquaint the student with the operation of a digital computer.

Since HYPO is a computer with a one-address instruction format — in addition to the various arithmetic, input/output and control instructions — various instructions specifying the movement between storage and the accumulator are required. Table 6-1 contains and describes the instructions HYPO can perform.

TABLE 6-1. Partial instruction set of the HYPO computer.

Operation Code	Operation	Description
00	HALT	Halt operation at this step; do not analyze any more instructions.
01	LOADAC	Transfer a copy of the contents of the storage location specified in the operand portion of the instruction to the accumulator, replacing whatever was previously in the accumulator.
02	STOREAC	Transfer a copy of the contents of the accumulator to the storage location specified in the operand portion of the instruction replacing whatever was previously in that storage location.
06	ADDAC	Algebraically add a copy of the contents of the storage location specified in the operand portion of the instruction to the contents of the accumulator, placing the result in the accumulator.
07	SUBAC	Same as ADDAC, except that an algebraic subtraction is performed.
08	MULAC	Same as ADDAC, except that a multiplication is performed.
09	DIVAC	Divide the current contents of the accumulator by the contents of the storage location specified in the operand portion of the instruction, placing the quotient in the accumulator and discarding the remainder.
10	JUMP	Transfer control to the storage location specified in the operand portion of the instruction. Interpret the contents of that location as the next instruction.
11	JACLEZ	Same as JUMP, except that the transfer is made only if the current contents of the accumulator is 0 or negative.
12	JACNZ	Same as JUMP, except that the transfer is made only if the current contents of the accumulator are not zero.
14	READ	Transfer the information contained on the data card currently located in the card reader to the storage location specified in the operand portion of the instruction. Position the next data card in the card reader.
15	PRINT	Transfer a copy of the information contained in the storage location specified in the operand portion of the instruction to the printer and print the information.

PROGRAMMING THE
HYPOTHETICAL
COMPUTER

Consider a program to sum five numbers. The program must obtain (i.e., read) the five numbers (data), calculate the sum, and make the result available. A program that accomplishes this task is:

PROGRAM 1: SUM FIVE NUMBERS

Address	Contents	Comments
000	+140013	Read the first number into Location 13
001	+140014	Read the second number into Location 14
002	+140015	Read the third number into Location 15
003	+140016	Read the fourth number into Location 16
004	+140017	Read the fifth number into Location 17
005	+010013	Transfer the first number now stored in Location 13 into the accumulator
006	+060014	Add the second number to it
007	+060015	Add the third number to it
008	+060016	Add the fourth number to it
009	+060017	Add the fifth number to it
010	+020018	Transfer the sum from the accumulator to Location 18
011	+150018	Print the contents of Location 18
012	+000000	Halt
013	+000000	
014	+000000	
015	+000000	
016	+000000	
017	+000000	
018	+000000	

In this program, the instructions in Locations 000 through 004 transfer the data into the computer so that it may be processed; the instructions in Locations 005 through 009 process the data, and the instructions in Locations 010–011 transfer and print the results.

This program illustrates the sequential operations of computers; once a program has started the instructions contained in consecutive storage locations are performed unless a transfer of control instruction is performed.

The program given to sum five numbers is not the only program solving this problem. The program given below is, in some ways, superior.

PROGRAM 2: SUM FIVE NUMBERS

Address	Contents	Comments
000	+140013	Read the first number into Location 13
001	+010013	Transfer the number from Location 13 to the accumulator
002	+140013	Read the second number into Location 13
003	+060013	Add the second number into the accumulator
004	+140013	Read the third number into Location 13
005	+060013	Add that number into the accumulator
006	+140013	Read the fourth number into Location 13
007	+060013	Add that number into the accumulator
008	+140013	Read the fifth number into Location 13
009	+060013	Add that number into the accumulator
010	+020013	Transfer the sum from the accumulator to Location 13
011	+150013	Print the contents of Location 13
012	+000000	Halt
013	+000000	

In this program, the data input and data-processing steps are intertwined.

Consider the total storage requirements for each program. Program 1 requires one instruction to input each number, one instruction to process each number, three instructions to output the result and stop, one location to store each number before processing, and one location to store the sum before printing. The total is $5*1 + 5*1 + 3 + 5*1 + 1 = 19$.

Program 2 requires one instruction to read each number, one instruction to process each number, three instructions to print the result and stop, and one instruction to temporarily store the current number and, later, the sum. The total is $5*1 + 5*1 + 3 + 1 = 14$.

Extending each program to sum 400 values increases the storage requirements for Program 1 to 1,204 locations and to 804 locations for Program 2. Since the storage size is 1,000 locations, Program 1 could not be used in this computer.

In actual practice, neither program would be considered adequate to sum more than a few numbers. Except for processing the first number, the same operations must be performed for each number (i.e., read the number, compute the partial sum). Under these conditions, it should be possible to simplify the problem by using a loop.

The sample programs shown here illustrate two important points:

1. The computer actually works or performs the indicated calculations in what is known as *machine language* (illustrated above). All computers actually work in machine language.
2. FORTRAN language is a way of writing a program familiar to the programmer. The FORTRAN program is then translated by an intermediate step into machine language.

We are here concerned with the writing of FORTRAN because it is a much more convenient way of instructing the computer, and because it is much easier and faster to write than machine language. Furthermore, the computer itself may translate FORTRAN into appropriate machine language.

QUESTIONS FOR DISCUSSION

1. A computer system consists of the five functional components listed below. Discuss each component.

   a. Input
   b. Output
   c. Arithmetic/Logical
   d. Control
   e. Storage

2. Some computers are called *fixed word-length* machines. Some are called *variable word-length* machines. What is the difference between the two?
3. What is a stored-program computer?
4. When a computer utilizes:
   a) nondestructive read,
   b) destructive write,
   what do these mean insofar as computer use is concerned?

5. A computer stores information as *data* the same way it stores the information as an *instruction*. How, then, is data distinguished from an instruction?

6. Define:

    a. Computer memory
    b. Algorithm
    c. Control unit
    d. Input/Output
    e. Peripheral storage

7. Follow this program and answer the question at the end.

```
FIRST   = 5
ABLE    = FIRST + 1
THIRD   = ABLE + 2
ABLE    = THIRD
FIRST   = ABLE
ABLE    = FIRST + 1
THIRD   = ABLE + 2
BAKER   = THIRD
ABLE    = BAKER
FIRST   = ABLE
LAST    = FIRST
STOP
END
```

What is the value of LAST?

7

Essex County Data
Edit — Summary Program

THE PROBLEM

One of the common problems for the historian and the economic historian who attempt to reconstruct the past efforts of human development and economic activity is the dearth of commonly usable measurable data. In the colonial period of American history, it was nearly 1800 before the government began to present statistical data series that are useful today in studying the process of economic growth and development. We know that Jamestown was founded about 1607, and that the Pilgrims stepped forth on Plymouth Rock sometime before 1620. From 1607 to 1800, however, the American economy is supposed to have just grown — presumably like Topsy. The question remains, however, whether there might be some consistent and continuous group of data that would be useful in developing the price and wealth indicators that are so badly needed in nearly all studies of history and economic history.

Our New England forefathers were extremely methodical in many things, one of which was the probate of estates preparatory to distribution of property to a descendant. The death records found in many of the old "quarterly court" records of the county courts are marvels of statistical detail. The present discussion concerns the information that could be derived from the Essex County Quarterly Court records as they were recorded between 1640–1682.

The purpose of this study was to attempt to develop a statistical series that would be useful in determining the following:

1. The progress of prices of individual commodities or assets between 1640–1690 (the early period of the British Navigation Acts).

2. To be able to develop, if possible, a consumer-goods or standard-of-living index and a capital-goods price index for Essex County.

3. To be able to examine wealth trends by year for that period, and to be able to answer specific questions such as those concerning the use of debt or credit instruments, the trend in holding various types of property, etc. While the general substantive conclusions are being published elsewhere, the methodology and the programming that went into the study may be of interest here.

THE DATA

If one is to examine estate asset inventories using a computer, then it is necessary first to keypunch the data into a form that is usable by the computer. Therefore, the first step was to establish a regular or standardized Hollerith-card layout for keypunching the raw data. The summary in Table 7-1 shows the form of the original data as it appears in the Essex County court records.

TABLE 7-1. Estate of John Huchison. (Taken from Salem Quarterly Court (November, 1676), pp. 230–31).

Inventory of the estate of John Huchison, who deceased about Aug. 2, 1676, taken Nov. 8, 1676, Nathaniell Ingersoll and Joshua Rea, and allowed, 29:9:1676, in Salem court: waring apparrell, 6li. 10s.; foure oxen, 18li.; five Cowes, 15li.; two three years old, 5li.; two yearling, 3li. 10s.; tenn sheep, 3li. 10s.; five Horsking, 5li.; one Horse, 4li. 10s; two Calfes, 1 li. 10s.; five Hogges, 3li .; sevenn pigges, 1 li. 15s.; two hundred ackres of land & medow & orcharde, one house & Barne - - - - ; in iron, 12s.; one friing pann, 1 iron pott, 13s.; tow axes & other tooles, 13s.; three parre Sheettes, 2li.; one wheell, tow pare pillowberes, 10s. 6d.; napkins, table cloth, 1 li. 2s.; Bassen & putter, 17s.; wooden ware, Cheste, 9s.; one fether bed, 3li. 10s.; woollen yarne & woole, 2li.; Rug, Blanketts new Cloath, 2li. 5s.; tow gunnes, 2li. 15s.; yokes, chaine, sheer, coulter, 1 li.; cleves & punn, foure pillowes, 1 li. 3s.; Engling corn & hay, 6li. 10s.; money, 7s.; 100 ackers of land with halfe the houseing in present possesion & 100 ackers of land, Revertion as appeareth By deed of giffte, 130li. Debts due to the estate, 7li. 14s.; 250 ackrs of land, 40li.; debts due from the estate, 15li. 10s.; total, 273li. 5s. 6d.

The first step was to keypunch the information onto cards in a standardized form so that the material would be available to the computer. Table 7-2 shows the form in which the information was keypunched. The table is interpreted as follows. Four cards were originally developed for each estate as indicated by Column 2 at the bottom of the table. The A-card showed the name of the decedent and the date of death. In this instance, one John Huchison died on the 8th day of November, 1676. The B-cards indicate the names of the persons who inventoried the estate. One of the interesting points developed from the inspection of the B-cards is that there was apparently some professionalism involved in inventorying the estates because the same names appeared quite frequently as the persons doing the estate inventory. This would tend to give a certain degree of consistency and uniformity to the estate records. The C-card shows the detail of the items of the estate. The D-card, later discarded as useless, showed the total value of the estate as shown in the clerk's inventory. This card was discarded because of some substantial errors noted in the

TABLE 7-2. Essex County Court Records (estate of John Huchison).

HUCHISON J	A JOHN HUCHISON		0811676
HUCHISON J	B NATHANIELL INGERSOLL		0811676
HUCHISON J	B JOSHUA REA		0811676
HUCHISON J	C001APPARRELL	WARING	100000000610000811676
HUCHISON J	C002OXEN		100400000180000811676
. . .			
HUCHISON J	C018PANN	FRIING	000100000000000811676
HUCHISON J	C019POTT	IRON	J001000000013000811676
. . .			
HUCHISON J	C053ESTATE DEBTOR TOTAL		100000000151000811676
HUCHISON J	D054TOTAL		100000027305060811676

1	1a2 3	4	5 6 7 8 9 10

arithmetic and because all estates did not have a D-card or total card. The C-cards then become the ones that we are primarily interested in in attempting to determine price and wealth trends in New England. The numbers at the bottom of the table refer solely to the C-cards.

The C-cards were divided into ten fields corresponding to the 80-column Hollerith card. Field No. 1, comprising the first 18 columns of the card, was for the last name of the decedent and the first initial. Field No. 1a showed the property type code — e.g., a number from 01 to 24 corresponding to the 24 types of property. The 24 types of property are shown in Table 7-3.

TABLE 7-3.   Essex estates property type codes.

Property Type	Code	Property Type	Code
Land	01	Dishware	13
Land & Realty	02	Household, NEC*	14
Real Property	03	Clothing	15
Farm Equipment	04		16
Farm Implements	05		17
Harness	06		18
Tools	07	Money	19
Livestock	08	Credit Assets	20
Food & Grains	09		21
Farm, NEC*	10		22
Household	11		23
Bed, bedding	12	Debts, Assets owed	24

*NEC = Not Elsewhere Classified

Field 2, which consisted of Column 21, was for the identification of the A-, B-, C-, or D-card. The items in each estate were numbered consecutively as they were punched. Therefore, each item in each estate has a card sequence number. The purpose of this was to give some control of the cards or items in each estate. This sequence number was punched into Field 3 of each card.

It may be well to mention a couple of techniques used (generally) to insure that all of the cards are present. In short, how can we insure that none of the cards have been lost or are out of place? This resolves itself into two problems:

1. Are all the cards that are supposed to be in each group actually there?
2. How many cards are supposed to be in each group?

This technique usually involves a "header" card for each estate, a "trailer" card for each estate, or some combination of both. We know, for instance, from Table 7-2, that the name changes each time that an estate changes. One technique would be to have the computer count the number of cards associated with each name, and to compare this count with:

1. The card sequence number in each card.
2. The card sequence number in the last card of the series.

This technique would not only show whether any cards were missing, but would indicate which ones were missing.

A second technique would be to place a header card at the beginning of each estate, with a field on the header card indicating how many cards were in that estate. A trailer card technique would work just as well.

The important thing to remember is that if it is important to your analysis to have the records available in a given sequence in a file, then it is necessary to insure the presence of all the cards through header and trailer cards and through program control. The development of Hollerith-card sequence numbers can be essential to this end.

The proper noun which named the asset or commodity item was punched into Field 4, which included Columns 25–58. Field 5 is a value code which was punched depending on the information given in the original inventory concerning the asset item. The original inventory of the estate had contained three types of items:

1) items which had a value associated with the named item,
2) items without a value associated with the named item,
3) items with a value for the named item and for certain previous items for which no value was given.

Items with a value, but not necessarily a quantity, were designated with a "1" in card Column 59, designated as Field 5. These, for instance, would include sequence Item 1 in Table 7-2. A number of the items appearing in the estate inventory had no given value. These items were identified with a "0" punch in card Column 59 and would include sequence Item 18 in Table 7-2. Some items, usually those items that were the final item of a series, contained a value that represented *not only* the named item but also all previous items that had no value associated with them.[1] This item is indicated with a "J" punch in Column 59 to indicate that the value contained in this card was for the indicated card and for all previous cards with a "0" in Column 59 (Item 19, Table 7-2).

Field 6 is designated as the quantity of the item or the measure of the item where indicated. The arrow in Column 6 shows that the indicated card column is a units digit and that any number appearing in the last two places of that field is a fraction. Field 7 indicates the value of the item in £ (pounds sterling). Field 8 indicates the value of the item in shillings, and Field 9 in pence. Field 10 (last seven columns of the card) indicates the day, month, and year of the date of death of the decedent. The field summary is given in Table 7-4.

TABLE 7-4.   Essex County study: Hollerith-card layout.

Card Field No.	Columns, Inclusive	Description
1	1–18	Name of deceased
2	19–20	Property class
3	21	Identifying letter
4	22–24	Card sequence number
5	25–58	Name of item or asset
6	59	Item control
7	60–64	Quantity (first three digits are units, last two are decimals)
8	65–69	Value, pounds
9	70–71	Value, shillings
10	72–73	Value, pence
11	74–75	Day
12	76–77	Month
13	77–80	Year (3 digits)

[1]This point was usually reasonably easy to determine, as semicolons (;) were used to separate grouped series items with a common value as well as to separate items with a given value for the named item. Reference is made to Table 7–1 for the interested reader.

Having keypunched the cards, and perhaps even verified them, it is now necessary to place the cards on magnetic tape or other mass storage devices. The process of placing punched cards onto a magnetic tape (form) is not necessarily completely without error. Therefore the immediate problem falls into two categories:

1. It is usually a good idea to edit the data as it is being placed onto tape.
2. It is usually a good idea to edit the tape to insure that all the cards supposed to be on tape are there, and that no extra records are present (no duplicates).

In the following discussion and questions, reference is to the data layout of the estate inventory records discussed in this chapter.

1. Write a program (or flowchart an algorithm) that would edit the data fields of record units being read from cards and being stored on magnetic tape. Refer to Table 7-2. The program should determine that:
   a) only numeric constants appear in numeric fields;
   b) only alphabetic constants appear in alphabetic fields;
   c) special characters appear where they are supposed to — if they are supposed to.

   In order to do this you will need a listing showing the way that the numbers, letters, and special characters are stored in the computer.

2. Once the data file is on magnetic tape, it is usually necessary to sort the file according to some desired scheme. One must then edit that file. While each person with his own data file would desire to edit it in his own way, let us recall the problem posed in this chapter. We have a relatively large data file on magnetic tape, say about 80,000 record units in the file. These are grouped by estate (decedent), and are in a prescribed order in the file, as described in the chapter. A header card may or may not precede each estate. What might be the purposes of this type of edit program? The following aims should be considered.
   a. The name on each of the estate cards should match either the name on the header card, or the name on the first card of the estate.
   b. The date on each estate record card should match the date on each other record unit or on the header card.
   c. None of the record units should be missing from any estate.
   d. There should be no duplicate record units for any estate.
   e. There should be no duplicate estates.
   f. There are as many record units in each estate as there are supposed to be.
   g. For each 0-card or cards punched, there is a J-group card.

   The point is, verifying the accuracy of information contained in large data files is a major problem for the social scientist. This is particularly a problem when the file is transferred from one form to another. The social scientist who simply assumes that his data file is correct is probably one who has done little work with data files on computers.

   Having considered the problems of editing data, let us proceed to some discussion of possible uses for the kind of data shown and the kind of programming needed to develop the data.

3. A historian using this data file may wish to know the following kinds of information:
   a. What is the total value of each estate?

      b. What is the average annual value and the annual aggregate value for the estates by year?

Discuss in class how such programs might be written to develop the required data. Write a flowchart (or an algorithm) that would develop such a program.

4. An economist using this data file may wish to know the changes in values and the rates of accumulation of capital — e.g., agricultural capital, commercial capital, money, etc. Assume that the economist is interested in the rates of accumulation of agricultural capital and commercial capital.

      Agricultural capital consists of property in code types 1,2,3,4,5,6,7,8,10.

      Commercial capital consists of property in code types 22,23.

Write a program (or an algorithm) to provide annual aggregate and annual average values for the two types of capital.

5. Ascertain the frequency of occurrence of agricultural property, commercial property, money, and ships in each year. Write a program or develop a flowchart algorithm to this end.

8

Historical Trade Analysis

The social science programmer is nearly always faced with three problems when working with large masses of data. *First*, when the data are too extensive to be placed in core, it is necessary to use some kind of peripheral-storage device. Magnetic tape is the cheapest form of mass storage and the most ubiquitous. Thus the social science programmer is nearly always faced with some kind of magnetic-tape data problem. *Second*, the social science programmer is faced with a problem of data coding. Whenever data are punched onto a Hollerith card there is nearly always some additional identification code put on the card for control purposes (as noted in Chapter 3). Often, however, the code initially put on the record unit is not the code that the programmer desires. Thus a problem of control codes appears, and must be solved. *Third*, there is the problem of efficient program utilization of data stored in core. This problem is related to the second problem, and we shall simply identify it as a problem of *pointers*.

For purposes of simplicity and appeal to diverse types of social science programmers, it is my intention to use a historical problem to help illustrate these three problems. It will be helpful if the reader remembers that social science data problems are always messy.

MAGNETIC-TAPE PROBLEM

One of the common problems for persons doing data work in the social sciences is the necessity to utilize magnetic-tape peripheral storage. The data are too extensive to place in the (random-access) computer core storage. It is necessary, therefore, to place the data on magnetic tape and to develop a program that will provide the necessary answers to specified questions.

There are two types of operations that a social scientist is likely to be concerned with when working with these kinds of large-scale data files:

1. The social scientist will want one or two "fields of information from *each* record in the magnetic-tape file.

2. The social scientist will want all the information from each record for only a few of the records from the magnetic-tape file.

Basically, the problem situation discussed in this chapter is a real historical situation, concerning English trade in the eighteenth century. The data constitute imports and exports — in constant sterling values — for England with every country or port involved in English trade. The time period is 1697–1801. This data file was relatively small, involving only about 7,000 cards which were placed on magnetic tape, illustrated in Figure 8-1.

The research problem, for the historian or the economist, might be as follows:

1. What were the changes in English trade volume in the eighteenth century, by country?
2. How did English trade with individual countries or ports of call — e.g., monopoly charter companies — change over time?
3. Did the percentage of English export or import trade change significantly over time? By country?
4. Did the various wars of the eighteenth century have a significant impact on English trade? On English trade with various ports or countries? On English trade with various regions?
5. Did the various Parliamentary acts (in England) significantly affect English trade with the various countries?
6. Group the trading areas by regions and proceed as above.

There are, of course a good many related questions that also could be asked. However, they would fall along the general lines shown.

The data source that would answer the kinds of questions considered above would be data concerning English commodity trade — both exports and imports — by country, for each year. It would be expected that the data would be expressed

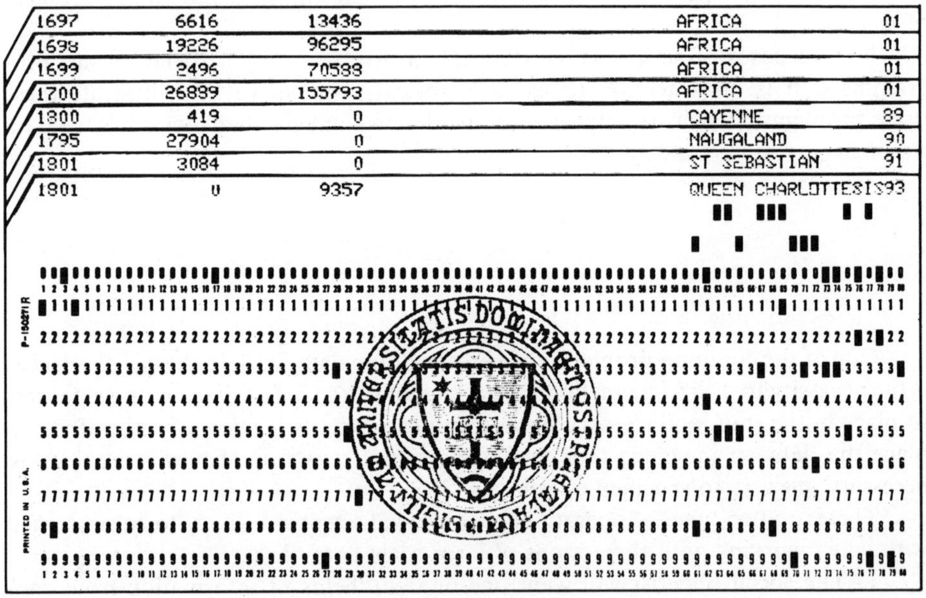

FIGURE 8-1.   Data input, English trade study. (The data file is ordered by country — 01, 02, 03, . . . 93 — by year.)

either in terms of physical commodities of goods *or* in terms of aggregate real values — e.g., values based on quantities times constant prices.

The data source used here assumes the values shown are real values of imports and exports. The data are punched into Hollerith cards as shown in Figure 8-1:

```
COLUMNS 1–4      YEAR
COLUMNS 5–17     IMPORT VALUE
COLUMNS 18–30    EXPORT VALUE
COLUMNS 31–159   BLANK
COLUMNS 60–78    NAME OF PORT OR COUNTRY
COLUMNS 79–80    PORT CODE. (A number unique for each port or
                             country trading with England.)
```

The data file is ordered by country and year, after the data are placed on tape, using a tape-sort program.

This problem is designed to focus on the English trade with the *old colonial system countries* — e.g., thirty of the countries (not all countries) that England traded with throughout the century as shown in Table 8-1. The problem, then, was to:

TABLE 8-1. Old colonial system trade.

American Colonies
    Carolinas
    New England
    New York
    Pennsylvania
    Virginia-Maryland
    Georgia

The Canadian Trade
    Newfoundland
    Hudson's Bay Company
    Nova Scotia
    Cape Breton
    Canada
    Belle Isle
    Quebec
    New Brunswick

The British West Indies
    Antigua
    Barbados
    Bermuda
    Jamaica
    Montserrat
    Nevis
    St. Christophers
    New Providence
    West Indies General
    Tortola
    Anguila
    Grenades
    Florida
    Dominica
    St. Vincent
    Tobago

1. Accept data from magnetic tape (see Figure 8-1):
   a. Accept some data from each record in the file.
      The data file would be read a record unit at a time. Data would be read from each record unit according to the appropriate field. The data would probably

be added into an accumulator or otherwise saved. The purpose of this part of the program is to develop appropriate base data for constructing index numbers. For instance, what percentage of the exports from England were exported in a given year?

b. Select certain records from the file and take information from those selected records.

The data file would be read a record at a time. Selection would be made on the basis of the PORT code, found in Columns 79 and 80 of each record; and on the basis of the YEAR, in Columns 1–4. Any desired calculations regarding trade volume for England, trade volume by country, significance of imports or exports in a country's trading pattern, etc. could then be developed.

2. Perform calculations on the data.

This would be approximately the same on any computer. If one desired to establish the percentage that the overall trade of New York was of the overall trade of *England* the procedure would be to:

a. Select the appropriate record units, and the appropriate data from each record unit (as in No. 1, above.)

b. Save the data in accumulators or defined areas as base data.

c. Make any needed calculations to find a percentage expressed as the relationship of a given datum as a fraction of the base value.

3. Print out desired individual port or country data (Table 8-1).

4. Label output data as indicated in Table 8-2.

The reader will have noticed that the discussion in this section of the chapter is set up more like a problem exercise than a narrative chapter segment. The reason is twofold. 1. Any dealings with mass data storage on magnetic tape is going to be messy. 2. Given the diversity of computer systems available to most programmers, and the variety of methods used by the various systems to handle files; there is really no right way to program this kind of problem.

TABLE 8-2.   Uniform column definitions.

ENGLISH IMPORTS:	The sterling value (in constant values) of goods imported into England from noted countries, ports, or colonies.
ENGLISH EXPORTS:	The sterling value (in constant values) of goods exported from England into noted countries, ports, or colonies.
IMPORT PERCENT:	The percentage of imports to England from a given location. Total English imports = 100 percent.
EXPORT PERCENT:	The percentage of exports from England to a given location. Total English exports = 100 percent.
INDEX PERCENT:	The sterling value of English Imports or English Exports from any location is expressed as a percent of a base. The base (100 percent) is the average of all years imports or exports for any location.
EXPORT BALANCE:	The amount of which English exports to any location exceed English imports from that location. If the number is preceded by a minus sign (—), the English imports from the location are greater than the English exports to that location.

In fact, the suggestion is that the reader or programmer concerned with magnetic-tape problems might well use the problem set up shown above and work out an algorithm for solving the problem on the computer system available to the user. For example, someone using a time-sharing system such as the GE DATANET 30 on a GE 635 computer system would solve the problem quite differently than someone using an IBM 360 series computer or someone using a UNIVAC 1108.

Having posed the problem, it is sufficient to leave it for the reader or programmer to decide how best the problem could be solved on the computer system available to the reader.

A PROBLEM OF CODING

The previous section concerned the manipulation of data for an individual country. Let us now consider the problem of aggregating the country data into regional patterns — e.g. American colonies.

TABLE 8-3. List of countries in the Whitworth Compilation: 1696–1801 (in order of initial entry.)

01 Africa	48 Cape Breton (Maritime Canada)
02 Canaries	49 Anguilla (Leeward Islands)
03 Denmark and Norway	50 Grenada (S. Windward Islands)
04 East Country (eastern Baltic)	51 Florida
05 East India	52 Dominica (Leeward Islands)
06 Flanders	53 Canada
07 France	54 Prize Goods
08 Germany	55 Scotland
09 Holland	56 St. Vincent (Windward Islands)
10 Ireland	57 St. Thome (variant of St. Thomas)
11 Italy	58 St. Thomas (Virgin Islands)
12 Madeira	59 Martinique
13 Newfoundland	60 Tobago (SE West Indies)
14 Portugal	61 Guadeloupe (Leeward Islands)
15 Russia	62 St. Eustatia (St. Eustatius; West Indies)
16 Spain	63 St. Lucia (Windward Islands)
17 Straits of Gibraltar	64 Havana
18 Sweden	65 Monti Cristi (Hispaniola)
19 Turkey	66 Belle Isle (off Newfoundland)
20 Venice	67 Quebec
21 Isle of Alderney	68 Isle of Man
22 Isle of Guernsey	69 St. John's Island
23 Isle of Jersey	70 St. Martin's (North Leewards)
24 Antigua (Leeward Islands)	71 Surinam
25 Barbados	72 Minorca
26 Bermudas	73 St. Domingo (Hispaniola)
27 The Carolinas	74 Cuba
28 Hudson's Bay	75 Curacao
29 Jamaica	76 Demerara (British Guiana)
30 Montserrat (Leeward Islands)	77 Malta
31 Nevis (Leeward Islands)	78 Trinidad
32 New England	79 New Brunswick (Canada)
33 New York	80 South Whale Fishery
34 Pennsylvania	81 New Holland (Australia)
35 Virginia & Maryland	82 Gibraltar
36 St. Christopher (St. Kitts; Leeward Islands)	83 Isle of Sark
37 Foreign Coin and Bullion	84 Yucatan
38 West Indies in General	85 St. Bartholomew (Leeward Islands)
39 Greenland	86 Falkland Islands
40 Georgia	87 Nootka Sound (Pacific Northwest)
41 New Providence (Nassau, Bahamas)	88 Buenos Ayres
42 Honduras Bay, Mosquito Shore	89 Cayenne (French Guiana)
43 Tortola (Virgin Islands)	90 Naugaland (Philippines)
44 Nova Scotia	91 St. Sebastian (Spain)
45 St. Croix (Virgin Islands)	92 Vera Cruz (Mexico)
46 British & Irish Linens, Foreign Trade	93 Queen Charlotte Island (Pacific Northwest)
47 British & Irish Linens, British Plantations	

TABLE 8-4.   English trade regions in old colonial system.

Country Code	Region and/or Subregion
	American Colonies
	Northern Colonies
32	New England
33	New York
34	Pennsylvania
	Southern Colonies
27	Carolinas
35	Virginia-Maryland
40	Georgia
	Canadian Trade
13	Newfoundland
28	Hudson's Bay Company
44	Nova Scotia
48	Cape Breton
53	Canada
66	Belle Isle
67	Quebec
79	New Brunswick
	British West Indies
24	Antigua
25	Barbados
26	Bermuda
29	Jamaica
30	Montserrat
31	Nevis
36	St. Christophers
41	New Providence
38	West Indies General
43	Tortola
49	Anguila
50	Grenades
51	Florida
52	Dominica
76	Demerara
56	St. Vincent
60	Tobago

We noted in Figure 8-1 that each year's data for each country was contained on a Hollerith-card image on magnetic tape. That card contained the name of the country, the year, the import and export data, and a country code. The names of the countries and the respective codes are shown in Table 8-3. The countries are grouped by region in Table 8-4.

The codes are arbitrary, in that they merely reflect the order in which the countries appeared in the original ledgers. The historian, in "following copy," has simply given each country a code number — e.g., Africa, 01, etc. — according to the position of the country in the document.

This poses a problem. The countries or country codes must be *converted* to a regional pattern as illustrated on Table 8-4. The problem is that there is no pattern to the coding that would be useful for regional data grouping. In order to accomplish the regional grouping the programmer has three options:

1. To distribute the countries to their respective regions using the existing codes in a computed GO TO statement.
2. To substitute a regional code for the country code in the main program.

3. To write a program that substitutes a new regional code for the country code on the magnetic tape.

Since we do not intend to write a complete program here, we shall simply indicate something about the alternatives. The reader may wish to expand one of these methods into a trial program or algorithm.

There are two specific problems involved here. The first is the computed GO TO statement to get each country into the correct region. There are 18 regions and subregions. The second problem is to provide storage for the regional data.

There are three types of data for each country, hence, three for each region:

A. Import values
B. Export values
C. Export excess

There are several ways to store the data in core for each region. A system of arrays may be used, with three arrays for each region.

It would be possible to set up three arrays for each region, one for imports, one for exports, one for excess or deficit exports. The computed GO TO statement is shown below:

```
GO TO (    11,    11,     8,     8,    13,     9,     9,     9,     9,     5,
1          10,    11,    12,    10,     8,    10,    10,     8,    10,    10,
2           5,     5,     5,    14,    14,    14,     7,    12,    14,    14,
3          14,     6,     6,     6,     7,    14,    13,    15,    13,     7,
4          14,    17,    15,    12,    16,    13,    13,    12,    15,    15,
5          15,    15,    12,    13,     5,    15,    16,    16,    18,    15,
6          18,    19,    13,    17,    17,    12,    12,     5,    13,    19,
7          19,    10,    17,    17,    19,    15,    10,    17,    12,    13,
8          13,    10,     5,    17,    18,    11,    13,    11,    17,    13,
9          10,    17,    13),ICODE
5 CALL DIST (BRISLI,BRISLE,BRISLB)
6,,,
```

There are 93 positions in the computed GO TO, one for each country. The label (number) appearing in each position is the statement number in the program that would control distribution of data for that country into the appropriate region. In this instance, a subroutine procedure could be used.

POINTERS

The use of so many arrays makes for extremely cumbersome programming. A simpler way to do this would be to define a table that has 54 columns, and 105 rows as suggested in Figure 8-2.

Three-column vectors would be assigned to each region: one for accumulating regional imports, one for regional exports, and one for regional export excess or deficit as shown.

The same type of computed GO TO would be required. However the program would handle only one data matrix, rather than 54 separate arrays.

A *pointer* would probably be used to keep track of the location of data in the matrix. The pointer would be three separate arrays that were 93 positions long. The location of each cell in the array would correspond to the number of the country. The contents of each cell would be the column number of the data matrix for the region.

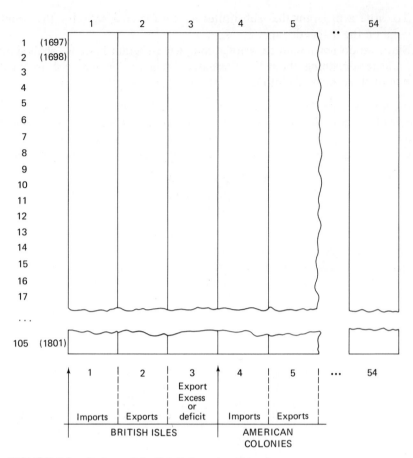

FIGURE 8-2. Data matrix: English regional trade.

For instance, we might have three arrays as on Figure 8-3. The three arrays show:

IPTIMP - Location in data matrix of regional imports for each country.
IPTEXP - Location in data matrix of regional exports for each country.
IPTBAL - Location in data matrix of regional export deficit or excess.

Figure 8-3 shows the three pointers. Each array is 93 positions (or cells) long, one for each country. In the illustration, country number 10 is Ireland. Ireland falls in the English trade region of the BRITISH ISLES.

As shown, all English imports from Ireland will be stored in Column 1 of the data matrix, the exports in Column 2, and the Irish export excess or deficit in Column 3.

Thus, from Figure 8-3, Ireland is Country No. 10. Therefore

IPTIMP (10)

gives the location in IPTIMP that tells the column vector number in the data matrix where the Ireland import data is placed. If the country code is read under the variable name ICODE, the designation would be:

IMPORTS: IPTIMP (ICODE)
EXPORTS: IPTEXP (ICODE)
EXPORT EXCESS: IPTBAL (ICODE)

This technique would shorten and simplify the program.

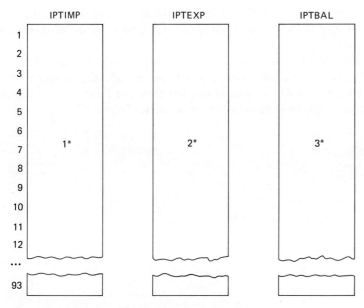

Refers to column vector in data matrix   (see Figure 8–2)

FIGURE 8-3.   Pointer: English trade regional data.

The contents of IPTIMP, IPTEXP, and IPTBAL would need to be set, either in the program or by a separate data section.

The reader may wish to work out this problem. The data matrix could be defined as:

DIMENSION DATAST (105,54) ·

QUESTIONS AND PROGRAMMING PROJECT

1. A third way of handling this problem would be to write a short program that would convert the country code on the magnetic tape into a more appropriate form.

    If we assume that the information is read from tape, the program would have to read the country code — e.g., Columns 78 and 80. Then the program would have to identify which region the country is in. The country code on the tape would then be replaced by a new unique code that
    A. Identifies the country.
    B. Identifies the region.

    Write a program that would recode the tape records. Refer to Tables 8-3 and 8-4. Use a four-digit code as follows:

    A. Regions and sub-regions numbered consecutively from 01 to 18. This regional code to go into Columns 77-78 of the tape "card" image.
    B. Countries within each region are to be numbered consecutively. This number to go into Columns 79-80 of the tape "card" image.

    If you don't like this code scheme, devise one of your own, and then write a program (algorithm) to change the codes.

2. The reader might wish to work out an algorithm to indicate how one could use only one array as the pointer (instead of three) to solve the problem noted in Part B, above.

3. The computed GO TO statement in Part B above permits a regional distribution (using subroutines) of all 93 countries. What modification would be necessary in the computed GO TO statement to analyze the three regions shown in Table 8-1, and to ignore data on all other countries (regions)?

9

Standardized Program Procedures[1]

What is a standardized or a "canned" program? It should be well understood that many of the problems of the social sciences have already been encountered. Therefore, it is reasonable to assume that programs have already been written to handle these problems. This type of program, when made general and acceptable to different types of social science research and computers, becomes a canned program. A canned program is a prewritten program supplied to researchers by some other individual researcher, research groups, or computer systems. Examples of some common canned programs are shown below.

Single-column frequency count

Frequently used in the social sciences, the single-column frequency count takes data that are coded on individual Hollerith cards and separates the card into columns which are classified as separate fields.[2] For the single-column frequency count to operate correctly, it is necessary that all the researcher's data — that is, *the answer to any individual question* the researcher has asked — must be coded in one column. After the program has separated each data card into columns, it will add up the number of like codes contained in each column. For instance, assume that Column 1 of data Card 1 contains a code from 0 through 9. Assume that there are 100 data cards. The program will now scan the first column of the hundred data cards and find out how many 0's are punched there, how many 1's, how many 2's, 3's, 4's, etc.

In Figure 9-1, there are five data cards. Each card has 10 data items punched in the first ten columns. If the reader will count the number of like codes in each column on the five data cards, he will easily recognize the purpose of such a program.

[1]Developed with Edward C. Piervallo, Manufacturers and Traders Trust, Buffalo, New York.,
[2]In this type of program, unless otherwise designed, single-column codes are assumed — i.e. each column a field. The reader may wish to review Chapter 3.

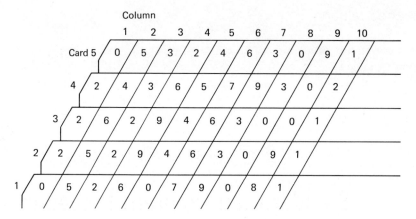

FIGURE 9-1. Frequency count.

The point is to indicate what answer to any particular question occurred most frequently. In Column 1 of each card in Figure 9-1 there are three 2's and two 0's. Therefore, in this example, the coded answer "2" appeared most frequently.

A frequency count may be obtained on any of the 80 columns as provided by the program. Programs may also be structured to handle more than one-column codes (fields) and more than 80 columns (in cases where there are more than one Hollerith card per respondent).

Two-column cross-tabulation

To explain the two-column cross-tabulation program, we will assume that an individual has sent out 100 questionnaires to 100 different universities and that each questionnaire contains 25 questions. The universities to which the questionnaires were sent ranged in size from 2,000 resident students to 25,000 resident students and included all male, all female, and coed classifications. We will further assume that upon receiving the return questionnaire, the individual researcher uses the first 10 columns of a Hollerith card to indicate the university from which the questionnaire was received. Columns 11 through 35 will then contain the answers to the questions with a coded answer which ranges from 0 through 9. Note that each card onto which the answers or the coded answers are punched will now contain 25 columns of information (Columns 11 through 35), and that each column will contain a coded digit from 0 through 9.

The purpose of the questionnaire was to ascertain the changing financial cost of sending a student through college. The hypothesis of the problem was that the small colleges, whether male, female, or coed, have increased their tuition fees proportionately more than the larger colleges. By cross-tabulating the columns which contain the code or type size of college with the column containing the amount of tuition increase at that particular college, we will have a good indication of whether or not the hypothesis was true. By cross-tabulation, we mean comparing the codes contained in each of these columns. We compare these columns, therefore, not only on the first data card but on all 100 data cards. Cross-tabulation, within limits, can be a good preliminary test of a hypothesis.

Linear correlation

Linear correlation is a commonly used statistical test to determine the relationship of one variable to another. It is a common proposition of economics that the general demand curve for any good is negatively sloped — that is, slopes downward to the right. If we wish to test this proposition, we could collect two types of data: first, the price of a good; and second, the amount of the good sold at each of the prices. Then, by using a linear-correlation program, we could correlate the cost of the good versus the amount of the good sold. If our proposition is correct, our curve should be negatively sloped, and our correlation should be very high, but negative (see Figure 9-2).

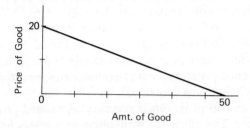

FIGURE 9-2. Linear Correlation.

As indicated by the above examples, a canned program is a computer procedure written by someone else, and that computer procedure (program) is available for use by others.

Why use them?

PURPOSE OF
CANNED PROGRAMS

Perhaps the best reason for utilizing a standardized program or a problem oriented language system is illustrated by the example of a statistics class at a well-known school. The students were given a problem consisting of two variables (X and Y) each with 80 observations. They were told to run a linear least-squares regression on the data and to calculate certain standard tests including the calculation for the slope of the line and the F-test. They were also told that they could use either an existing computer standardized program or they could use an electric or electronic calculator. They could work individually or together. For those students who used the electric calculator it took a total of 36 man hours to do the problem. For those who used the canned program on the computer, it took a total of 30 minutes (three tries) to punch the cards correctly, to make up the control cards, and 36 seconds for the computer to complete the run.

Thus, the economics of the situation seem clear. There is a considerable saving in time if one uses the computer in preference to doing work by hand.

Time affects both the individual with the ability to program and the one without. Obviously, the person without the ability to program does not have time to learn how to program. The person with a programmer's ability, depending upon the vastness of his research project, may not have the time to write a program. Therefore, the most advantageous alternative is to use a canned program. From the above discussion, it is apparent that the most important reason for using a canned program is time: *it takes advantage of computer technology and other people's labor*. Furthermore, it permits an individual to devote his time to the analysis of his final data, rather than preparing raw data for final analysis. There are other reasons for using canned programs, such as the type of research that requires a complex mathematical analysis. An individual may have the knowledge, ability, and time to program. However, he may not have the background knowledge to do a complex mathematical analysis. If there exists a canned program which incorporates this type of analysis, it is to the advantage of the researcher to make use of it.

Advantages and disadvantages of canned programs

One of the primary advantages of a canned program is the capability of performing repetitive operations on different combinations of the same data. This type of program is set up to handle any specific piece of data from a Hollerith card; it is not limited to just one, two, or three columns of Hollerith coded data. Many research projects, although guided toward one hypothesis, are capable of producing definitive results. The generality of canned programs makes available the repetitive use of data and the generation of more than one conclusion.

A second advantage inherent to canned programs is accuracy. A canned program has been used many times before. The efficiency with which it operates has been objectively tested. Therefore, it eliminates the possibility of error which might be encountered if an individual attempted to write his own program. This is an important aspect of the canned program. Any written or published results of a research project are highly scrutinized, thus, the possibility of error must be minimized. The use of a canned program effectively reduces one element of possible error.

A third advantage of the canned program is the ease with which it permits an individual to explain the methodology of his analysis. Many types of written reports on research projects require an explanation of a technique used. Much of this explanation will be up to the individual researcher. However, the person using a canned program can utilize the written explanation of the program in explaining the methodology he followed. This written explanation does not in any way explain any preliminary adjustments that were done to the data. It only explains the techniques for the final analysis.

The basic disadvantages in using a canned program are to be found in the limitation of the program itself, that is in the quality of the standardized program used, and the accuracy of the results to be expected.

The first point concerns the quality of the standardized program being used. The user must be aware of the formula used to develop the computer routine.

A standardized program is primarily a program that has been written by someone else for his own use and has then been generalized for wider use. For any given type of statistical study there are many statistical formulas and many computer programs for calculating the formula in slightly different ways. It is important, therefore, to have some idea of the nature and quality of the program you are using.

Let us give a very simple explanation. Following are two formulas for the calculation of standard deviation:

1. Unbiased Estimate of Standard Deviation (Standard deviation from sample variance):

$$s = \sqrt{\frac{\Sigma(X_i - \bar{X})^2}{N - 1}}$$

2. Maximum Likelihood Estimate of Standard Deviation (Standard deviation for population variance):

$$\hat{\sigma} = \sqrt{\frac{\Sigma(X_i - \bar{X})^2}{N}}$$

In the first instance the divisor is $N - 1$; in the second instance it is N. These are both estimates of a standard deviation of an unknown probability distribution from which the data were taken. Even people supposedly quite competent in a field may use the wrong standard deviation because the program's output is incorrectly or vaguely labeled. Furthermore without studying the program itself it is impossible to establish precisely which formula is used.

Thus, first you must know your data and the specific formula used in the canned program. An additional half-hour or hour spent in making sure of the nature of the canned program will not seriously disturb the economy of using standardized programs. One final point is that at times standard program procedures will use a very general labeling notation to identify the output of programs. This can lead to confusion and the user should always investigate if there is doubt concerning the meaning of a label.

The second point concerns: a) The algorithm by which the answer is computed; and b) The number of digits (significant digits) used by the computer in carrying out the calculations.

The point concerning the algorithm is illustrated by referring to the following two algorithms for calculating:

$$\sigma = \sqrt{\frac{(X_i - \bar{X})^2}{N}} = \sqrt{\frac{X_i^2}{N} - \bar{X}^2}$$

Theoretically the two algorithms give the same result. The second one develops much larger numbers before the final answer is obtained. The number of significant digits carried by the computer determines the accuracy of either (any) algorithm.

A third problem with standardized program procedures concerns the structure of data used as input to the program. For example, a cross-tabulation program may be set up only to handle *one-column coding;* in any one column of a Hollerith card, letters, numbers, or symbols can be punched. The coding scheme on any given research project, thus, cannot incorporate more than one column for any individual piece of data. If a coding scheme for a given project incorporates more than one column and this type of cross-tabulation program is utilized, the results will be meaningless. In such a case as this, if an individual wishes to use *the canned program,* he either must recode his data by hand, or write a program which will do it for him.

This technique of writing a program to convert data into a form which is usable for a canned program is a very common occurrence in social science research. If this situation of code field length arises, it can be handled by writing a small program to convert the data to suitable form. This would be easier than attempting to write the complex analysis already done by the canned program in order to handle two-column coding. The type of data conversion depends upon the individual and the type of canned program to be used. Once the limitations of the canned program are known, the individual can decide on a conversion method of his own.

Feeding data to, or converting data so that it can be fed to a canned program, is only the beginning of research analysis. The final stages of analysis require the interpretation of the results generated by the program. A canned program will write out or punch, according to a specified form, the results that are generated by the analysis of a particular set of data. Note that this form is specified and that it may not be to the liking of the individual using the program. In fact, it may very be difficult to interpret. This is a fourth disadvantage of canned programs. However, given time, most outputs are written so that they can be interpreted.

The only time that the method of output becomes extremely prohibitive is when the individual intends to use the printed output as part of a research report. *First*, it may require excessive explanation to those to whom the report is being presented. The person or persons to whom the research report is being submitted may not be familiar with research programming techniques. Therefore, the output included in the report must be explained in detail. This can cause confusion and occupy a lot of time. *Second*, the disadvantage of this type of output occurs when the researcher intends to use the program output directly as part of a publication. The method of output may not be suitable for book printing. In this case, it may require writing a specific program rather than using the canned program in order to acquire the type of output necessary.

TYPES OF CANNED PROGRAMS: OPEN AND CLOSED FORMATS

The FORMAT statement — its purpose

In order to properly use a canned program, the FORMAT statement of the FORTRAN language should be well understood. In its simplest form, the purpose of the FORMAT statement is to describe to the computer, in an understandable way, how data is to be read in or written out of an intermediate storage area. However, the use of the FORMAT statement is one of the most complicated and sophisticated parts of FORTRAN programming. By learning all the possible means of using a FORMAT statement, a programmer can make work much easier for himself, both in data input and data output. Canned programs are of two types: *open format* and *closed format*.

Open-format programs

An open-format program is one that is capable of reading a number of different forms of coding — that is, one-column, two-column, three-column, etc. Furthermore, it may be capable of accepting a variable number of format types. For a program which carries out mathematical calculations, only real numbers will be acceptable. In cross-tabulation, possibly real, integer, and alphanumeric will be acceptable. However, in the case where only real values are used, the variables may be acceptable in fields involving several columns, including signs and decimal points.

At this point, the reader is probably asking himself how a program, when it is canned, can handle different types of formats. The program cannot possibly contain every FORMAT statement that a researcher might use. There must be a more convenient method, and there is. It is known as *object formatting*. This particular type of formatting permits the programmer to read into the program, under a specified program-control-card format, another format *as data*. Referring to the program segment below in Table 9-1, the reader will find that the two READ statements read the variable FORM1. It reads this variable under FORMAT Statement 93. FORMAT Statement 93 says 12A6; that is, read 12 6-column fields and accept alphanumeric code — numbers, letters, or symbols. Furthermore, the variable FORM1 is in a

DIMENSION variable, being dimensioned to 12 words. The programmer would punch on a card the format exactly as he would punch it for the program, starting in Column 1 but omitting the word "FORMAT." This card would be placed as the second data card for this program. The second READ statement would assign these particular symbols — that is, parentheses and whatever other format types are listed between parentheses to the variable FORM1. When this is completed, the program continues. The computer, rather than having to reference a format statement number when executing the third READ statement merely scans the characters assigned to the variable FORM1 which occupies the position of a FORTRAN format statement number in the third READ statement. Data will be read in — according to the characters assigned — just as if a specific format for this purpose were contained in the program.

TABLE 9-1.   Open-format routine.

```
DIMENSION FORM1 (12)
        .
        .
        .

READ    (5,90) INPUT, LENGTH, COMP, ITERM
READ    (5,93) FORM1
        .
        .
        .

READ    (5, FORM1), (NAME(J, N + 1), J = 1, LENGTH)
        .
        .
        .
        .
        .
        .

93 FORMAT (12A6)
        .
        .
        .

        STOP
        END
```

Canned programs, even though generalized to handle many types of data and to provide for different types of output, cannot handle all possible situations; they have limitations. A program that is going to utilize statistical calculations cannot handle integer type formats. Most statistical calculations involve division. If this is done, an integer truncation occurs. It is not permissible for reasonable accuracy. Format flexibility is the most encompassing problem of canned programs. There are many other limitations with most canned programs. However, most of these limitations are inherent in the particular computing system and programming language being used. The size of a computing system will restrict the number of variables and observations of variables that can be analyzed. The language in use as well as the computing system will restrict the size of a data field which can be read (this minimizes permissible coding schemes for research).

Objective-time formatting is not acceptable to many programming languages, and all languages restrict the number of format cards that can be read as data. Even with these and their limitations, canned programs have become an effective and usable tool for the social sciences.

Closed-format programs

The closed-format program, as the name indicates, permits only one type of data in a specific coding form. It has a particular advantage, but not for the user. The advantage of this type of program is for the programmer. He does not have to anticipate any of the many possibilities of data types that a user will encounter. He only has to find the most general and incorporate that into his program. This permits ease in writing.

As an example of this type of program, a series of statements have been extracted from a closed-format program (Table 9-2). Note the READ statement which reads the data into the computer. It designates one FORMAT statement, but does not use a variable name. The FORMAT statement designated is particular to the program. The FORMAT is (8F10.5). All data must be punched in this form, as the program will accept no other. If the data are punched in another form, most computer systems will indicate that an error is involved. If it is punched in F-type format, however, and not in the proper columns, errors will result in the answers. The program will read in the wrong numbers, and will read in the numbers it is told by the fixed-format statement. If they are not punched in this manner, the numbers used in the calculations carried out by the program are in error.

TABLE 9-2. Closed-format routine.

.
.
.
.

15 FORMAT (8F10.5)
.
.
.

105 READ (5,15) (Y(J,I),J = 1,N)
.
.
.

STOP
END

Along with the disadvantages of poor data-input flexibility, there are several other disadvantages of closed-format programs. First, if it is the only program of its type available to a researcher, it can cause problems in data coding or in the conversion to fit proper coding. Second, statistical analysis very often requires extreme accuracy. If the program is not set up to handle double-precision elements, then certain amounts of accuracy are lost, and, for a particular research situation, the program may not be of value. Third, since data input cannot be manipulated in such a way that fits the desires of the user or researcher, then the output may not contain the particular series of results that are desired. Or, if the output does contain these results, it may contain them along with a list of other output which is unnecessary for the research being done. This requires, in the first case, either using another program, or writing your own; and, in the second case, the separating of the valid output from the invalid output.

At this point, the reader may be wondering how a general canned program originates. One source of canned programs is from those individuals who have done social science research. When their research was carried out no canned programs, or at least not the canned programs necessary for the research, were available. Thus, individuals were required to write their own programs. The result was, in many cases, the conversion of these individual programs into canned programs.

A second source of canned programs is from research groups. The programs supplied by 1) International Business Machines Corporation, 2) IBM Users Group, and 3) Biomedical Computer Programs written by the Health Sciences Computing Facility (Department of Preventative Medicine, Public Health School of Medicine, University of Los Angeles) are perhaps the best examples of this source.

With the advent and use of electronic data processing, most research groups have, as part of their membership, a staff of programmers. The programs written by this staff of programmers to carry out the operations of the research groups may result in a situation similar to that of the individual programmer. Many of the programs are versatile and can be generalized and are therefore supplied to other people doing the same type of research. The primary difference in having a research staff is that if a particular problem of social science is very common, this staff can be immediately assigned the task of writing a generalized program which can be supplied to other researchers working on the same type of problem.

Some canned programs are those supplied by a particular computing system. This type of canned program is supplied as a library routine and is part of the computing facility installed at any school or research center.

When a particular researcher is at a point where he wishes to use a canned program, he must both locate the proper program, and know how to properly instruct the program. There are a series of definite instructions which must be followed, and are known as the control portion of a canned program. Specifically, these are referred to as *program-control cards*. They constitute the instructions to the program itself. Each column of each control card has a designated use, and must contain that portion of control code which is designed to be punched there. The control cards for a canned program are passive instructions. They are read as data by the program and will precede and follow the actual data file to be analyzed.

The discussion below illustrates types of canned programs available to computer users, and illustrates something of the nature of the program control cards.

Programs originating from individual programmers

Single-column frequency count

Operationally, this type of program is set up to separate and count the punches contained in any individual column or columns of Hollerith cards. After totaling each of these codes, most frequency-count programs will determine what percent each code type represents of the total number of codes contained in any column of all cards. Note that, with some limitation of the number of columns that can be handled by the program, it will carry out this operation for all the designated data columns. Functionally, for research, this type of program has several purposes.

First, it can be used as a data sort. Since the program separates data by column, card, and code, it can indicate to the researcher the exact pattern of the data he has collected. The result is usually a better understanding of the type of analysis that has to be done.

Second, this type of program can be used as an indication of the proper collection of data. In the social sciences, when attempting to extract a sample, one generally will try to make a selection at random. However, the selection, due to poor methods, often tends to be biased. The frequency-count program, because it separates data, permits visual examination of the type of data selection. If the resulting data is biased in any way, it will become apparent. This results in the researcher having to eliminate some of his data or possibly begin again and make another selection of a hopefully random sample.

Third, the frequency count can be used as evidence of the direction of the hypothesis. By knowing the number and percentage of the different types of data appearing on the different data categories, one can make a preliminary estimation of the direction of his hypothesis. Frequency count would not indicate the final validity of a hypothesis. Other statistical tests are necessary for this; however, as is the case with the first example, it can and usually does indicate the direction of analysis or the statistical technique to be used.

In Figure 9-3, the reader will note a series of four cards for a single-column frequency-count program.[3] The four listed cards are what are known as the control cards for a canned program. If we look at the first card, we note that it contains a title — the name of some research project. This particular program is set up to label any individual sets of data read in. By consistent execution of the program, it can read in and do frequency counts on many sets of data files in sequence. This is the reason for providing a title for each data run. It gives a better understanding of the output in that it lets the researcher know what data source this particular output refers to. The second card included as an example contains the word CARD punched in the first four columns, and the numbers 0, 8, and 0 in the next three columns. This particular program is set up to read either card or tape. If we punch CARD here, it will refer control to that section of the program that expects the data to be entered from cards. If we had punched TAPE here, the program would refer control to that section of the program that will read tape. The three numbers punched in the next three columns indicate the number of columns on which we want frequency counts. Note that 080 columns refers to one data card. This means that we have one data card per respondant; that is, we asked, at most, 80 questions of each person who received a questionnaire. The program now knows the number of columns it must take frequency counts on.

The third card in Figure 9-3 is a presentation of a data card. The last card listed contains a star. This is an END-OF-FILE marker for a card deck. The program tests for the END-OF-FILE card by examining the first data field for an asterisk.

It should be understood that in many instances there are more than 80 columns per data record. In such cases, the program listed above would require one blank card after the END-OF-FILE card (Card 4, Figure 9-3) for each additional set of 80 columns or fraction thereof. The reason becomes apparent when one understands that the number of columns designated on the control card (Card 2, Figure 9-3) refer to the number of data items of each record. All these columns are read on one READ statement. Therefore, for each set of 80 columns, the program reads a data card. If there are more than 80 columns and there are no blank cards after the END-OF-FILE card, the program will fail.

---

[3]Program used at Social Science Training and Research Laboratory, University of Notre Dame, Notre Dame, Indiana.

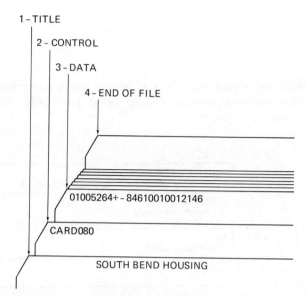

1 - TITLE
2 - CONTROL
3 - DATA
4 - END OF FILE

01005264+ - 84610010012146

CARD080

SOUTH BEND HOUSING

FIGURE 9-3. Standardized program: Program-control cards, single-column frequency count.

In cases where more than one data file is to be analyzed, the user only needs to repeat the system execute card and the control and data cards specified by Figure 9-3. The program deck need not be repeated.

Nonrepetitive lists

The function of a nonrepetitive list program will not become readily apparent to the reader unless he has had experience with vast amounts of data. Vast refers to situations in which each investigation involves more than 10,000 Hollerith cards. When one is involved in such a data bank, the possibility of repetition becomes prevalent, although it is obvious that the repetition is necessary for some analysis. The nonrepetitive list program is geared for just such a situation. It can readily eliminate repetition in data types without necessitating visual scanning.

To explain, an example of the above situation will be given. Assume that we have as a data bank all the ships that entered and left New York harbor from 1820 to 1860. This particular data bank would involve a large number of ships. Assume, secondly, that we are interested when writing up our analysis to know *not the number of ships*, but the *rig types* of the sailing ships that entered and left New York harbor. If this data is contained on the cards, it will be repetitious. Many ships under many different names and different captains were of the same rig type. To go through the bank of data by hand would be virtually impossible. The nonrepetitive list program, however, will go through the program rapidly and efficiently and select the rig types involved. If a second ship under a different name and different captain is of the same rig type as some other ship that has already been encountered, it will not be entered in the output. Therefore, we can rapidly determine the number of rig types that entered and left the New York harbor. The user's write-up for this standardized open-format program appears below.[4]

[4]Program used at Social Science Training and Research Laboratory, University of Notre Dame, Notre Dame, Indiana.

Nonrepetitive list

The problem

In general, a nonrepetitive list is generated for the records which comprise a data bank. Tests for repetition are made across as many as 80 data fields.[5] The program-control cards are shown in Figure 9-4.

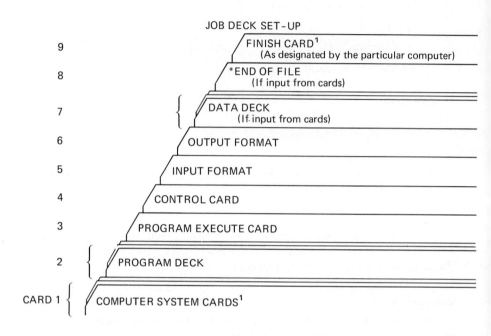

JOB DECK SET-UP

9   FINISH CARD[1]
(As designated by the particular computer)

8   *END OF FILE
(If input from cards)

7   DATA DECK
(If input from cards)

6   OUTPUT FORMAT

5   INPUT FORMAT

4   CONTROL CARD

3   PROGRAM EXECUTE CARD

2   PROGRAM DECK

CARD 1   COMPUTER SYSTEM CARDS[1]

1. Furnished by individual computer system and varies with each system.

FIGURE 9-4. Nonrepetitive list program-control cards.

The program

The program operates by setting up a blank array. The first set of data fields of the first record (as designated by the user) are read into this array. Each of the remaining data fields of the remaining records are read and compared with those data fields already appearing in the array. If the data fields of the record being read are the same as the data fields of some record already appearing in the array, they are eliminated; if not, they are entered into the array. As program execution continues, each record contained in the nonrepetitive array is printed.

Input

Program-Control Card (Card No. 4, Figure 9-4). A program-control card is necessary to designate to the program:

1. The source of data input (*tape* or *card*).
2. The number of data fields being read (max: 80, 1 column = 1 field).
3. The first data field on which the test for equality is to be made.
4. The last field on which the test for equality is to be made.

[5]A character or series of characters on a Hollerith card or magnetic tape which are assigned to some variable name; here 1 column = 1 field.

The control card is punched as follows:

Columns	Content
1–4	CARD or TAPE (depending on the source of data input)
5–6	The number of data fields per record being read in e.g., (80)
7–8	The first field to be used in the comparison e.g., (05, 03, 65, 41)
9–10	The last field to be used in the comparison e.g., (64, 48, 78, 42)

Data

As stated above, data can be entered from card or tape. A maximum of 80 data fields per record are permitted. The length of a data field must remain within the allowable limits of the particular computer system in use, and must be read under I or A-type format.

Format cards

This particular program utilizes object-time format. It permits the user to read in the input and output formats as data. In doing so, certain restrictions are placed on the user:

1. Both the input and output formats must appear in the first 72 columns of a Hollerith card.
2. Both input and output formats must be of A or I type.[6]
3. The format must be punched in the same way as a normal FORTRAN IV format, with the statement number and the word FORMAT eliminated (Detail Cards No. 5, 6, Figure 9-4): (80A1), or (A1, I2, A4, 16A1).
4. Only two format data cards are permitted. The first designates the input format; the second, the output format (Cards No. 5, 6, Figure 9-4).
5. If input is from cards, the format must read a 1-column alphanumeric character as the first data field (Detail Card No. 5, Figure 9-4): (A1, I2, A4, 16A1) or (80A1).[7]

End-of-file-card

When data is read from cards, it is necessary to place a card at the end of the card deck to mark the end of the data file. This card is punched as the last data card (Card No. 8, Figure 9-4) as follows:

Column	Content
1	* (Asterisk)

Program limitation

Due to the memory capability of the particular computer in use,[8] a nonrepetitive list will be only 300 records in length on output. Each record can consist of a maximum of 80 data fields. If there are more than 300 nonrepetitive items in the data bank being analyzed, then repetition will (or can) appear between each set of 300 records which are printed on output.

Output

1) Nonrepetitive list of the data records under consideration, based on the first and last fields for comparison, designated by the user on the control card.

---

[6]The test for the end of a data file is based on the character which appears in the first column.

[7]Note that all the fields are one-column alphanumeric characters.

[8]If the computer to which the user has access has larger memory capability, then the program can be easily modified to produce a larger nonrepetitive list.

2) Message indicating that the maximum of 300 records were entered into the array used for comparison.

RECYCLE TOO MANY ENTRIES

3) The total number of records which were printed as being nonrepetitive, even if there are more than 300.

As indicated above, the nonrepetitive list program is subject to limitations.[9] This is primarily due to the available storage in a computer. The amount of data that can be stored in a nonrepetitive list matrix is limited. In this program we store a matrix that is 80 by 300. Note that this takes up 24,000 locations of memory. To attempt to make the matrix larger could take up too much memory. This fact presents a problem since our matrix can only contain 300 columns, our nonrepetitive list can only involve 300 nonrepetitive records. In the case of this program, if the matrix is full, that is, if all 300 columns are full, control will refer to Statement 90 which will print out RECYCLE TOO MANY ENTRIES. It will then refer back, set the column number to 0, and start again. If there are more than 300 items which are nonrepetitive, the program will represent a minor amount of repetition. Depending on the amount of nonrepetitive items, the program can be said to be relatively efficient.[10] It will generally permit visual examination of the output which will, in turn, allow the researcher to eliminate them by hand if there are more than 300.

Programs originating from research groups

The BMD package

The BMD Package, or Biomedical Computer Programs, is a set of statistical programs available for any size computer from the Department of Preventative Medicine, Public Health School of Medicine, University of California, Los Angeles [11] The BMD Canned Programs are the standard statistical programs available today. Table 9-3, following, shows a list of the programs available in this package and a reference to the description of each of the programs.

It is well to note here that there are two primary disadvantages to the BMD Package. First, it does not allow for the output of one program to be immediately fed to another. It requires that there be an intermediate storage area, primarily, magnetic tape. Second, most of the BMD programs do not allow for punched output. The result is that if one has a program that is not set up to handle tape or some other form of peripheral storage, he cannot use the data available from the BMD program immediately. Rather, it must be repunched by hand onto cards.

Princeton standardized routines

P-Stat is an evolving user-oriented language for the statistical analysis of social science data.[12] This describes P-Stat tapes, Version 51.

[9]This is generally true of all canned programs and is discussed in more detail below.

[10]Input data files should be sorted before using the nonrepetitive list program. This will eliminate repetition in the output units.

[11]BMD, Biomedical Computer Programs, (Los Angeles, Health Sciences Computing Facility, Department of Preventive Medicine and Public Health, School of Medicine, University of California) p. 35. Program development (for the BMD) was accomplished on the IBM 7090/7094 using the IBM FORTRAN II Monitor System. Many other systems can accommodate programs written in FORTRAN II. Programs may be converted for FORTRAN IV.

[12]All requests for further information on these routines should be addressed to Dr. Roald Buhler, Director, Computer Center, Princeton University, Princeton, New Jersey.

TABLE 9-3. Biomedical computer programs

Description and Tabulation

    Simple data description
    Correlation with transgeneration
    Correlation with item deletion
    Alphanumeric frequency count
    General plot including histogram
    Description of strata
    Description of strata with histograms
    Cross-tabulation with variable stacking
    Cross-tabulation, incomplete data
    Data patterns for dichotomies
    Data patterns for polychotomies

Multivariate Analysis

    Principal component analysis
    Regression on principal components
    Factor analysis
    Discriminant analysis for two groups
    Discriminant analysis for several groups
    Canonical analysis
    Stepwise discriminant analysis

Regression Analysis

    Simple linear regression
    Stepwise regression
    Multiple regression with case combination
    Periodic regression and harmonic analysis
    Polynomial regression
    Asymptotic regression

Special Programs

    Life table and survival rate
    Contingency table analysis
    Biological assay: Probit analysis
    Guttman scale preprocessor
    Guttman scale #1
    Guttman scale #2, Part 1
    Guttman scale #2, Part 2
    Guttman scale #2, Part 3
    Transgeneration
    Transposition of large matrices

Time Series Analysis

    Amplitude and phase analysis
    Autocovariance and power spectral analysis

Variance Analysis

    Analysis of variance for oneway design
    Analysis of variance for factorial design
    Analysis of covariance for factorial design
    Analysis of covariance with multiple covariates
    General linear hypothesis
    General linear hypothesis with contrasts
    Multiple range tests
    Analysis of variance

A collection of statistical programs written for the IBM 7094 and the IBM System 360 (128 K and 256 K versions),[13] P-Stat has the capability of handling large amounts of data. However, at present, the system cannot handle much more than approximately 10,000 rows in a matrix. A matrix of more than 15,000 rows may not fit on a 2,400-foot tape. The system operates most efficiently with a matrix of 2,000 or fewer rows. Matrices may include up to 150 columns.

Currently, P-Stat includes approximately 80 different operations including matrix operations, various types of intercorrelations, and statistical operations such as regression, factor analysis, rotations, etc. It is not claimed that P-Stat can handle all statistical or other operations at present; however, the system is open-ended and may be modified.

To get an idea of how the P-Stat system works, consider a card file drawer with perhaps 80 programs in it. Each of these is separately bound with rubber bands. Consider another drawer which has a number of separate sets of data in it. A user decides that he wants to perform some single operation using two of his sets of data. He selects the programs that he wants from the one drawer and the data from the second drawer. He then goes to the computer and performs the desired operations, and takes the output from the computer as punched cards. The user labels the punched output and adds it to the existing data file drawer and returns the programs to their drawer. He then returns to his notes to see what the next operation is, and performs this next operation the same way that he performed the last; that is, he gets the new programs from the one drawer, and the newly desired data, and returns to the computer.

The important point to be noted here, from a user's point of view, is that the output data from one program may be used as the input data for the next, or the original data may be reused.

In some ways the P-Stat system is like the file drawer with the 80 separate programs in it. The P-Stat tape is in fact a FORTRAN chain tape with 30 separate links on it. The 80 operations are created from these links in various combinations. The basic principle in P-Stat is that the output from any operation can be the input for any other operation. The file drawer of data is simulated by the user's permanent data tape, which at any point may be a mixture of matrices of input data and matrices of intercorrelations of other results of operations from a number of different runs. The program is machine independent and written in FORTRAN II

Programs supplied by computing systems

Printer-plot routine

The purpose of the printer-plot routine is quite simple. It is meant to plot, in two-dimensional form, calculations done by the user or researcher. The fact that it is a printer plot means that it will be done with the normal symbols available to a particular computer system and handled by the on-line printer. This is as opposed to several other methods of graphing, one of which is a plotter which does not use

[13]The work leading up to the development of P-Stat in its present form was aided by a National Science Foundation grant, NSF GP 579. These studies were also aided by a contract (NR 301–921) between Princeton and the Office of Naval Research, Department of the Navy. Not all of the FORTRAN programs included originated at Princeton. Details of the various components and contributers can be obtained from Roald Buhler, Princeton University, by requesting the manual describing P-Stat, Version 51.

symbols, but rather draws what is asked for in line form. This would be available for most standard computer systems from the respective company or user group.[14]

User routine: program-control cards

In the introduction to this chapter, a cross-tabulation program was described.

The cross-tabulation program, as explained, is to compare two or more separate columns of data for all the data respondents involved and match the different types of codes. In a two-column cross-tabulation, two columns as designated by the analyst or user are picked up by the program and cross-tabulated according to the code contained in those columns. If there are more than two columns and the program is set up to handle more than two columns, then the user would designate the number of columns he wishes to cross-tabulate and the program would carry out this function in the same manner that it handled the two-way cross-tabulation. As an example of the use of a cross-tabulation program, let us assume that we wish to know which bank in a particular city has the most accounts (and why). Further, assume that we handle the research by means of a questionnaire to a group of people. The two important questions on this questionnaire, for our example, would be, "What bank do you bank with?" and "Why?" giving a list of conveniences offered by banks.

The person answering the questionnaire would mark the bank at which he has an account and then select those conveniences which persuaded him to use this particular bank. We place the data from the questionnaire on cards including the two columns of data from the two questions referred to above and we could use a cross-tabulation program to make a preliminary judgment on the reasons why some banks have more accounts than others. We could cross-tabulate the column containing what bank is used *with* the column containing the conveniences offered by a bank. This would give a reasonable estimate of the most influential convenience offered, as well as the descending order of influences. It would do the reader well to remember that the use of cross-tabulation is generally not a final basis for accepting or rejecting a hypothesis; it only gives a preliminary estimation.

Normally, statistical or other analytical tests must be used to make a valid judgment. It is known that in North Africa the number of children who die increases rapidly as a percentage of population during the heat of the summer. It is also known that the heat of the summer has a tendency to melt the tar on the streets. If these two things are placed on data cards and a cross-tabulation program is run, the result would be that heat and melting tar are the cause of dead children. If the person doing the research thought the cross-tabulation program was a final judgment, he would make a grave error.

Cross-tabulation is a common and effective tool of the social sciences. This is particularly true with questionnaire research. However, as explained above, it should be used with caution and for purposes other than a final analysis. Many of the purposes, as described under frequency-count programs, are the same for the cross-tabulation. Only if a research report is a preliminary study should a cross-tabulation program be considered a final means of estimation.

[14]There are several examples of plot routines:
Daniel D. McCracken, *A Guide to Fortran IV Programming* (New York; John Wiley & Sons, 1965), pp. 93–101.
IBM Systems Reference Library, *IBM 1620–1627 FORTRAN Plotter Subroutines*, File Number 1620–25, Form C26–5841–1. A sample program is shown for the plotter for use with FORTRAN II and FORTRAN IId. The sample program is shown on pp. 6 and 7 of the noted IBM manual.

So far we have discussed what a canned program is, what its sources are, what the types are, and how to use them. However, in the course of explaining these statements, we mentioned that it is sometimes necessary to convert data as might be the case if a closed-format program is being used or if the limitations of an open-format program require it. An example of the need for data conversion is discussed below under "Multiple linear regression, a standardized routine."

Multiple linear regression, a standardized routine[15]

Problem description
Multiple linear-regression analysis is performed for a set of independent variables and a dependent variable. Selection of different sets of independent variables and designation of a dependent variable can be made as many times as desired.

It is often necessary to convert one's data in order to fit into the schematic format of a canned program. This can be the result of several different "factors." First, the person carrying out the research may have no prior knowledge of programming and therefore no way of knowing how to code his data on the Hollerith cards. If he attempts to do this without prior consultation, it may result in having to revamp the data before doing the actual analysis. Second, the data used in a particular research project is often not collected by the person directing the research. It may have been collected by some other research group or person and have already been set up in a separate coding scheme. If the researcher now using this particular set of data wishes to use a canned program, it may be necessary to adjust the data to fit the particular program desired. Third, even if data are coded in such a way that it could be handled by a canned program, the data may not lend itself to proper analysis; that is, it may be written in such a way that even using the canned program would yield meaningless results.

Assume that we desire a multiple-regression analysis on four variables. Assume also that the program to carry out this analysis is set up to handle at least eight observations of one variable on each input card, continuing until all the observations for that variable are concluded. A new card is used for each of the remaining variables, as shown on Figure 9-5.

Before any type of conversion can be made, it is important to reiterate the nature of the test being used. The regression analysis here indicates direction (of change) and *dependency* of one variable on another. If a shift occurs from one factor or variable to another, that shift will be noted.

A preliminary hypothesis in a research project involving an underdeveloped area might suggest that there is a shift in the nature of economic activity from the (less advantageous) agricultural activity to the (more advantageous) commercial production.[16] It is supposed that this will be shown by the increase in the (relative) volume of commercial capital over a 40-year period, by the increase in the value of

[15]International Business Machines, *IBM Application Program*, System/360 Scientific Subroutine Package, Programmers Manual (New York, 1966), pp. 95ff. Multiple Regression Program.

[16]The complete analysis being developed by this research project is beyond the scope of this book. However, before any of the analysis could be carried out, a preliminary test had to be made to determine whether the hypothesis being considered had any element of validity. The reason for this preliminary test stems from the type of data and the type of result being considered. If the hypothesis is not reasonably true, then the model being worked on has only a low probability of success. Therefore, the preliminary test will indicate to the researcher whether this model or some other model might be better suited for the type of data available (see Chapter 13).

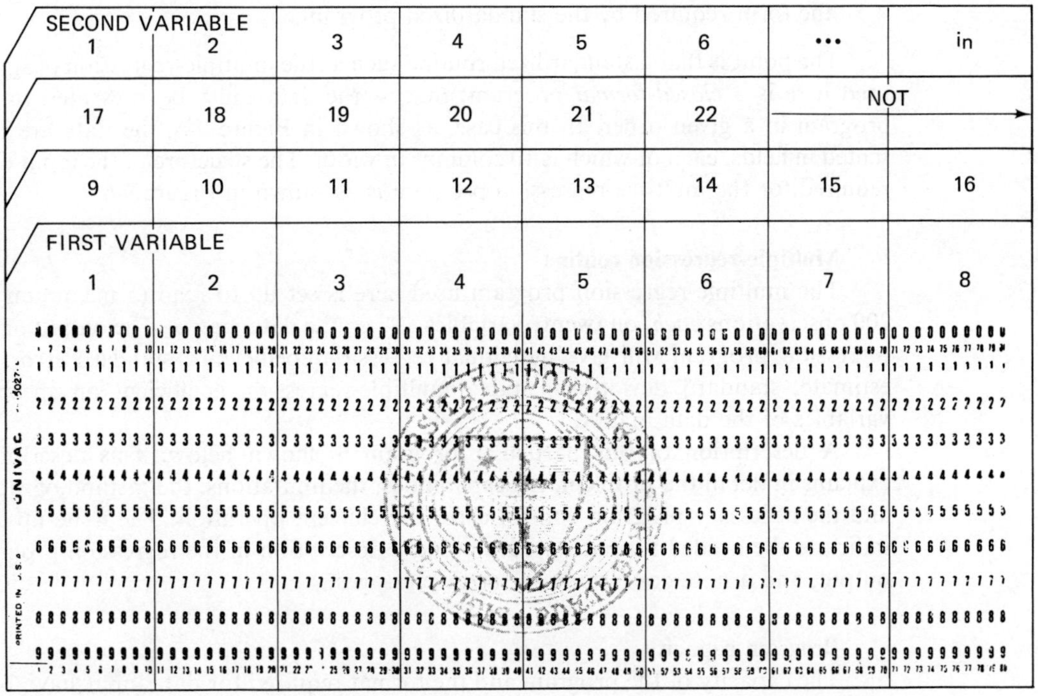

SECOND VARIABLE 1	2	3	4	5	6	•••	in
17	18	19	20	21	22	NOT →	
9	10	11	12	13	14	15	16
FIRST VARIABLE 1	2	3	4	5	6	7	8

FIGURE 9-5. Sample: Hollerith-card format — data structure for multiple regression. NOTE: Data are entered on eight 10-column fields for each card. Multiple cards are used as indicated. In the example here, we are assuming that the multiple-regression program requires that observation for each variable be presented with no more than eight observations to a card, using as many cards as are needed to contain all of the observations for each variable. The fields (8 to a card) are shown as spaces, separated by vertical lines. Each field (for each observation) is numbered.

commercial capital, and by the amount of credit, debts, and currency (cash) encountered in the period.

A regression model operates by examining direction of change and the dependency of one variable on another. In this instance, agricultural capital is one variable, and commercial capital is a second variable. If agricultural capital (one variable) is presented to the program in the data *form of average annual values*, then commercial capital (the second variable) must be presented in the same way.

The data must be presented to the multiple-regression program, eight observations per Hollerith card on six Hollerith cards per variable (file). If the data are available on a file, one observation per record, then these data must be converted to the required form of eight observations per card. This second conversion may occur either by writing a program to place the data card values from one form to another, or by keypunching the data in the required form.

The problem of converting data from its original or primary form to that required by the multiple-regression standardized routine consists of two steps:

1. Getting the raw data into uniform and homogeneous categories — i.e., land or money, agricultural capital, etc. — and into the same value form — i.e., average annual value.

2. Getting the uniform grouped data — i.e., money or agricultural capital — into the form required by the standardized program.

The point is that a standardized routine such as the multiple-regression program used here is a *closed-format* program; that is, the data must be presented to the program in a given order. In this case, as shown in Figure 9-6, the data are presented in fields, each of which is 10 columns in width. The structure of the input data required for the multiple-regression program is as shown in Figure 9-6.

Multiple-regression routine

The multiple-regression program used here is set up to read (a maximum of) 200 observations *each*, on twenty variables — i.e., the data matrix. The output of the regression program will give individual regression coefficients, standard errors of estimate, standard deviations, and a multiple-regression coefficient on specified variables of the data matrix.

A description of this particular program is shown below. This description explains in detail the problem, the capabilities, the limitations, the method of input, and the necessary program control cards for efficient operation. The write-up also indicates the needed format for data input, a description of the regression program output, and a note concerning the error messages.

Program capacity

The capacity of the program and the format required for data input have been set up as follows:

1. Up to 20 variables including both independent and dependent variables.
2. Up to 200 observations per variable.

Input

Control card: One control card is required for each problem. This card is prepared as follows:

Columns	Contents
1–6	Problem number (may be alphanumeric)
7–11	Number of observations (right justified)
12–13	Number of variables
14–15	Number of selection cards (see below)
16–17	01 if punched output is desired (predicted value of dependent variable).

Leading zeros are not required to be keypunched.

Data cards

Input data are read into the computer one variable at a time; i.e., if 42 observations are available, the first variable is read in on five cards plus two fields on the sixth card. Begin a new card for each variable.

Selection card

The selection card is used to specify a dependent variable and a set of independent variables in a multiple linear-regression analysis. Any variable in the set of original variables can be designated as a dependent variable, and any number of the remaining variables can be specified as independent variables. Selection of a dependent variable and a set of independent variables can be performed over and over again using the same set of original variables.

The selection card is prepared as follows:

Columns	Contents
1–2	Option code for table of residuals 00 if it is not desired, 01 if it is desired.
3–4	Dependent variable designated for the forthcoming regression.
5–6	Number of independent variables included in the forthcoming regression (the subscript numbers of the individual variables are specified below).
7–8	First independent variable included.

FIGURE 9-6. Input data: Multiple-regression program (4 variables, 42 observations each).

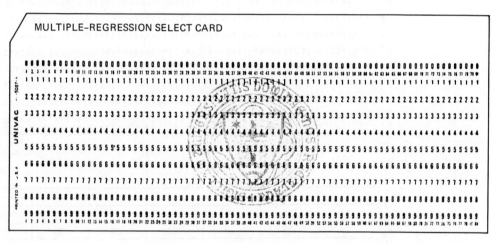

Credits*

FIGURE 9-6. (continued)

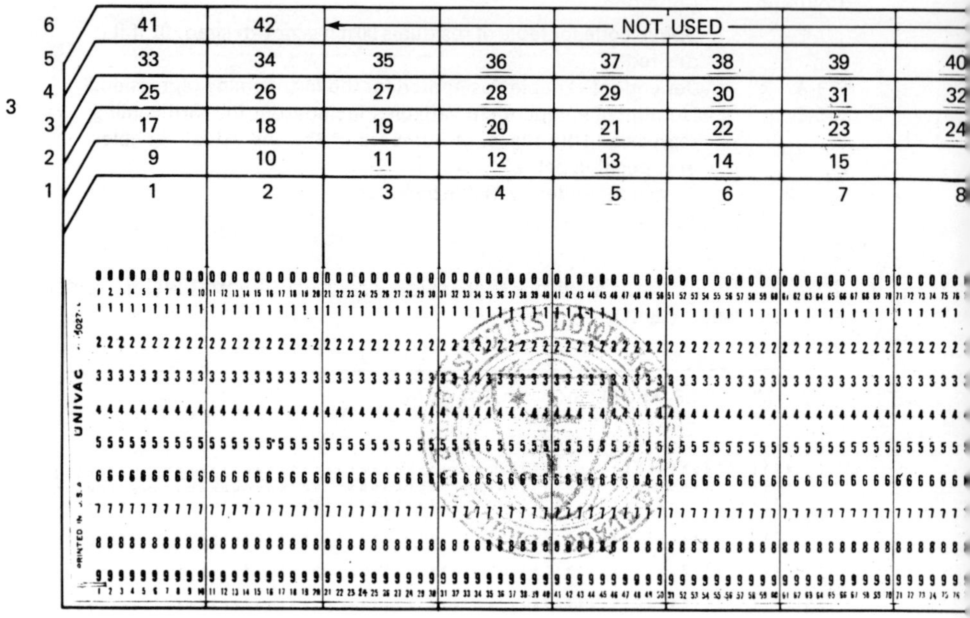

6	41	42	←		NOT USED			
5	33	34	35	36	37	38	39	40
4	25	26	27	28	29	30	31	32
3	17	18	19	20	21	22	23	24
2	9	10	11	12	13	14	15	
1	1	2	3	4	5	6	7	8

MONEY*

6	41	42	←		NOT USED			
5	33	34	35	36	37	38	39	40
4	25	26	27	28	29	30	31	32
3	17	18	19	20	21	22	23	24
2	9	10	11	12	13	14	15	16
1	1	2	3	4	5	6	7	8

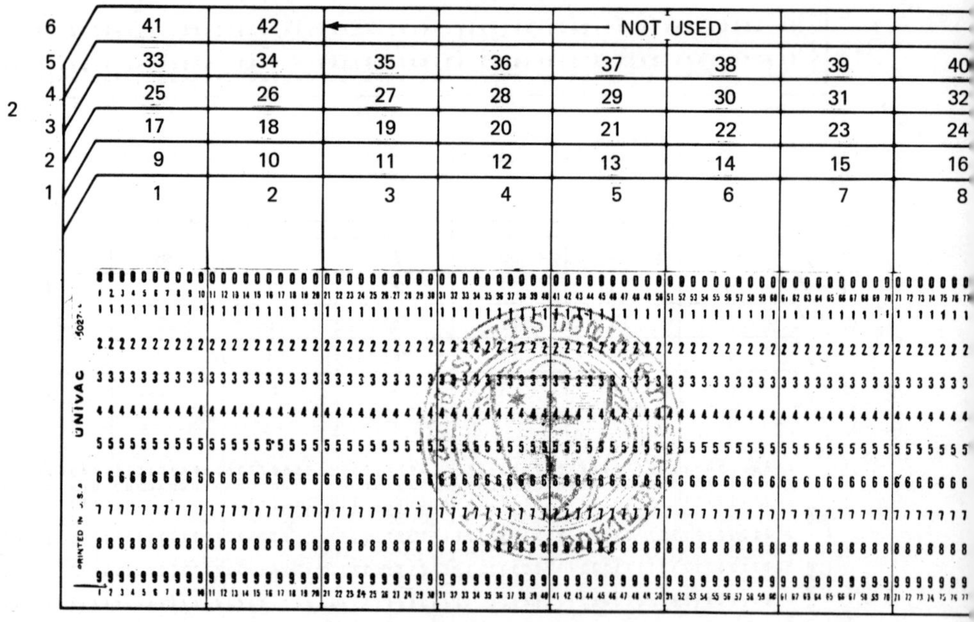

COMMERCIAL CAPITAL*

FIGURE 9-6. (continued)

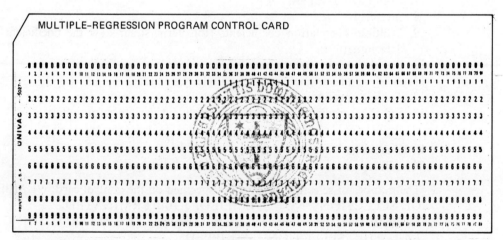

AGRICULTURAL CAPITAL*

MULTIPLE-REGRESSION PROGRAM CONTROL CARD

*All variables in £ Sterling — e.g., Average Annual Values — are uniform and rounded to nearest £ value. The value in Field 1 for each variable is the value for 1641. The value in Field 42 is for 1682. The program-control cards assign 42 observations for each variable, or 6 cards. Variables may be arranged in any desired order.

Columns	Contents
9–10	Second independent variable included.
11–12	Third independent variable included.
13–14	Fourth independent variable included.
15–16	Fifth independent variable included.
etc.	

The input format of (22I2) is used for the selection card.

Deck set-up

The control card follows immediately behind the system cards. This control card is followed by the data cards which, in turn, are followed by the selection cards. To utilize more than one set of data, merely start the process over again by using a control card, data cards, and selection cards, and so on.

Output

Description: The output of the sample program for multiple linear regression includes:

1. Lower triangular correlation matrix.
2. Means.
3. Standard deviations.
4. Correlation coefficients between the independent variables and the dependent variable.
5. Regression coefficients.
6. Standard errors of regression coefficients.
7. Computed T-values.
8. Intercept.
9. Multiple correlation coefficients (this term squared is the coefficient of determination).
10. Standard error of estimate.
11. Analysis of variance for the multiple regression.
12. Table of residuals (optional).
13. Punched predicted values of the dependent variables (optional).

Error message

The following error conditions will result in messages:

1. The number of selection cards is not specified on the control card: NUMBER OF SELECTIONS NOT SPECIFIED. JOB TERMINATED.
2. The matrix of correlation coefficients is singular: THE MATRIX IS SINGULAR. THIS SELECTION IS SKIPPED.

Error condition No. 2 allows the computer run to continue; however, error condition No. 1 terminates execution of the job.

The description of the control and input to the program and the closed format of the multiple-regression program explains the reason for the input structure of the data. Furthermore, the hypothesis being considered results in the need for two considerations:

1. The aggregation — of different types of assets into general *capital* categories — e.g., agricultural, commercial, money, etc.
2. The selection of the proper program to handle the analysis.

The multiple-regression program used here gives a statistically correct answer to the validity of the hypothesis. Since it is a multiple regression, it permits regression of more than one variable upon another. The research project being discussed uses more than one variable. The multiple regression (canned program) involved here, even though it is a closed-format program, permits easy conversion of the Essex raw data to the regression input format requirement. The program is capable of selecting any one variable of the independent variables on which to do the regression. Finally, the program is set up to handle more than one set of data which makes it convenient for us to handle total yearly quantities and evaluations as well as yearly averages and evaluations in the same program run.

The relative effectiveness of raw data conversion for use in a canned program is primarily dependent upon the time given to the valuation, the type of analysis, and the understanding that the researcher has of the desired statistical test to be done. If, as in the case presented, the type of analysis is well understood and the type of canned programs available is known, then data conversion becomes relatively simple.[17]

[17]See Chapter 13 for additional discussion of this type of model analysis.

three

COMPUTER APPLICATIONS IN THE
SOCIAL AND BEHAVIORAL SCIENCES

10

Urban Renewal: A Sociological Problem[1]

THE PROBLEM INVOLVED

Urban renewal was one of the more widely discussed and argued domestic issues of the 1950's and early 1960's. Many different groups were affected — realtors, contractors, politicians, businessmen, social workers, civil rights groups, political scientists, sociologists, city planners, architects, local housing authorities, and several Federal agencies — not to mention the home owners and residents in the path of the "Federal Bulldozer."[2] Such a broad and diverse constituency also meant that urban renewal had a ready stock of critics. Civil rights groups protested that urban renewal was "Negro removal." Social workers suggested that relocating families from areas to be renewed was simply moving the slums from one part of the city to another. Economists noted that urban renewal programs substituted high-income rental units for the prior low-income rental units and that the problem of poverty was not solved by this method. The Federal Urban Renewal Administration and the cities involved were hoping that residential renewal would retard the flow of middle-income white families to the suburbs. The city planning agencies were hoping that this would halt the continuing decline in property values in the central city and would improve the quality of housing available to Negroes.

Critics have asserted that renewal has failed in one of its major objectives — that of decreasing the stock of substandard and overcrowded housing in a city and of attracting middle- and upper-income residents back to the city. Others, such as the Housing and Home Finance Agency, warned that slum clearance "could result in a worsening instead of the desired improvement of the housing conditions of Negro and other racial minority families if the administration of these programs resulted in decreasing the living space presently available in any community to such groups."[3]

The purpose of the present study was to evaluate, as nearly as possible, the actual results of major renewal efforts on the changes in the population charac-

[1]Miss Carole Wolff (Ph.D., Michigan State University) is Associate Professor of Sociology at Sacramento State College, Sacramento, California. She was previously a research analyst at the Bureau of Social Science Research, Washington, D.C.
[2]Anderson, Martin, *The Federal Bulldozer: a Critical Analysis of Urban Renewal, 1949–1962* (Cambridge, Mass., M.I.T. Press, 1964).
[3]"Living Space Available to Racial Minority Families," Housing and Home Finance Agency, Local Public Agency Letter, No. 16, February 2, 1953.

teristics of cities and in the condition and extent of the housing supply.[4] Answers were sought to questions posed by the critics of renewal and by those who spoke in its defense. Did cities that engaged in major urban renewal improve the quality of housing in their city? Did overcrowding decrease in these cities? Did urban renewal accelerate or retard the exodus of whites to the suburbs? Did urban renewal result in better or worse housing for members of minority groups?

THE DATA

The sample

Three cities were chosen for the research: two experimental cities and one control city. St. Louis, Missouri, and Washington, D.C., the experimental cities, had engaged in sizeable urban renewal projects during the 1950's. The control city, Cincinnati, Ohio, had done little in the way of urban renewal in the 1950's.

The sample consisted of all the census tracts within these three central cities. The two "experimental" cities were classified as "leading urban renewal cities" between 1949 and 1960 by the Federal Housing and Home Financing Agency based on the amount of federal funds spent for renewal activities. Washington, D.C. ranked fourth in total federal funds spent, fifth in federal funds reserved but unspent, and third in funds spent per capita. St. Louis was eighth in total federal funds spent, sixth in federal funds reserved, and seventh in per capita expenditures. Thus, these two cities were designated as "experimental" because they had been exposed to the specified experimental condition — that is, to urban renewal. The control city did not undergo the experimental condition, hence the term control city.

In the classical experiment, the subjects should be as much alike as possible. In a natural experiment of this sort, it is only possible to match the subjects on a few crucial variables. If the renewal (experimental) cities do not differ in any systematic way from the control city on the basic variables related to population and housing, then a possible relationship between different patterns of change *and* the experimental condition may be entertained. If the renewal program has had a unique impact on housing and population changes in the city, it would be expected that the patterns of change in the experimental cities would differ from the patterns observed in the control city.

The three cities are roughly similar in size, are above average in the percentage or proportion of the population that is Negro, and all are "border" cities between North and South. They all receive fairly constant streams of new migrants from the South. In 1950, Washington, D.C., had a total population of 802,000; St. Louis, 857,000; and Cincinnati, 504,000. All three cities had a greater percentage of Negroes than the average for the 25 largest cities in the United States. In 1950, Washington, D.C., was 34.5 percent nonwhite, St. Louis was 18.0 percent nonwhite, and Cincinnati was 15.6 percent nonwhite. The 25-city average for 1950 was 13.9 percent nonwhite. In 1960, Washington was 54.8 percent nonwhite, St. Louis was 28.8 percent nonwhite, and Cincinnati was 21.8 percent nonwhite. In 1960, the 25-city average for nonwhite population was 20.7 percent. Similarly, the three cities were *below* average in the growth rate of their Negro population. While nonwhites in the 25 largest cities (in the United States) increased by 55.3 percent on the average (between 1950 and 1960), the increase for Washington, D.C., was 47.3 percent; for St. Louis, 39.9 percent; and for Cincinnati, 39.4 percent.

[4]The hypothesis and findings discussed here were part of a larger study done in partial fulfillment of the Ph.D. Degree in Sociology at Michigan State University by the author.

Changes in the population and housing characteristics of a city could be related to many different factors, among them the age and condition of the existing housing structures in the city, the occupational make-up of the city, and the educational and income level of the residents. In 1950, the cities were not identical on these characteristics, but St. Louis and Cincinnati were quite similar. This means that one experimental and one control city are not substantially different on these variables. The second experimental city differs from both of them, which would only strengthen the conclusion that renewal is an important independent variable if both St. Louis and Washington, D.C., show similar patterns of change despite their differences in occupational distribution and housing characteristics.

St. Louis was similar to Cincinnati in the relative age of its housing supply, the condition of the existing housing in 1950, and the make-up of its work force. Between 80 and 90 percent of the housing in these two cities was built prior to 1930, while in Washington, D.C., 40 percent of the housing was built after that date. Washington, therefore, was a newer city in terms of the age of its housing. The housing in St. Louis and Cincinnati was in worse condition with approximately a third of the housing in the two cities classified as substandard in the 1950 census. Both St. Louis and Cincinnati are primarily manufacturing centers, with the largest portions of their labor force in manual occupations. The District of Columbia is primarily an administrative center with the bulk of its labor force in clerical, professional, and administrative positions.

The basic sources of data were gathered from the census publications of 1950 and 1960, with the basic unit of analysis being the census tract. Two types of information were gathered for all census tracts in each of the three central cities:

1. Data describing the population in the tract including race, median family income, median education, etc.
2. Data which show the characteristics of the housing units in the tract including the percent of all units classified as substandard, the percent of all units classified as overcrowded, and the percent of all nonwhite occupied units that are substandard and overcrowded.

Census information was chosen because it was the most complete set of data available; it was collected by a standardized sample method, and the data are comparable for the two points in time — 1950 and 1960. This permits a *before and after* comparison with the experimental condition occurring in the interim period.

Three of the major hypotheses of the study were:

1. Urban renewal would improve the housing stock in a city; therefore, the percent of all housing units classified as substandard (by the Census Bureau) would decline from 1950 to 1960 in the experimental cities. The percent of all housing units classified as substandard would remain approximately the same in the control city.
2. The percent of overcrowded housing would decline in the renewal cities as a result of the clearance projects and would increase in the control city.
3. These changes would be most noticeable in the nonwhite occupied housing, since urban renewal has disproportionately involved the clearance of neighborhoods of predominantly Negro residents.

One way to test these hypotheses is to compare, for example, the percentage of substandard housing units in 1950 and 1960 for each census tract in the city. The differences can be summed (Census Tract No. 1, 1950 — Census Tract No. 1, 1960) for all tracts, divided by the number of tracts, and the result will be the mean difference. Then the mean difference of changes in the percent of substandard and of overcrowded housing from 1950 to 1960 can be compared for the three cities, as shown in Table 10-1.

TABLE 10-1.   Changes in substandard and overcrowded housing (1950–1960).

Item	Washington, D.C.	St. Louis, Mo.	Cincinnati, Ohio
Mean difference in percent Substandard: All census tracts	2.99	7.55	—13.22
Mean difference in percent Overcrowded: All census tracts	1.49	4.23	—0.134
Mean difference in percent Substandard in Negro-occupied housing units: All census tracts	9.83	3.39	—8.11
Mean difference in percent Overcrowded in Negro-occupied housing units: All census tracts	3.31	0.79	—2.16

A positive value in the table indicates that the percent of substandard or overcrowded housing *declined* from 1950–1960. A negative value indicates that the percentage increased. It would appear, then, that the three hypotheses are confirmed by the data. In both of the experimental cities, substandard and overcrowded housing decreased on the average. In the control city, the percent of substandard and overcrowded housing increased (on the average). In Washington, D.C., both trends were accentuated in nonwhite occupied housing. In St. Louis, the improvement in housing quality was not as great in nonwhite occupied units as it was for all housing units.

Data-card layout

The information collected on each census tract required three 80-column Hollerith cards. Each card of information for all census tracts in a particular city was labeled a "deck." Decks 1 and 2 dealt with housing characteristics. Deck 3 dealt with population characteristics. Each city had a Deck 1, 2, and 3 for both 1950 and 1960. This meant that the same information could be found in the same deck and in the same columns for two points in time, 1950 and 1960. Each deck is identified in Figures 10-1, 10-2, and 10-3, respectively. Column 78 shows the deck number as either 1, 2, or 3; Column 79 shows the year. A "0" (zero) in Column 79 is used for 1950, and a "1" in Column 79 indicates 1960. Column 80 identifies the city. An X in Column 80 indicates Washington, D.C.; a Y, St. Louis; and a Z, Cincinnati.

In Figure 10-1, Card 11X (in Columns 78, 79, and 80, respectively) is Deck 1 (Housing Characteristics), 1960, for Washington, D.C. Card 10Y is Deck 1 (Housing Characteristics), 1950, for St. Louis, Missouri. Thus, using Columns 78–80, each card in each deck of input data may be specifically identified.

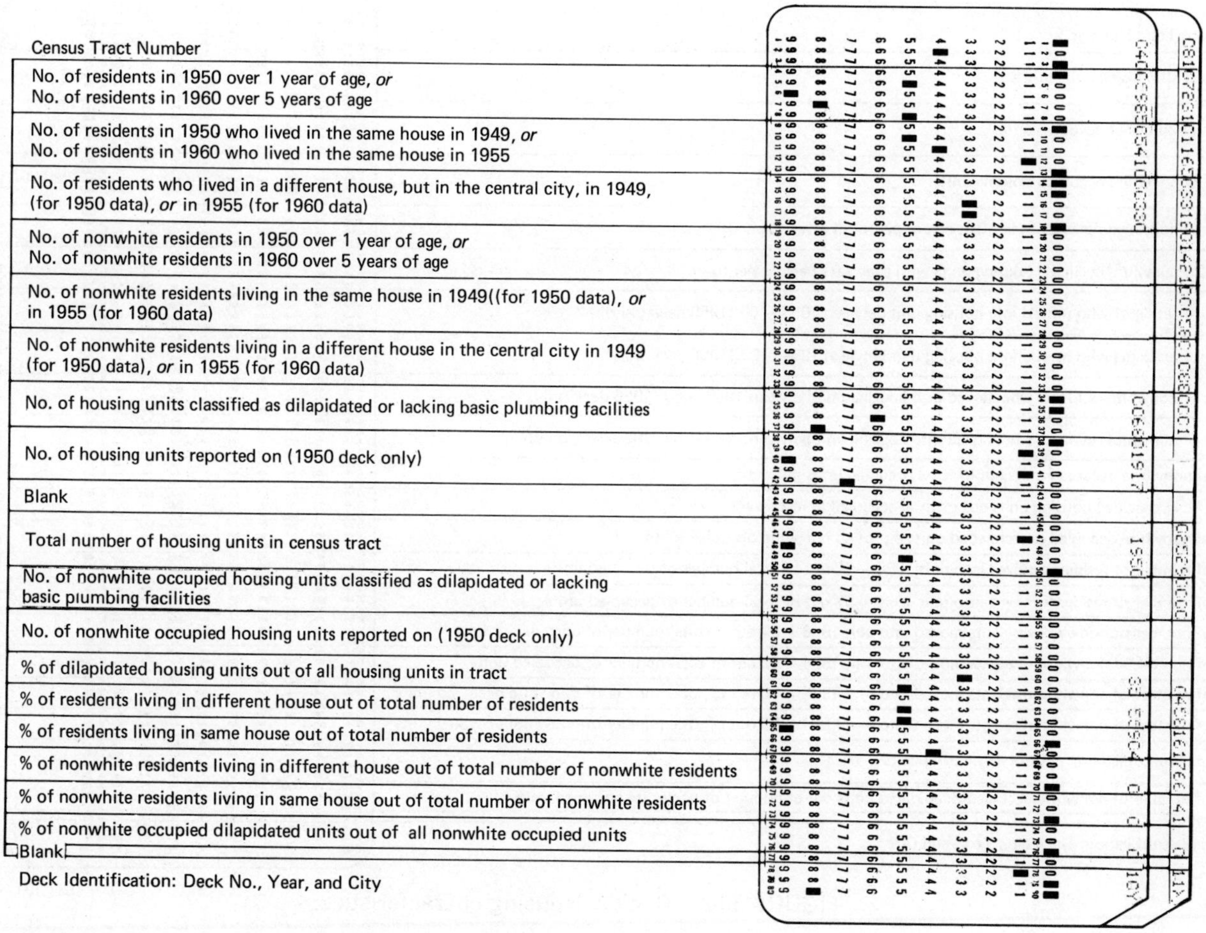

FIGURE 10-1. Deck 1: Housing characteristics.

The cards are so constructed that the raw data — that is, the census information — is punched into the first half of the card. Computed information is punched into the second half of each card. For instance, in Figure 10-1, Deck 1, Columns 34–37 show the number of housing units that were classified as dilapidated in 1950. Columns 38–42 gives the number of housing units that were reported on for that census tract in 1950. These data were taken from the census information. Columns 59–61 show the percentage of dilapidated housing for 1950. This was obtained by dividing columns 34–37 *by* columns 38–42. A FORTRAN program was used to compute the percentages from the data in the cards and to print the answer in Columns 59–61.

From the various tables, it is apparent that considerable information can be placed on each card. In this instance, the decks, year, and city were identified in Columns 78–80. Columns 1–3 contained the census tract number. Census Tract 081 is shown in Figure 10-1 for Washington, D.C., 1960 census. Census Tract 040 refers to Tract No. 40 for a particular city for a particular year. The fields in each card are explained in each of the tables. In some instances, the data collected by the census in 1950 was somewhat different than the information collected in 1960 — that is, given fields were not comparable for the two years. This, however, is more a problem of analysis than of programming.

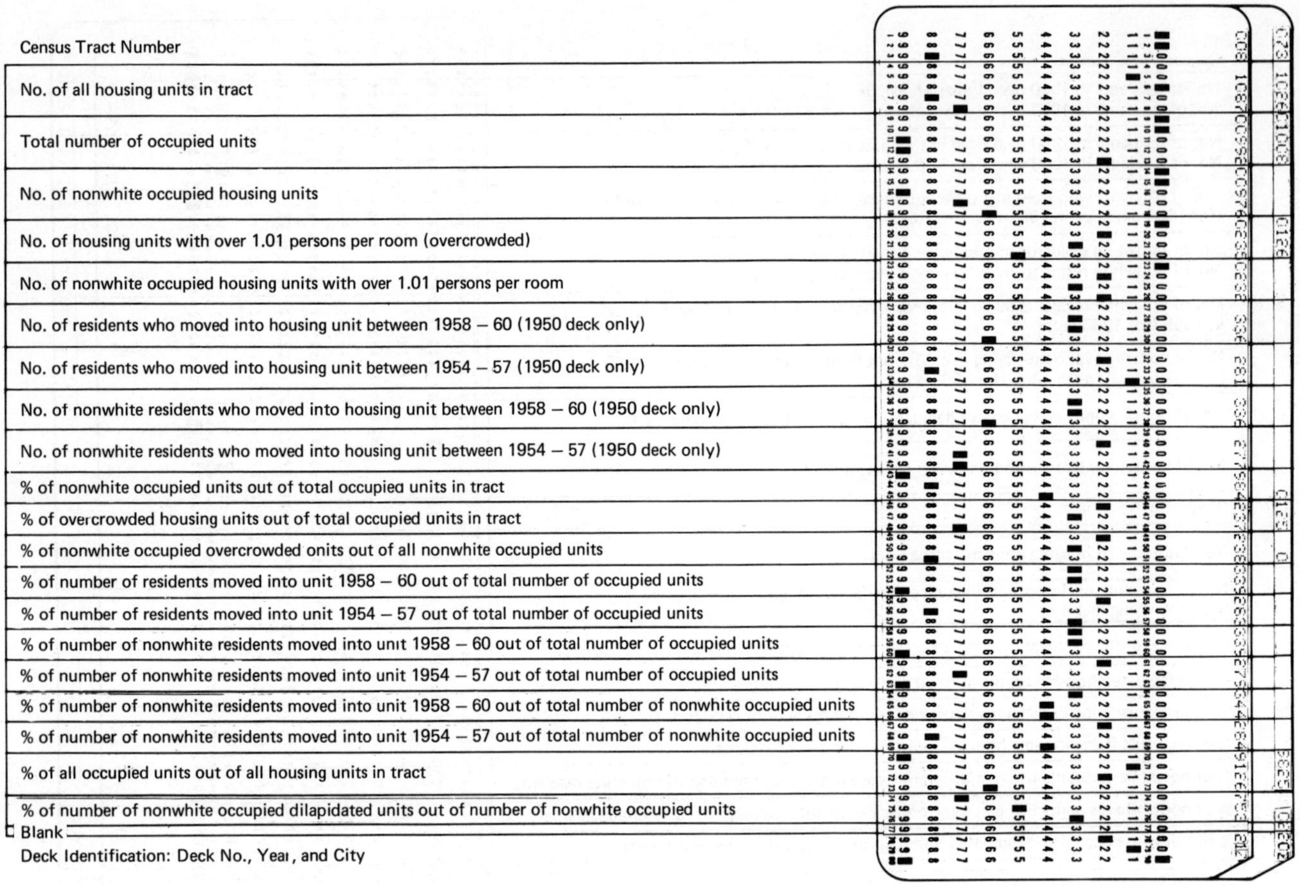

Census Tract Number

No. of all housing units in tract

Total number of occupied units

No. of nonwhite occupied housing units

No. of housing units with over 1.01 persons per room (overcrowded)

No. of nonwhite occupied housing units with over 1.01 persons per room

No. of residents who moved into housing unit between 1958 − 60 (1950 deck only)

No. of residents who moved into housing unit between 1954 − 57 (1950 deck only)

No. of nonwhite residents who moved into housing unit between 1958 − 60 (1950 deck only)

No. of nonwhite residents who moved into housing unit between 1954 − 57 (1950 deck only)

% of nonwhite occupied units out of total occupied units in tract

% of overcrowded housing units out of total occupied units in tract

% of nonwhite occupied overcrowded units out of all nonwhite occupied units

% of number of residents moved into unit 1958 − 60 out of total number of occupied units

% of number of residents moved into unit 1954 − 57 out of total number of occupied units

% of number of nonwhite residents moved into unit 1958 − 60 out of total number of occupied units

% of number of nonwhite residents moved into unit 1954 − 57 out of total number of occupied units

% of number of nonwhite residents moved into unit 1958 − 60 out of total number of nonwhite occupied units

% of number of nonwhite residents moved into unit 1954 − 57 out of total number of nonwhite occupied units

% of all occupied units out of all housing units in tract

% of number of nonwhite occupied dilapidated units out of number of nonwhite occupied units

Blank

Deck Identification: Deck No., Year, and City

FIGURE 10-2. Deck 2: Housing characteristics.

Figure 10-2, Deck 2, describes the housing units themselves — that is, the number of housing units that were overcrowded, occupied by nonwhites, and substandard, and how recently the present resident moved into the unit (1960). Some of the information gathered in 1960 would be blank in 1950, and some of the information in a given field for 1960 would not be comparable with the information in that field for 1950. This, again, is a problem of analysis. If the instructions are properly set forth, this will cause no problems for the programmer.

Figure 10-3, Deck 3, describes the characteristics of the population in each census tract. Again, the last three columns identify the deck number, the data, and the city. The raw data fields and the calculated information fields are explained in the table itself.

PROGRAMS USED[5]

To count cards

The first program to be discussed simply counts the cards in a given deck. This was required because the computer center used in this analysis has a sorter with no

[5]See review questions at end of chapter. Programs illustrated in this chapter were written in FORTRAN II on a variable word-length machine, an IBM 1620.

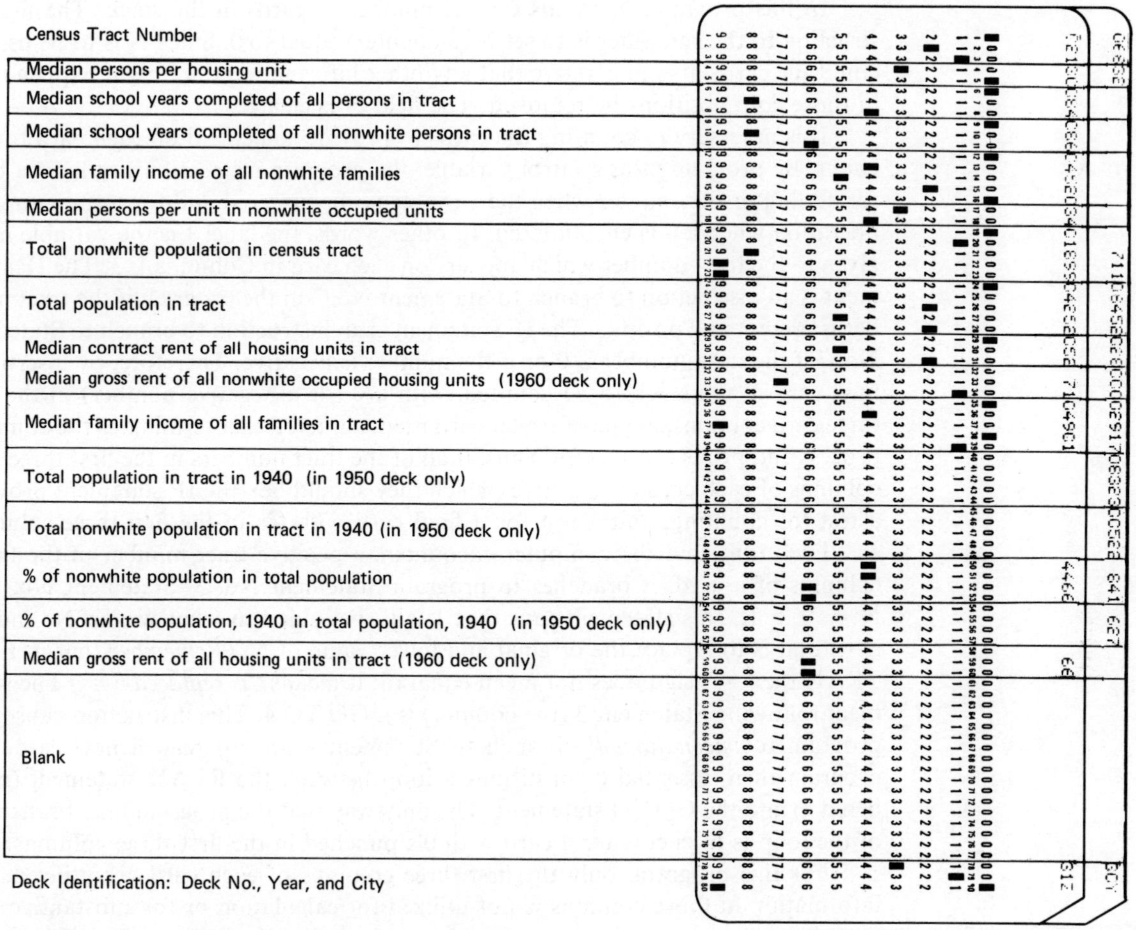

Census Tract Number

Median persons per housing unit

Median school years completed of all persons in tract

Median school years completed of all nonwhite persons in tract

Median family income of all nonwhite families

Median persons per unit in nonwhite occupied units

Total nonwhite population in census tract

Total population in tract

Median contract rent of all housing units in tract

Median gross rent of all nonwhite occupied housing units (1960 deck only)

Median family income of all families in tract

Total population in tract in 1940 (in 1950 deck only)

Total nonwhite population in tract in 1940 (in 1950 deck only)

% of nonwhite population in total population

% of nonwhite population, 1940 in total population, 1940 (in 1950 deck only)

Median gross rent of all housing units in tract (1960 deck only)

Blank

Deck Identification: Deck No., Year, and City

FIGURE 10-3. Deck 3: Population characteristics.

counter. Therefore, if a person wanted to know how many cards there were in a given deck (perhaps to check the number of cards punched for a given city against the number supposed to be available), it would be necessary to count the cards by hand or to write a program to count the cards. Or if one wanted to know how many census tracts in a given city in a given census year were over 50 percent nonwhite in their population, one referred to Columns 50–53 of Deck 3. Sorting on Column 50 would divide the deck into two stacks: those where the nonwhite population was 50 percent or over, and those where the nonwhite population was 49 percent or less. Each stack could then be counted. If over 100 cards are involved (for the three cities in each of two years), the computer is considerably faster and more accurate than the person, even considering the time in writing a program. The first or "counting" program is shown below (FORTRAN IID):

```
        N = 0
    4 READ 1, J
    1 FORMAT (I3)
        IF (J) 7, 7, 3
    3 N = N + 1
        GO TO 4
    7 PRINT 1, N
        END
```

In this program, N stands for the number of cards in the stack. The first instruction to the computer is to set N (a counter) equal to 0. Since N is to be used to count the cards, it is imperative that any other information that might happen to be in those core positions be removed. The field N is cleared.

It is necessary in counting the cards to provide some field on each card for the count. By providing this control variable, the program instruction can have a basis for adding to the counter when the variable is encountered and for terminating the operation when a 0 is encountered. In other words, the label J is the variable name given to the tract number which appears on each card in Columns 1–3. The IF statement is an instruction to branch to Statement No. 3 in the program if the tract number is present and positive. The IF statement is an instruction to branch to Statement No. 7 if the tract number is 0 or if the number is negative. Therefore, by inserting a final card in the stack to be counted, with a 0 (or a negative number) in the first three card columns, a type of trailer card is encountered that terminates the counting process and prints the answer. Thus, if all of the tract numbers in the first three card columns of each card are positive (which they should be), the IF statement provides a test for counting, and a test for a final card with 0's in the first three columns.

Each time that the computer encounters a positive tract number in the first 3 columns of a card, it branches to program Statement No. 3. Statement No. 3 is: $N = N + 1$. This statement says that 1 is to be added to what was in N, and the new total is to replace the original and lower value of N. (*Remember* that in FORTRAN the "$=$" sign does not mean equal to; it means "*is replaced by*.") The statement following Statement 3 (the counter) is a GO TO 4. This instruction causes the program to *unconditionally* branch to Statement 4 and to read a new card. The program then, essentially constitutes a loop between the READ statement (numbered 4) and the GO TO statement. The only way that the program may branch out of the loop is to encounter a card with 0's punched in the first three columns.

For this program, only the first three columns of each card are utilized. The information in those columns is not utilized for calculation or for substantive data purposes. The number in the three columns is used only for counting (if positive), and for terminating the counting (if zero or negative). The information in the first three card columns (I3) is stored in the computer in a three-position field which is labeled J.

To calculate percentage

While the first program illustrates the use of programming and the computer for tasks normally performed by other data-processing machines (the sorter), the second program below illustrates the use of the computer for certain elementary tasks involving data manipulation and calculation. The purpose of the second program was threefold:

1. To sum the total number of substandard housing units in all census tracts. This information was contained in Deck 1, Columns 34–37 (Figure 10-1).
2. To sum the total number of housing units for all census tracts. This information was contained in Deck 1, Columns 46–50 (Figure 10-1).
3. To calculate a percentage of substandard housing units for the city as a whole: the sum of Deck 1, Columns 34–37, divided by the sum of Columns 46–50.

For ease of handling, let us call the substandard housing units in Columns 34–37
Field *A*. Let us also call the total housing units in Columns 46–50, Field *B*

The program to accomplish these calculations is shown below:

```
5   SUMA = 0.
    SUMB = 0.
4   READ 1, A, B
1   FORMAT (33X, F4.0, 8X, F5.0) ──────6
    IF (A − 9999.) 3, 7, 3
3   SUMA = SUMA + A
    SUMB = SUMB + B
    GO TO 4
7   PER = (SUMA/SUMB) ∗ 100.
    PRINT2, PER
2   FORMAT (5X, F8.2)
    PAUSE ────────────────────7
    GO TO 5
    END
```

The first statement of the program, labeled 5, tells it to clear the defined area
SUMA and set that to 0. The second statement provides for setting the area SUMB
to 0. Statement No. 4, the READ statement, provides for the reading of the data
card and the storage of the data in the card into Areas A and B. The information
placed in Area A is that concerning substandard housing from Columns 34–37 on
the data card. The information placed in Area B is that concerning total housing
units from Columns 46–50 in the data card.

Since these two fields are the only data fields on the card that are of concern,
the FORMAT statement tells which columns on the card are to be utilized and
placed in A and B respectively. Since the first data field begins with Column 34, the
first part of the FORMAT statement is an instruction to skip the first 33 card columns (33X). The first data field is four columns in length (Columns 34–37) and is
therefore read under an F4.0, the F indicating that REAL notation is used, and the
4 indicating that beginning with card Column 34, four columns are included in this
field. Since the next field begins on Column 46 in the card, the 8 columns from
Column 38 through and including Column 45 are skipped (8X). The second card
field is 5 columns in length, hence is picked up or read as F5.0. The READ statement
indicated that the first field is placed in defined Area A, and the second field on the
data card is placed in defined Area B in the computer storage. The computer will
automatically ignore the remainder of the card. In short, the FORMAT statement
directs the computer to skip the first 33 columns, and to treat the next four columns
as a four-digit number, which will be called A. The computer is then directed to
skip the next 8 columns and treat the next five numbers (or columns) as a five-digit
whole number which will be called B.

The percentage required is for the entire city, not for each tract. Therefore, a
test is necessary to determine when all the census tracts for a particular city and for a
particular year have been read. In this instance, it is assumed that the cards are in
order for each city by year. At the end of each city, for the given year, is a trailer

---

[6]On the IBM 1620 (compiler system used), it was not necessary to terminate the FORMAT
statement with a slash mark (/), if less than the full 80-column record has been READ. On many computers, the FORMAT statement would have to be as follows: 1 FORMAT (33X, F4.0, 8X, F5.0/)

[7]The PAUSE statement is a rarely used statement that is provided on few machines — usually on
those with, basically, only a card capability. In this program, when the read hopper has exhausted a
data deck and printed out the results, the PAUSE causes the computer to stop. When the hopper has
been refilled and the start button pressed, the program continues by executing the statement: GO TO 5.

card with a number 9999 punched in Columns 34–37. The card with the number 9999 indicates that all of the data cards have been read and that the percentage should now be calculated. The IF statement will keep the process reading cards and adding the card fields into the total (or accumulator) fields until the 9999 card is encountered. When the 9999 card is encountered, the program control branches to Statement 7. That is, when the data in Field A (value of A) minus 9999 is equal to zero, the program control branches to the Statement No. 7.

Statement No. 7 divides whatever is in SUMA (the value of SUMA) by whatever is in SUMB and multiplies it by 100 to properly position the decimal for a percentage notation and deposits that number in Field PER. The final statements instruct the computer to print the answer in PER. At this point, the immediate job is done and the computer operation, encountering the PAUSE statement will stop.

Since there were a total of 6 stacks of cards (1950 and 1960 for each of the three cities), the PAUSE statement allows the operator to insert the next set of cards into the read hopper of the computer card reader if necessary. By pressing START on the computer console, the next stack of data cards may be read without reloading the program. Thus, the statement following the PAUSE is a GO TO 5. The program instruction branches to Statement No. 5 which resets the SUMA and the SUMB to 0 and then proceeds to accept the data cards. In this program, no last card or trailer card or job card is provided, and the program is completed when the computer comes to the sixth pause, having printed out its sixth answer.

The printout for the program showing percentage of overcrowded units was:

13.5	(DC 1950)
11.9	(DC 1960)
20.3	(SL 1950)
15.5	(SL 1960)
17.5	(CN 1950)
14.7	(CN 1960)

The parentheses indicate that the data was printed out in a particular order, but that the data were not labeled as to city and year. If the data available are strictly ordered — and the output simple so that there is no possibility of confusion — this type of program which does not label the data is usable. If there is any possibility of confusing the output data and if it were necessary to test the cards as read in, to test the output, and to label the output specifically for city and year, the program would be a good deal longer than it is now.

The output for the same study showing percentage of substandard housing was as follows:

12.1	(DC 1950)
9.7	(DC 1960)
27.0	(SL 1950)
19.0	(SL 1960)
29.5	(CN 1950)
19.7	(CN 1960)

To calculate mean difference and standard deviation

The third program illustrates a still more complicated programming operation, but it is one that is typical of one of the major uses which social scientists make of computers. Descriptive statistics and tests of statistical significance (means, standard deviations, and correlations) are increasingly important in the social sciences and particularly in sociological, psychological, and professional education work. Most of these tests are time-consuming to do by hand, particularly if the sample involved is a large one. It is time-consuming to write a FORTRAN program, but the computer can run the data and perform all the required calculations in a very few minutes.

In the present program, two descriptive statistical ideas were needed: the mean difference, and the standard deviation of the difference. The mean difference simply gives the average change (positive or negative) over all census tracts of a particular variable from 1950 and 1960. The standard deviation of the difference is the average deviation (or variation) of each difference from the mean difference or from the average difference. Thus, if some tracts changed very little and others changed a lot, the (average) deviation from the average difference will be high. However, if most tracts changed about the same amount (regardless of whether that change was large or small) the average deviation from the average difference would be low.

The formula for the mean of the difference is:

$$\bar{X} = \sum \frac{(X_i 1950 - X_i 1960)}{N}$$

The symbol $\bar{X}$ stands for the mean difference. The symbol Σ means "sum of." $X_i 1950$ refers to the value of a particular variable for a particular census tract in 1950. $X_i 1960$ refers to the value of that same variable for the same census tract in 1960. N refers to the number of census tracts or number of 1950–1960 comparisons on the given single variable.

The formula for standard deviation of the difference is:

$$\sigma = \sqrt{\frac{\Sigma d^2 - \frac{(\Sigma d)^2}{N}}{N - 1}}$$

In this formula, d refers to the value of the difference. The sum of d^2 means tha you want to square each 1950–1960 *differences* and then add them up. The (sum o d)^2 means that you want to sum up all the differences and then square that figure.

In order to perform these operations, we tell the computer how to arrive at each part of a formula and then instruct the computer (through the program) how to put each part together at the proper time. The program is shown in Table 10-2.

The first substantive statement in the program is the DIMENSION statement: DIMENSION E(128), EZ(128). These are the two main variables that the computer has to keep track of. E is the percent of substandard housing in any particular census tract in 1950. EZ is the percent of substandard housing in any particular census tract in 1960. Variable E is found in Data Deck 1 — 10Z for Cincinnati; 10X for Washington, D.C.; 10Y for St. Louis (Figure 10-1). Variable EZ is the same variable, for the same cities, but for 1960 — 11Z, Cincinnati; 11Y, Washington, D.C.; 11Y, St. Louis. The number in the parentheses following each variable name (128) is the number of values of E or EZ for each variable. In this instance, the (128) refers to the number of census tracts in the city.

The next six statements simply set certain defined areas to zero for either fixed or floating point notation or set some value equal to a predetermined quantity. In this instance, SUMD5, SQD5, XD5, and SIGMA5 were all set to equal to 0 (REAL notation). SQSUD5 was set equal to 0 (REAL notation). The area CN was set equal to 128 (REAL notation), the maximum number of census tracts.

TABLE 10-2.   FORTRAN program to calculate "standard deviation."

```
    DIMENSION E(128), EZ(128)
    SUMD5 = 0.
    SQD5 = 0.
    SQSUD5 = 0.
    XD5 = 0.
    SIGMA5 = 0.
    CN = 128.
    READ 1, (E(I), I = 1, 128)
    READ 1, (EZ(I), I = 1, 128)
  1 FORMAT (58X, F3.1) ——————————————————————— *
    DO 4 I = 1, 128
  4 SUMD5 = SUMD5 + (E(I) − EZ(I) )
    DO 5 I = 1, 128
  5 SQD5 = SQD5 + ( (E(I) − EZ(I) ) * (E(I) − EZ(I) ) )
  6 SQSUD5 = SUMD5 * SUMD5
    XD5 = SUMD5/CN
    SIGMA5 = SQRTF ( (SQD5 − (SQSUD5/CN) ) / (CN − 1.) )
    PRINT 100, SUMD5, SQD5, SQSUD5
100 FORMAT (4X, 11HSUM OF DIFF, 5X, 10HSQ OF DIFF, 1X, 14HSQ-SUM OF DIFF / /
 13 F15.4/ /)
    PRINT 999, XD5, SIGMA5
999 FORMAT (15HDECKS 20Y − 21Y/ /16H MEAN OF E − EZ = F10.3/ /16HSIGMA OF
  1 (E − EZ = F10.3)
    END
```

*Since the actual program shown here was tested and run on an IBM 1620, it was felt that the FORMAT statement should be left as shown. However, this FORMAT statement form would not necessarily be correct for other computer systems or FORTRAN compilers. On many FORTRAN systems, it would be necessary to rewrite the statement as follows:

1 FORMAT (58X, F3.1/)

Shorthand titles were given to each segment of the formula for easy reference. These shorthand titles are the variable names used in the computer:

SUMD = The sum of the differences (the numerator in the formula for the mean of the difference).
SQD   = Each difference squared (the first term in the formula for the standard deviation).
SQSUD = The sum of the differences, squared (the numerator of the second term in the formula for standard deviation).
XD   = The mean of the differences (SUMD/CN).
CN   = The number of census tracts or values of E and EZ.
SIGMA = The standard deviation or square root of

$$\frac{SQD - SQSUD/CN}{CN - 1}$$

The first READ statement directs the computer to read variable E where I successively has the values from 1 to 128. In other words, there are 128 cards, each with a value on it in certain columns. That field, or the data from that field, is designated E. Thus, the cards are read, and the data on the first card is placed in the Array E at E(1). The data in that field from the second card is placed in the E-array at E(2). This is all provided for by the READ statement: READ 1, (E(I),I = 1, 128). The second READ statement instructs that the same function be performed for the data which is labeled EZ.

The FORMAT statement provides that the first 58 columns of the data card are to be ignored, and the next three columns constitute the data field which is to be stored in the computer storage as E(1),E(2), . . . E(128). The variable E is a three-digit number with one digit to the right of an (implied) decimal point. The sequence of data (input) cards is such that the 128 cards for 1950 are stacked first and the 128 cards for 1960 are stacked behind them. The READ statement is also a control statement that instructs that 128 cards be read and the data deposited in E; a second 128 cards will be read using the same FORMAT statement and the data will be deposited in EZ(1), . . . EZ(128). This type of controlled READ statement is a combination READ statement and DO statement,[8] where the READ is the instruction to the computer and the DO controls the number of cards read. All the desired raw data is now in the computer storage in the two-dimensioned arrays.

The DO statements were then used to begin the calculations needed. The first DO statements, DO 4 I = 1, 128, provided that Statement 4 be accomplished 128 times. In carrying out the DO statement, the I of the DO statement takes an initial value of 1, and each time the loop is completed, it is incremented by 1 until the I equals the terminal value of 128. The thing that is *done* 128 times is to subtract the value in the EZ(I)-array (where I can equal from 1 to 128) respectively, from the E(I)-array (where the I can equal from 1 to 128). The first time the operation (Statement 4) is performed: E(1) − EZ(1). The data in the first position of the EZ-array is subtracted from the data in the first position of the E-array, and the difference between the two is placed in SUMD5.[9] The second time the operation occurs, the data in the second position of the EZ-array, EZ(2), is subtracted from the data in the second position of the E-array, E(2), and the result is added to that already in SUMD5.

In a similar manner, the operations in Statement 5, controlled by the second DO statement, are carried out and the results are consecutively added into SQD5. The operation carried out in Statement 5 is to *first* take the difference of E(1) − EZ(1); *second*, square that difference; *third*, add the squares into SQD5.

One final operation has to be carried out before the mean and standard deviation formulas may be calculated by the computer. It is necessary to square the sum of the differences. This is accomplished by Statement 6:

$$SQSUD5 = SUMD5 * SUMD5$$

SUMD5 was one of the first calculations performed. This instruction provides that the computer multiply that value, which is stored in the core by itself. This product is labeled SQSUD5.

The computer now contains all the data required to perform the actual operations necessary to solve the formulas for the mean and standard deviations. All the necessary data is stored in memory in the computer and all stored data has the necessary labels attached. The operations or parts of the program which we have discussed up to this point might be called the preparatory part of the program. The last part of the program solves the formulas and presents the answer desired.

The final part of the program is the actual solution of the formulas using the data developed. The first statement is:

$$XD5 = SUMD5 / CN$$

This says that the mean of D (or $\overline{X}D$) can be obtained by dividing the sum of D by CN.

The next statement is:

$$SIGMA5 = SQRTF ((SQD5 − (SQSUD5/CN)) / (CN − 1))$$

[8]Usually called an *implied* DO.
[9]SUMD5 is added to the difference each time the statement is executed.

This statement notes that the standard deviation of D (SIGMA) can be obtained by taking the square root (SQRTF) of the operations in the first pair of parentheses. The computer evaluates the equation to arrive at a single value. It then takes the square root of that single value. The instruction SQRTF is a function, a type of subprogram that is performed automatically by the computer whenever it encounters the words SQRTF.[10]

The work of the program is largely over with the formula solved. The program instructs that three things be printed. The three things that it was important to obtain in the program were:

1) sum of the differences (SUMD),
2) square of the differences (SQD),
3) sum of the differences, squared (SQSUD).

These are indicated by the designation following the number of the FORMAT statement in the PRINT statement. The FORMAT statement tells the computer to skip 4 spaces (4X),[11] use the next 11 columns to print the words: SUM OF DIFF. Then five spaces are skipped (5X) and the next ten spaces are used to print the words: SQ OF DIFF. One space is skipped (1X) and the next 14 spaces are used to print the words: SQ-SUM OF DIFF. The two slash lines (//) indicate that there is to appear one blank line or row between the line just printed and the information that is to be printed following the slash lines. The format notation following the two slash marks (//) is: 3F15.4//. This indicates that the three values are to be printed, allowing fifteen positions for each one with four positions allowed to the right of the decimal place: then, two more blank lines or rows are to appear after the data. When this operation is completed, the computer encounters another print statement to provide the values for the mean difference $\overline{X}D$ and SIGMA, or the standard deviation. The output for this is accomplished according to FORMAT Statement No. 999. Again, a combination of Hollerith statements to provide labels and regular output statements to provide information is used.

The printouts were to provide information on substandard housing. It indicates that the average difference, on a census tract basis, for Cincinnati was a 13.22 percent increase in substandard housing over the decade. The printouts for the same variable for St. Louis and Washington, D.C., indicated that these two cities experienced an average decrease in substandard housing. One of the printouts is shown below:

1. Cincinnati:

SUM OF DIFF	SQ OF DIFF	SQ-SUM OF DIFF
—146.9000	53531.2700	2151795.6100

DECKS 10Z — 11Z
MEAN OF E — EZ = —13.215
SIGMA OF E — EZ = 17.510

Similar printouts were provided for St. Louis and Washington, D.C.

---

[10]Some FORTRAN compilers require that some function names end in "F."

[11]Some compilers use the first column of the output format record for control; thus, the (4X) on some compilers would cause only 3 columns to be skipped. The reader should check his own computer FORTRAN manual on this point.

REVIEW QUESTIONS AND PROBLEMS

1. The programs discussed in this chapter were actually written *and run* on an IBM 1620, using a FORTRAN IID compiler. They have been shown here because they not only illustrate the use of the computer in developing statistical tests of significance, but also because they can be used as problem studies. In most instances, the student is given *1*) the problem, *2*) the logic used by the author in constructing the program, and *3*) the answers obtained. The programs are quite simple and illustrate many of the basic problems of social science programming. The output is simple, and the basic problem is that of converting a statistical formula to FORTRAN.

   The best review question and problem at this point would be to rewrite the program so that it would compile and run on the computer available to the student or reader. Even though the original data decks are not available, they could be constructed in facsimile easily; and these programs provide the beginning student with the practice needed to become familiar with his computer in relatively standard programming exercises.

2. The second exercise would be for the student to modify the program (shown in Table 10-2) or construct a similar one of his own that would handle two variables at a time. The student may wish to add to the program sufficient Hollerith statements so that the output is more completely and more appropriately labeled. Start by writing an algorithm of the problem and then rewrite the program for your computer.

11

Death of a Dream:
The Closing of Studebaker[1]

THE STUDY

On December 9, 1963, the word leaked out that Studebaker had decided upon the immediate and permanent shutdown of its South Bend auto plant. The last American-made Studebaker car was scheduled to come off the assembly line on December 20th — five days before Christmas. The effect of the closing on the community was devastating.

Studebaker had long been the area's largest employer and its shutdown wiped out a 45-million-dollar annual payroll and over 9 percent of South Bend's jobs. The community just could not believe that it had really happened — Studebaker had experienced its ups and downs before, but the firm had always pulled through. Now it was gone. By February 1964, the Department of Labor estimated the South Bend unemployment rate to be 9.1 percent of the work force as compared to the low point of 2.1 percent the previous Fall.

Typical of many situations similar to the shutdown experienced by South Bend, a number of beliefs were expressed which might be interpreted as "consolations" to some segments of the community not directly or adversely affected by such major plant closings. For example, one belief was that since the average age of the Studebaker workers was on the older side, such employees would, therefore, have few children and thus the burden of deprivation would not be too serious. Other similar beliefs, none of which were based on any concrete empirical knowledge, further muddled the situation. Such beliefs might be a kind of "defense mechanism" serving as a sort of comforting device for those who wish to evade the serious nature of the impact of the Studebaker closing. The degree to which such beliefs are adhered to can affect the nature and extent of community action necessary for meeting the impact. For this and many other reasons, Dr. Harold Sheppard, federal coordinator of government assistance in South Bend, urged that research be undertaken to clarify these beliefs.

[1]This chapter was written by Frank J. Fahey, Associate Professor of Sociology and Associate Director, Social Science Training and Research Laboratory, University of Notre Dame; and J. John Palen, University of Wisconsin—Milwaukee. Financial support for original research was provided by: Area Redevelopment Administration, USDC.

124

The lack of knowledge regarding the effects of job displacement in South Bend were compounded by the fact that little research had been done anywhere on this problem. Students of the American industrial scene seem to take it as axiomatic that one of the most serious problems facing the economy in the near future will involve its ability to absorb large numbers of workers who have been displaced by technological change or plant shutdowns. There is little doubt that factors such as plant relocations, industrial mergers, automation, and shifts in product demand will lead to more rather than to fewer "redundant" workers. Perhaps the long-run reabsorption of displaced workers into the system may be solved by increasing population and consumer demand; however, the picture with regard to short-run adjustment is far less sanguine. Our success or failure in dealing with these problems of job displacement is directly related to our knowledge of the displaced worker, his potentialities, and his limitations.

This study attempts to respond to both the above shortcomings by providing information on the impact of a major plant shutdown on the workers who are displaced. The effects of the closing were particularly severe on the 80 percent of the labor force who are paid hourly rates. There was no severance pay for such workers. Salaried workers received severance pay on a sliding scale that ranged from one week's pay for less than six month's employment, to 3 month's pay for ten or more years experience.

DATA: SAMPLE

This section focuses on the techniques used to gather information on the displaced worker. Particular attention is directed to the use of the computer and how it assisted in developing the overall methodology.

The original research design called for interviewing 650 Studebaker or former Studebaker workers. The immediate problem was how and where to select 650 names so that the interviewing could proceed as scheduled. The Studebaker Corporation cooperated with the authors by providing a complete list of all workers employed by the corporation as of October 1, 1963, when there were 8,391 employees. The data were supplied by Studebaker on two Hollerith cards for each worker. The first concern was to transfer the information on these cards to magnetic tapes so that they could be processed by the computer. It should be noted that at this time the University of Notre Dame had recently acquired a UNIVAC 1107 computer which was so new that few people knew what its limitations were. We soon became aware of its limitations. Our first attempt to transfer the data from cards to tape was an abysmal failure. No one had taken the time to figure out how many cards could be transferred to a single tape. Approximately 85 percent of the data was transferred from card to tape when we hit the end of the tape. And here we were faced with our first major problem.

It should be mentioned at this point that the Hollerith cards that Studebaker used were not exactly the same size as the Hollerith cards that were used by UNIVAC. They were somewhat thinner and had a tendency to jam the card reader of the computer. It took considerable time, therefore, to read 16,000-plus cards into the computer in order to transfer the data to tape. You can imagine our disappointment when we thought the job was almost completed and discovered that it had to be repeated. It is often possible to transfer data into a more compact data-set image. The information we desired did not require 160 columns (2 cards), but could be reduced to 120 columns thus providing us with a saving of 25 percent in space on the magnetic tape. We also wanted the data to be transformed as it went from cards to tape so that we would not have to do subsequent transformations with the data. There were two major transformations that we wished to do. One was a simplified job classification scheme and the other a code for determining the geographical residence of each employee.

The information that was used directly included social security number, name and address of each employee, birthdate, seniority date, sex, marital status, number of dependents, and clock number. The data transformations mentioned above were particularly necessary because the sample of 650 was to be a job-stratified random sample. If a simple random sample were used we would be greatly overrepresented with nonskilled workers and find very few skilled or salaried workers in our sample. The corporation had already provided a simplified coding scheme for classifying the salaried workers but a 6-digit number was used to classify all hourly workers. Our procedure was to list the job-classification number of all skilled workers and change it to a 1; to take the job-classification numbers of all semiskilled workers and set it to 2; and all other numbers would be set to 3 to represent the nonskilled worker.

The geographical transformation was somewhat more complicated. We decided that we would use the following code for geographical residence; 1, would represent South Bend; 2, Mishawaka; 3, other St. Joseph County; 4, Marshal County; 5, Elkhart County; 6, Berrien County, Michigan, etc. We were thus able to get three classifications for St. Joseph County and one each for the counties which surrounded South Bend so that we might know the magnitude of the effect of the shutdown on these outside areas. To do this it was necessary to punch out the name of each city and transform it to the appropriate number. With the transformations written and the shorter number of columns per record we were now ready to transfer our data from card to tape.

It was not that simple. The transformed scores were each assigned to an empty column. There was one error in the program that we had not anticipated: cities listed in the address of the workers were not always spelled in the same way and in several instances they were mispunched or spelled improperly. We had a subroutine written into our program so that if none of the addresses matched the transformations which we asked the computer to make, it would print out the name of the city. In going through the difficult procedure of putting the cards through the card reader we again discovered that we had to do it one more time. There were five errors in the addresses of the Studebaker workers and we had to make the appropriate change in order to get the data on tape in proper form.

With these changes made, it was then finally possible to have a usable tape with the name and address plus other pertinent information on each and every Studebaker worker. This procedure took approximately one week. Table 11-1 indicates the Studebaker job-classification distributions by frequency and percentage. Our sample was drawn quite rapidly. This is the procedure that was used: we took every tenth name in the skilled category; every 13th name in the semiskilled category; every 14th name in the non-skilled category; every 8th name in the supervision category; and every 8th name in the administrative category. This yielded a 7.91 percent sample containing 664 workers.

The sampling technique was modified slightly from a straight, stratified random sample, but, due to the size of the sample, it should be as unbiased as a truly random sample. The workers were listed sequentially according to social security number. This modification proved necessary so that it would conform as closely as possible to the 650 interviews allowed for in the research design. This procedure also enabled

TABLE 11-1. Studebaker job classification distributions by frequencies and percentages.

	Frequency	Percentage
Skilled	511	6.1
Semiskilled	1182	14.1
Nonskilled	5255	62.6
Supervision	717	8.5
Administrative	726	8.7
Total	8391	100.0

us to measure characteristics of the sample with characteristics of the population to see whether the sample was truly representative. The weighted sample deviated only slightly from the universe and not beyond the 5 percent confidence limit.

The advantage of having all Studebaker employees listed on one magnetic tape provided useful information on the population parameters. It also proved extremely useful for practical reasons. Shortly after the research began, a project designed to aid older workers was inaugurated in South Bend under the auspices of the Department of Labor. There was no list of older workers available other than the list we had on tape. It was a simple procedure to specify to the computer by means of programming that every person 50 years of age and older be listed for the older worker project. This undoubtedly made their approach very efficient in attempting to reach older workers since they would have had no other way of knowing who all these workers were.

THE ANALYSIS

The workers in the sample were a good cross-section of the Studebaker labor force. Many of the workers were older men with high seniority since these were the men most likely to be retained over the lean years prior to the shutdown. Only one fifth of those working for Studebaker at the time of the closing had been first employed by the company during the preceding five years. At the other extreme, over 10 percent had started with the firm before 1928 — 35 years before the shutdown. The average worker had more than 20 years seniority at the time of the closing. In age, 65 percent of the workers were over 45 while half were over 50. Only 15 percent of the workers were under 35 years old. In terms of the pay they had been receiving, they were the cream of the South Bend labor force, although their educational and skill levels were relatively low. One third had not gone beyond grade school, while 9 percent had some college. Sixty percent of the sample were rated nonskilled by the Studebaker Corporation records. This fact reflects the nature of assembly-line production — that is, heavy reliance on repetitive performance of a single operation by a worker possessing minimal training.

The average Studebaker employee was thus an older worker who had been receiving relatively high wages but who did not have skills that could be easily transferred to other jobs. His high seniority also meant that he had no recent job-hunting experience and was generally unfamiliar with the job market. In some cases he had worked his entire adult life at Studebaker. He was ill-equipped emotionally and occupationally to begin all over again. We were interested in determining what success such workers had in finding reemployment. Who among the Studebaker workers were those most likely to find new jobs? What were the factors that contributed to the success or failure of their reemployment efforts? Which of the predisplacement factors were the most important for the displaced Studebaker workers? Which were the most likely to contribute to his reemployment?

The data for this research were obtained from an interview schedule administered to the stratified random sample previously discussed. The interviewing took place in April 1964, and was conducted by 22 trained interviewers of both sexes. To minimize response bias, Negro respondents were usually interviewed by Negro interviewers, and interviewers who spoke Polish, Hungarian, and Flemish were also used. One interview was completed with a deaf worker. The worker's mother, who did not understand English, converted the sign language for her son into Hungarian for the interviewer and in this manner the interview was successfully completed. This was the only interview conducted in a foreign language, which is interesting since many workers gave difficulty in speaking English as one of the more important reasons for refusing to participate in interviews in other studies.

In this phase we utilized the traditional variables of age, education and skill level. We also included the variables of income level, race, political party preference, and religion. Multivariate and regression techniques were used in the analysis of data in addition to the more commonly employed percentage distributions. None of these would have been feasible without the use of the computer.

THE HYPOTHESES TO BE TESTED

From a wide range of hypotheses about the Studebaker shutdown we will be concerned only with a few in order to show how these were tested. The hypotheses are 1) what predisplacement factors are the best predictors of employment status following a permanent plant shutdown, 2) what effect did the Studebaker closing have on the attitudes and beliefs of displaced workers in terms of alienation,[2] radicalism,[3] and particularly economic deprivation.

It was necessary to construct indexes of alienation, radicalism, and economic deprivation from the data that had been coded from the interview. The data from a seventeen-page interview were coded on three Hollerith cards for each Studebaker worker interviewed. Each column corresponded to a question in the interview schedule. A code book was developed which explained or translated the code for the interview schedule. This codebook ran thirty-five pages. When punching data on more than one card it is necessary that each interview be numbered and this corresponding number put on each Hollerith card that was used to code data from the interview. In our study we used the first three columns of each card for this identification number, and in Column 80 of the card we put which data card it was — number 1, 2, or 3. These data were then transferred to magnetic tape. Each data set then consisted of two hundred and forty columns. This means that the first column of the second card became Column 81 and the first column of the third card in the data set became Column 161. There were approximately 40 blank columns at the end of the third card of the data set which we were able to utilize in constructing new variables from the data that we had already collected.

---

[2]A measure of the emotional adjustment of the worker to society.
[3]The attitude of the workers toward the degree of government control of economic life.

Economic deprivation

For example, in order to achieve a better understanding of the actual extent of economic deprivation and to discover who was most likely to suffer its consequences, an index of economic deprivation was constructed. The index probes three dimensions of economic hardship, 1) the change in amount of savings over the past year, 2) the number of expenditures cut down on since the shutdown, and 3) application for surplus-food relief.

The index of economic deprivation was constructed by assigning to the answer on the question about the amount of savings, 2 points for a decrease in savings, 1 point for "same" response, and 0 points for an increase in savings. On the question on cut-down and expenditures, a positive response to a decrease in two or more expenditures was assigned 2 points, a positive response to a decrease in one expenditure was assigned 1 point, and a reply of no cut-backs was given a score of 0. For the question on surplus food, the application for food was assigned 2 points, while not applying for surplus commodities was assigned 0 points. This scale measures the discrepancy or dissonance between one's needs and one's means for satisfying them. In spite of our equalitarian norms, those in different social strata clearly have differing minimal levels of expectation. This scale thus measures relative economic deprivation.

The mechanics of scoring this question was to take the answers given in Column 90 (savings), Column 100 (cut-down in expenditures), and Column 108 (surplus food recipient) and to place the summated scores from these columns into Column 201. To do this it was necessary that we construct a new tape by going from the original tape to a second tape.[4] As we transferred the data from the first tape to the second tape, the scoring on the index of economic deprivation was computed and placed in Column 201. At the same time we were also putting a summary score into Column 202 which was scaled as follows: a score of 0–1 point was coded as low economic deprivation, a score of 2 points as medium-to-low deprivation, a score of 3–4 points as medium-high deprivation, and finally a score of 5–6 points as high deprivation. The index was constructed in such a manner that only those who applied for surplus food could possibly receive a score of high economic deprivation. Twenty-six percent of the workers had low economic deprivation, 16 percent had medium-low deprivation, 45 percent had medium-high deprivation and 14 percent had high deprivation.

At the same time that the index of economic deprivation was being constructed in going from the original magnetic tape of the data to a new magnetic tape, two other indexes were constructed. The index of alienation was placed into Columns 205 and 206, and the index of radicalism was placed in Columns 207 and 208. The scoring procedure or the method of translating the points for these indexes was similar to the procedure used in constructing the index of economic deprivation and placing it into new positions on magnetic tape.

The importance of the computer in constructing these indexes cannot be underestimated. If a computer were not available these would never have been constructed — or if constructed would have taken many many man hours to accomplish. Without the computer a relatively simple analysis of the data would be available while with the computer it was possible to do much more sophisticated analysis.

To construct Table 11-2 we ran separate cross-tabulations between economic deprivation and the independent variables of employment status, age, race, educa-

[4]Characteristic of the UNIVAC tape system.

	Low Deprivation	Medium-Low Deprivation	Medium-High Deprivation	High Deprivation	N	Probability	Contingency Coefficient
Employment Status							
Not reemployed	12.8	12.8	48.1	26.3	156		
Reemployed	30.1	20.3	40.6	9.0	133	P 0.001	0.358
Still working at Studebaker	43.0	12.7	44.3	0.0	79		
Age							
34 or younger	30.2	20.8	41.5	7.5	53		
35–49	23.7	16.8	43.5	16.0	131		
50–59	21.7	11.7	53.3	13.3	120	NS	0.179
60 and over	32.8	15.6	32.8	18.8	64		
Race							
White	28.8	16.4	43.3	11.5	323	P 0.001	0.256
Negro	2.2	8.9	53.3	35.6	45		
Educational Level							
8 yrs. or less	17.1	10.6	50.4	22.0	123		
9–10 yrs.	18.3	19.7	47.9	14.1	71		
11–12 yrs.	31.5	16.8	41.3	10.5	143	P 0.001	0.270
13 + yrs. (College)	48.4	19.4	29.0	3.2	31		
Job Classification							
Nonskilled	18.3	14.7	46.9	20.1	224		
Semiskilled	23.1	15.4	50.8	10.8	65		
Skilled	33.3	16.7	50.0	0.0	18	P 0.001	0.337
Supervision (foreman)	52.4	4.8	38.1	4.8	21		
Tech., Off., and Adm.	52.5	25.0	22.5	0.0	40		
Wage Level (1963)							
Less than $3,999	19.1	20.6	45.6	14.7	68		
4,000–4,999	13.5	12.2	48.6	25.3	74		
5,000–5,999	16.8	10.9	50.5	21.8	101		
6,000–6,999	30.0	18.0	48.0	4.0	50	P 0.001	0.399
7,000–7,999	45.9	19.7	34.4	0.0	61		
10,000 and over	78.6	14.3	7.1	0.0	14		
Political Party							
Democrat	20.8	11.5	47.4	20.3	192		
Republican	40.8	22.4	34.7	2.0	49	P 0.001	0.336
Other	26.8	18.9	44.1	10.2	127		
Religion							
Protestant	27.6	15.1	44.7	12.6	199		
Catholic	23.2	14.2	45.2	17.4	155	NS*	0.076
Other	21.4	35.7	35.7	7.1	14		

*Based on Protestants and Catholics only (N = 354) — the "other" category did not achieve acceptable theoretical cell frequencies.

tional level, job classification, wage level, political affiliation and religion. These separate tables were constructed simultaneously in one computer run. Then we punched cards from these data for each contingency table. A program was written to compute the chi-square and the contingency coefficient for each table.

The relationship between economic deprivation and the various social and economic characteristics of the Studebaker workers is given in Table 11-2. Employment status, as would be expected, was strongly associated with the worker's extent of economic distress. Those still at Studebaker had the lowest deprivation while those unemployed had the highest. The workers who had found reemployment were in the middle. None of those still at Studebaker had high economic deprivation, while over a quarter of those unemployed did. A full three-fourths of the unemployed workers were found in the high or medium-high deprivation categories. As a sidelight, it is interesting to note how many of those still at Studebaker fell into the medium-high deprivation category. Although this group of workers was still employed, they had already begun to cut back on expenditures in anticipation of their expected layoffs. In a sense, this constitutes a form of anticipatory socialization to the unemployed worker role.

The variable of age, on the other hand, was not statistically significant and had only a low correlation with economic deprivation. This was in spite of the fact that age has a strong association with employment status. The difference appears largely because the oldest age group, which is the one most likely to be unemployed, did not exhibit the expected high degree of economic deprivation. To the extent that any age group had higher deprivation, the middle-aged respondents appear to have had the greatest financial difficulty. This is because these workers, in most cases, still had dependents to support, as well as other financial obligations — such as mortgages.

Among the three socioeconomic status variables, the one that demonstrates the strongest association with the workers' deprivation was his wage level at Studebaker prior to the shutdown. With the expected exception of the aberrant lowest-wage category, there was a marked inverse relationship between income and economic deprivation — the higher the income level, the lower the deprivation. However, while the pattern is striking, it can hardly be called unexpected. Those in the highest income brackets are more likely to have other sources of income and they are also more likely to secure reemployment more rapidly than are those in the lower wage levels.

The respondent's job classification, likewise, is clearly associated with the degree of economic distress experiences. This, of course, is to be anticipated, given the fact that the socioeconomic status variables are not independent of one another. In any case, far more of those with low-skill levels have higher deprivation than do those with more skilled or white-collar jobs. The distribution is also similar for educational level, although the contingency coefficient is somewhat lower. Those with the lowest educational level have the fewest respondents in the low-deprivation column and the greatest number in the high-deprivation column. There is a clear pattern of low education relating to high deprivation.

The difference in economic deprivation between whites and Negroes is quite considerable. It was expected that nonwhites among the Studebaker workers would have far more economic problems than would whites. However, the degree of difference is striking — almost 90 percent of the Negroes have medium-high or high economic deprivation — and, only 2 percent of the Negroes have low deprivation compared to 29 percent of the whites. Nonwhites are not only more likely to be unemployed, but they are also far more likely to suffer severe economic distress. It is also possible, however, that Negroes feel less stigma about receiving surplus food.

The relationship between the worker's political affiliation and his level of economic deprivation is also quite definite. Republicans have the lowest economic deprivation while Democrats have the highest. This finding can be attributed largely to differences in socioeconomic status levels of the respondents and of the two major parties. In our sample, Republicans as a general rule have higher income, occupation, and educational levels than do Democrats. Thus political party differences generally reflect socioeconomic status differences.

Causes of economic deprivation

We now turn our attention from a concern with the existence or strength of statistical relationships to the related question of what variable or variables are the best determinants of economic hardship. The relative predicative abilities of employment status, age, job classification, education, income and race are given in Table 11-3. The table gives the multiple-correlation coefficient, R squared, plus the beta weights which are the standardized partial-regression coefficients.

In order to run a multiple regression (discussed in greater detail in Chapter 9), it was necessary to punch new data cards for each person interviewed. This was accomplished by transferring data from the original tape to punched output. One data card was generated for each respondent. For the multiple-regression program to work properly, all punched output was in floating point — i.e., a decimal point was added to each number transferred.

Table 11-3 indicates quite clearly that the worker's employment status is the best predictor of economic deprivation following dismissal. This finding supports the results of the correlational analysis. As anticipated, those who had not found new jobs suffered the greatest hardships, while those who had found some type of reemployment suffered less. The age of the worker, in spite of its importance in predicting employment status, was of practically no value in determining the extent of economic hardship encountered by the worker. Age was the weakest of all the predictions. While the oldest workers have the highest amount of unemployment, this is balanced by the fact that middle-aged and younger workers tend to have more dependents and greater financial responsibilities.

The three socioeconomic status factors of education, income, and occupation are, at best, of limited predictive utility. Knowing any of these predisplacement

TABLE 11-3. Standard partial-regression coefficients (beta weights). In a series of multiple regressions predicting economic deprivation (N = 289)*

	Independent Variables					Multiple Correlation Coefficient	R²
Age	Occupation	Education	Income	Race	Employment Status		
-0.043[a]	-0.107[a]	-0.122[a]	-0.144[a]	0.197[a]	-0.250[a]	0.449[b]	0.201
	-0.112	-0.134	-0.127	0.195	-0.260	0.447	0.200
		-0.167	-0.150	0.193	-0.254	0.435	0.189
			-0.167	0.201	-0.292	0.404	0.163
				0.226	-0.274	0.369	0.136
					-0.292	0.292	0.085

*The independent variable contributing least was dropped in each successive regression.
[a]Beta weights with all other independent variables controlled.
[b]F significant at the 0.001 level for all regressions.

factors does not enable us to add much to our predictive knowledge of the extent of economic deprivation encountered. This discovery of the minor utility of these variables is particularly interesting since the percentage differences are considerable in some cases. Another change from the correlation data is in the relative ordering of the three variables. The regression analysis indicates that educational level is somewhat more important than the earlier (correlation) contingency coefficient would suggest. Finally, race is moderately important as a predictive variable; nonetheless, while percentage differences between the white and Negro responses is marked, knowing a respondent's race in itself does not allow us to adequately predict his degree of economic difficulty. Further analysis of the data indicates that alienation and radicalism are predicted better by economic deprivation than by variables such as employment status, education, age, etc.

CONCLUSION

The significance is that by the use of a computer and sophisticated statistical techniques it is possible to get a better understanding of why people behave and think in the way that they do. The important findings in this study would not have been possible without using the computer in developing new variables such as economic deprivation and then by being able to run extremely sophisticated statistical tests such as multiple regression.

12

The Historian and the Computer[1]

HISTORICAL METHODOLOGY AND THE COMPUTER

For the historian, the computer is particularly useful whenever something can be learned by counting. An equally great advantage of the computer is that it may be used for processes other than counting. It may store and retrieve alphabetized data on command. It may find, sort, and arrange variantly spelled words or information about variant spellings. In short, one of the great advantages of the computer is that it can deal with verbal as well as with numerical problems. It is well to illustrate this through applications to economic history because this kind of history deals mostly with things that can be counted — whether bushels or codfish, ton-miles or insurance premiums, tax dollars or porterage fees, values-added or freight-car loadings. The computer, of course, has value in any kind of history — whether military, political, linguistic, medical, or other — which deals with multitudes of facts in recognizable categories. Here, however, we shall confine ourselves to economic history.

The obvious advantage of the computer is that it can handle enormous quantities of facts at the rate of a million separate operations per second. A less obvious advantage, but certainly as great, is that it forces the student to ask precise questions. One cannot carry on an unprepared dialogue with a computer; for the computer itself is of no help. It will not refine vague curiosity into sharp and penetrating inquiries; it will only give specific answers to specific questions. In its ability to think original thoughts, the computer is a half-wit. Computers can be given responses to chess moves, but, as yet, there is no possibility that a computer could beat a player who is better than the one who composed the responses, or one who, by games theory, randomizes more skillfully. The computer, which the humanist or social scientist will use, works with the arithmetic of an infant, saying only "yes" or "no," "right" or "wrong." But the computer can combine and recombine yes-no reactions and in minutes produce results that would take a large number of people and many centuries to calculate.

---

[1]The first half of this chapter evolved from materials developed and published by Marshal Smelser and William I. Davisson, "*The Historian and the Computer: A Simple Introduction to Complex Computation*", Essex Institute Historical Collections, CIV, No. 2 (Salem, Mass.: The Essex Institute © 1968), pp. 109ff.

A few generalities will help before getting down to cases. To learn the scientific answer to a question, the question must be sharply defined. The quality of the definition will depend on the quality of the mind which defines. Sharpening the question may be the hardest part of the whole study. Having arrived at a question which will lead to the answer sought, the seeker is still faced with a methodological problem — that is, with finding the right way to get the answer, whether he is using the computer or a pencil and paper. Almost always the inquirer will have to divide his problem into parts and solve each part separately. To put it more conventionally, for humanists, he will have to break his problem into elements, collect data about each, construct hypotheses about each of the elements, test these hypotheses, and draw the conclusions into one defensible answer. Certainly the use of the computer or any other system of calculation is here subordinated to the human mind, which must evaluate at every stage, from the formulation of an answer derived from mute facts which speak not of themselves but with the voice of their master.

At the risk of repetition, the process can be explained this way: (1) shaping the correct question out of the nebular gases of creative curiosity; (2) developing a method of answering the question defined; (3) applying the method to data which bear directly on the question, an application of method that is a) bibliographical and archival, and b) mining the sources for their ore; (4) studying or "processing" the facts to put them in an order in which they can be understood; and (5) phrasing the answer.

The computer is of use only in the fourth step; but if one wishes to be scientific or definitive about things that can be counted or measured, the computer is indispensable. Without it one is reduced to generalizing from scraps of information. Such generalizations from scraps are often very durable in historical literature. Their durability is probably in direct proportion to their agreement with what logically ought to or could have been the case rather than with what really happened. This is not to adopt the positivist view that if man cannot measure, man cannot know; but to urge the conviction that what can be measured should be measured.

The economic historian has the problem of trying to draw valid answers from questions put to enormous masses of facts, usually expressed in statistics. So large are many of these collections that one student, using pencil and paper, or a small desk calculator, can neither distill nor arrange the total of facts in any way which can be understood, even by him. But the computer is so fast and so accurate that it can produce simple one-page answers to questions which are put to the very largest collections of figures expressing quantities. These brief answers can be produced as tables and graphs, both easily printed by the computer at the command of its user. With the computer all the data can be assimilated. It is no longer necessary to write economic history from scraps and dubious samples.

For example, the inventories of estate in the records of Essex County, Massachusetts, 1641–1700, can be reduced to approximately 130,000 data cards which together tell us all that can be known now of the wealth of the county in those sixty years. To learn the answer to pointedly defined questions about the economy of the county, the manner of holding property, the types of property held, the nature of the wealth of the county and how it grew, the computer, starting at the beginning, can print seven one-page tables and eighteen explanatory graphs in about ten minutes. Such tables and graphs may distill to only one sentence each, but if the author has a good mind each sentence will be the definitive sentence on its subject.

A manual worker would have had to organize and make perhaps 1,000,000 calculations from the estate records — or, more likely, from notes on the estate records — and then draw his graphs and compile his tables. How long would it take? At least two thousand clock hours. Put another way, let it be assumed that two scholars, equally informed and of equal ability, approached the study of seventeenth-century Essex County. The man who used the computer would finish his study of all the data before the manual worker finished a fractional sample. Because of the labor involved and the sheer impossibility of organizing a huge mass of data by hand or by desk-size mechanical calculators, the constant tendency of writers has been to generalize broadly from narrow spans of data drawn from statutes, from personal memoirs and account books, from such short series of statistics as come readily to hand, and from the tendentious economic writings of contemporaries who were trying to influence public policy. The results can be provocative, even entertaining, but they convey no certitude. One may estimate a man's riches by his manner of life, but one could do more than guess if he could total the figures in the memoranda of his tax accountant.

The special value of the historian is that he knows the field of facts, or universes of data. William O. Aydelotte has pointed out that there have already been many quantitative studies in history. He himself has applied the method to voting patterns in the British House of Commons, and he names nearly a score of such studies that have either upset established generalizations or have provoked intensive restudy by skeptical scholars.[2] These questions could not have been left to computer scientists; only historians know which superannuated generalizations rest on inadequate statistical support.

The use of high-speed electronic data-processing is not limited to that which can be measured, but may be most useful to the historian of quantities. In the sources, what can be measured is usually, but not always, expressed in statistical tables for the researcher. There are no special problems of the reliability of quantity sources that differ from those of other sources. A list of quantities can be as false as a list of qualities. The historian will use the same standards of critical scholarship to evaluate quantitative sources as he uses to evaluate any other sources. A bitter old general, writing his memoirs to revenge the blighting of a career, could fake or forget his strength reports or the strength of the enemy army; just as he could lie about the morals of the civilian directors of strategy, or omit their successes. Actually, the study of quantitative information may offer less critical difficulty than the study of other sources, because it is usually compiled for other than forensic purposes. In economic history it is usually compiled to make money — whether by taxation or profit; thus, it is to the interest of the compiler to take pains to be accurate, in a mood often foreign to the writer of the narrative of a crucial political struggle in which he participated.

Methodologically, there are several caveats which must be kept in mind while applying quantitative methods, whether by hand or by machine, to economic history. 1) Although quantities as quantities can be tabulated for very early periods, even from Babylonian records, statistical tables are not numerous and continuous from a time much earlier than the late seventeenth century. The most reliable economic records which predate the last decade of the seventeenth century are estate records, which, incidentally, lend themselves to many interesting inquiries. 2) The names of places, weights and measures, and commodities differ from age to age; these differences pose critical problems which historians are professionally obligated to solve and cannot be accepted as obstacles. 3) Polemic writers, attempting to justify or to change policy, have not been above producing deliberately biased series of quantities for the purposes of persuasion rather than instruction; this

---

[2]William O. Aydelotte, "Quantification in History," *American Historical Review*, **LXXI** (1965–66), pp. 803–825, an excellent and persuasive study.

problem of tendentiousness is found in all works of advocacy and is no greater in quantitative studies than in other kinds of historical study. 4) In early economic history all the arithmetic of the Western world seems to have been done manually, even after the abacus and Pascal's wheels were available. Inevitably, clerical errors have crept into records, even the honest records of zealous government departments. Some of these errors of calculation have been quite large. The computer provides a happy remedy; unlike the manual worker, it can recalculate the addition, subtraction, multiplication, and division at a rate which occasions no appreciable loss of time. On the other hand, if the customs' clerk noted down 132 barrels of molasses, when he meant to write 123, the error is unknowable to posterity. And since it was unknowable before the invention of the computer, there is no objection to electronic data-processing.

To use the computer for economic history the historian need not change his habits of thought very much. In individual cases, the principal difference may be that he has been used to formulating a question and then roving in search of data to answer the question. To use the computer correctly the opposite technique is used. First, he peoples the relevant universe with all its data, then he asks the questions. Traditionally there have always been two ways of learning history. One student will ask, "Why did A do B?" and then look for a body of sources which contains the answer. Another will come upon a trove of documents which have not been previously exploited and ask himself, "What questions does this collection answer?" The second method must be used in studying history by means of the computer. The facts must be assembled to answer every conceivable question that may ever be asked of a given universe. The inquirer never starts with a specific question and proceeds to assemble the data, but starts with the whole body of data and asks questions. After all, what is a collection of historical data but a collection of answers waiting to be questioned? If the questions are unanswerable the answers are unknowable.

It follows that the investigator must have a prior classification scheme and be lavish, profuse, unstinted, even excessive and extravagant in cross-referencing, so that every conceivable future pairing of categories will be possible when the time comes to ask questions. The prior classification scheme is essential, but the data will shape it. In existing statistical tables the original compiler has already suggested the scheme. If one wishes to convert verbal documentary series into tables, one will find that the original clerk will usually have followed a set form — whether for tax assessments, wills, estate inventories, notes of hand, or whatever.

Traditionally, historians have perhaps unconsciously felt that a data sample is satisfactory proof. Why not sample this data? In the first place, it is unnecessary — the computer can digest it all. In the second place, it is bad methodology. In early economic history there is no easy way to extract valid random samples. Historical data is incomplete to begin with. What is left to study is but a sample. Even a private diary entry of the twentieth century is only a sample of a day's data. If there were an adequate series of historical facts, identically complete from start to end, it would be possible to take a preset sample which would give very accurate results, as opinion pollsters do at one specific contemporary instant. But there are no such series of past recorded quantities. Each series is a sample. Useful results cannot be obtained in history by sampling samples. The invariable rule must be, get all. The point is illustrated by Table 12-1, which was prepared by Professor Lawrence A. Harper, Department of History, University of California, Berkeley.

The table shows graphically every quarter of a year for which complete port information is available. For example, it is arithmetically impossible to find even a ten-year interval with complete data for each tenth year; the closest one can come

TABLE 12-1.   Colonial Naval Office Lists (C. O.5 for the Port of New York (PRO, C. O.,5/ 1222–1228).

Available Naval Office Lists by Years and by Quarters
Quarters change as noted below:

Quarter 1   Dec. 25 to Mar. 25
Quarter 2   Mar. 25 to June 25
Quarter 3   June 25 to Sept. 29
Quarter 4   Sept. 29 to Dec. 25

After 1752, quarters change as follows:

Quarter 1   Jan. 5 to Apr. 5
Quarter 2   Apr. 5 to July 5
Quarter 3   July 5 to Oct. 10
Quarter 4   Oct. 10 to Jan. 5

In the chart below completed squares indicate full years. Missing quarters in partial years are shown by missing sides in the squares, numbered by quarters, as follows:

```
      2
   1 □ 3
      4
```

Year New York I E	Year New York I E	Year New York I E
1715	1734	1753
1716	1735	1754
1717	1736	1755
1718	1737	1756
1719	1738	1757
1720	1739	1758
1721	1740	1759
1722	1741	1760
1723	1742	1761
1724	1743	1762
1725	1744	1763
1726	1745	1764
1727	1746	
1728	1747	
1729	1748	
1730	1749	
1731	1750	
1732	1751	
1733	1752	

to it is the series 1724, 1734, 1743, which is anomalous because 1744 is wholly absent. Yet the table is a graph of all the data available from which the historian can generalize about the trade of the port of New York from 1715 to 1764 inclusive. The impossibility of valid sampling seems plain. Even the making of this graph to determine what is available required analysis and organization of all the data.

If the reader is still attending to this matter, at about this point he will properly ask, "How do you do it?" He does not need to be able to operate a computer but it helps to have a notion of how it operates. First, the researcher draws a sharp boundary around his finite universe of facts — for example, every fact collected in the census of 1880 in the state of California was collected on a predesigned form which the researcher cannot improve upon. If he is dealing with less intelligently collected data, he will design a form of his own and will have research assistants transfer the facts from the source to his form. Third, these facts are recorded on Hollerith cards or on magnetic tape (according to the kind of computer used). This produces a data bank, before programming, and is called peripheral storage.

To take a specific case, all the individual estate inventories of Essex County, Massachusetts, for the years 1640–1682, total 430. In a preliminary study of these inventories the author found about 26,000 individual items — assets or liabilities, tangible property and intangible property. Each of these individual items could be written as a simple sentence; for example, "In 1666, John Smith had a horse worth six pounds."

Remember, "Horse plus modifiers equal sentence." That horse and his modifiers went on one card, punched there by a keypuncher. Thus the known wealth of Essex County for those forty-two years was recorded on 26,000 Hollerith cards. It so happened that these particular estate inventories had been printed, so the keypunchers worked directly from the bound volumes. They found about 1,500 archaic spellings of words representing over three hundred kinds of personal property. If wanted, these spellings can be accumulated by categories and reduced to standardized spellings by the computer.[3] If they had been in manuscript or on microfilm only, the data would have been transferred by hand by clerical workers to a form devised for the purpose — a form simple enough for the keypuncher to follow without being vexed by the necessity for making his own decisions.

This illustration from Essex County, Massachusetts, is drawn from the experience of research in progress. In the course of the study, a methodological lesson was driven home painfully. A colleague came upon an essay arguing the literacy of seventeenth-century New England. The computer was commanded to print all the signatures of the appraisers of the estates of Essex County, from 1640 to 1682, in alphabetical order, with a parallel column of the estates appraised and the dates of their signatures. In only one instance did the phrase "his mark" occur. This seemed to show a rather high level of literacy. A quick scanning of the source showed that the editors of the published documents had indicated in footnotes whether the signatures were autograph or not. Where the words "his mark" occurred in the body of the text they had stood, but if absent were not inserted by the editors. Because the nature of the signature did not appear to be an economic fact, the economic historian did not tell the keypunchers to include the footnotes. Hence the degree of literacy of the men appointed appraisers of estates in seventeenth-century Essex County remains a mystery. The methodological moral was clear — get all the data.

A few unexpected facts, however, justified the computer's few seconds of effort. Two women were thought wise enough to appraise estates. Bearers of honorific titles were rather diffident about signing them in their own hand or else were remarkably few — an "ensigne," a captain, a major, and three misters comprised the peerage. Only two sturdy characters signed themselves with the straightforward title of "goodman." And poor Giles Corey, the one of the few men in American history to be tortured to death as part of official judicial process (when he refused to plead guilty or not guilty to a charge of witchcraft), was accounted meritorious enough to appraise an estate in November, 1666.

A good deal of time has been profitably spent on the quantitative study of the wealth of Essex County[4] in the seventeenth century as a microcosm of the colonial economy.

The study of economic history, by studying all the data of its several subdivisions, can lead both to new discoveries and to revisions of old concepts which have been accepted from generation to generation without skepticism. Probably the first

---

[3]For example, "chair(s)" appeared as: *chayre(s)*, *chayrs*, *chaires*, *chayer*, *chares*, *chaiers*, *cheares*.

[4]William I. Davisson, "*Essex County Price Trends: Money and Markets in seventeenth-Century Massachusetts*" (April, 1967) and, "*Essex County Wealth Trends: Wealth and Economic Growth in seventeenth-Century Massachusetts*" (October, 1967), Essex Institute Historical Collections.

task is to reexamine the old generalizations that rest on rather narrow data. One of the most enduring of shibboleths in American historical writing has been the phrase "triangular trade," which has been used to explain the economic growth of the northern colonies which had little to sell directly to Britain. The idea is that, in ports from Philadelphia northward, merchants loaded their ships with local products, sold them abroad at an apex of the triangle, bought what was normally available at that apex, proceeded to the third apex, and sold the second cargo for a profit which was then used to buy a third cargo. The third cargo was brought home and sold. The cash was then used to buy British manufactures. This explanation has persisted in the conventional wisdom for decade after decade without question. It has been "proved" by descriptions of particular voyages which followed this pattern. The "proof" sufficed to produce a universal truism. Although the above description is a trifle oversimplified, triangle after triangle has been described.

The author has accumulated a data-bank from the Pennsylvania Gazette (Philadelphia), which lists every ship arrival and departure, every entry and clearance, for the two three-year periods 1733–1735 and 1749–1751. The port-of-entry (naval office) revenue records of Philadelphia for those periods have been destroyed by fire. The press is the only surviving comprehensive source for populating this particular universe of data. Davisson, and Lavonne Coffeen (Sacramento State College Computer Center), queried the Sacramento State College IBM 1620 computer about the triangle or triangles. The computer, so to speak, shook its head firmly. On the basis of all the surviving data, the computer provided tables from which the author could only deduce the following.[5]

1) There was no triangular trade which could be associated with Philadelphia in these two three-year periods. 2) Philadelphia shipping ran three shuttle lines: a coastwise North American trade extending to Canada, a trade to and from the Caribbean, and a trade to Europe — usually to British ports. 3) Philadelphia was the entry port for the distribution of goods from Europe and the collection of goods for shipment to Europe. (A corollary finding, for the benefit of maritime buffs, was that practically all the coastal traffic consisted of the movement of sloops and schooners, while no specific kinds of rig dominated any other aspect of the sea-going trade of Philadelphia.)

Was this a triangle? No, it was more of an "H-trade," with the horizontal line representing the transatlantic shuttle.

Admittedly, this one study of two three-year periods was not the funeral of the concept of the "triangular trade," but surely it is unsettling when an age-old generalization fails to survive its first full-scale statistical reexamination. The generalization of the "triangular trade" deserves no more than hypothetical standing until stabilized by a method that can be duplicated. Such a method will require the historian to do more than to present his impression derived from scrutiny of a few ship logs. To count the number of deep-water sailing ship passages under the Union Jack, from 1741 (when the first comprehensive list begins) until American independence, is beyond the capacity of the unaided human mind. At a guess, they could hardly have been fewer than half a million. When they have been counted, tabulated, and analyzed by electronic data-processing, historians of the economy can begin to generalize in a specific sense, instead of searching for what they hope are a few characteristic traits and tendencies which adequately answer the perennial question of history, "What happened?"

[5]See William I. Davisson, *"The Philadelphia Trade"* (Abstract), Western Economic Journal, **III** (1965), n.p.

In summary, the computer can be used in economic history to manage vast masses of quantitative data — that is, facts about things that can be usefully measured or counted. At a million operations per second it can reduce the reply to any answerable question to a single sheet, either as a table or a graph, or both. Having as many of these answers as he believes he needs, the art of the historian is brought into play to interpret; the merit of the interpretation is his, not the computer's. Computer science and its technical language need not directly concern the scholar except insofar as he needs to be able to talk with the operator of a computer, who will serve as interpreter between inquirer and machine.

Economic history, because it can now bring to bear all relevant data, can become a science at least as exact as astronomy or paleontology, both of which concern themselves with the past, and both of which develop despite the knowledge that there are gaps in their sources which may never be filled. It may sound a little pretentious, but it is tempting to call economic history, as studied by high-speed electronic data-processing machines, by the precise name "paleoeconomics."

THE HISTORICAL DATA BANK

Traditional economic history

Considerable historical research and writing has gone into the examination of problems of economic development in Great Britain and in the American Colonies. Considerable additional effort has gone into the examination of a possible relationship between the scope and the nature of economic development in Great Britain and the Colonies (plantations). The Navigation Acts represent a major attempt to integrate the metropolitan and colonial economies. Essentially, the Navigation Acts provided for the following:

1. Goods specified in the Statutes (enumerated products) exported from the plantations had to go to Great Britain even though they were to be reexported.
2. Certain types of goods to be imported into the plantations had to come from or by way of Great Britain.
3. All goods had to move in ships owned, manned, and built in the Empire.
4. Certain goods and products could not be produced in the colonies, but had to be imported from Great Britain.
5. Gold could not be exported from Great Britain (with some narrowly defined exceptions).
6. Certain colonial products (those that competed with English manufactures, agriculture, or fisheries) could not be sold in Great Britain.

In short, mercantile theory, as expressed in the Navigation Acts, was designed to control the economic development of the plantations and of Great Britain by controlling oceanic commerce.

Hitherto the general approach in writing economic history of the British Colonial System has been a documentary one rather than a statistical one. This traditional approach assumed that legislation — a Navigation Act — was needed, enacted and enforced. For the most part, the history of trade and economic development of this period has been written from the traditional point of view.

This traditional point of view is illustrated by two of the standard works of this period:

1. Charles M. Andrews, *The Colonial Period of American History: England's Commercial and Colonial Policy*, Vol. 4 (New Haven: Yale University Press, 1964)

    2.   Lawrence A. Harper, *The English Navigation Laws* (New York, Columbia University Press, 1939)

These volumes have been written from literary and legal sources — that is, from parliamentary debates, private memoirs, statutes, and colonial legislative materials. Professor Harper himself recognized the deficiency of this approach and was instrumental as early as the 1930's in starting to modify this traditional approach to the economic history of this period.

Origin of the data-bank approach

During the 1930's, Professor John H. Cox and Lawrence A. Harper (Department of History, University of California, Berkeley, California) received a grant from the Works Project Administration.[6] The objective of Professors Cox and Harper was to acquire the raw economic data needed in order to describe and analyze the economic history of the British Empire in the eighteenth century. The opening paragraphs of the Cox-Harper report, comprise the best statement that we can find illustrating the need for developing raw quantitative data. Quoting from the report:

> This filmbook[7] is the first of a series dedicated to the task of making basic data available for a better understanding of the past. It is intended to supply the actual statistics of what happened, without which general conclusions concerning economic history are merely hypotheses.

Professors Cox and Harper did not go beyond the compilation of the filmbooks because the data available was too voluminous to handle without the computer technology. Now that the needed computer technology is at hand, the filmbooks developed by Professors Cox and Harper are being transferred to machine readable form. Each filmbook is a summary of trade for one American and one Caribbean port.[8]

What can be done

This new approach would study the economy of the British Empire in the eighteenth century by using a comprehensive data bank. The study of economic growth and of economic change would be in terms of trade and commodity movements. It was not possible to undertake this type of research seriously until the computer and computer technology made possible the utilization of the total relevant quantifiable data (for each area of investigation). Thus the overall enquiry would involve two phases:

1.   Development of an economic history data bank available to economists, historians, and other interested in problems of economic growth and development.

---

[6]This grant was: Official Project No. 65-1-08-62 under the auspices of the Works Project Administration.

[7]A filmbook is a typed manuscript summary of the Naval Office records, one volme for each American and Caribbean port, taken from available records.

[8]These data are being keypunched and are in Hollerith card form and in magnetic tape form at the University of Notre Dame. The Customs 17 and Customs 3 are also being keypunched.

2. Development of a "model" that can be useful to scholars working in other disciplines. One of the most important aspects of our project would be methodological. The restudy of the economic history of the old British Empire by using computer technology would test traditional generalizations. Any "new approach" to economic history cannot rely solely on quantifiable data and data bank. There must, in fact, be a merger of this new approach with traditional approaches to economic history. Thus the "model" would deal with this problem of integrating traditional methodology and computer methodology.

The data bank

The primary operation involved in establishing a computer or machine-readable historical data bank is to place in suitable form — e.g., magnetic tape — the relevant data for any field of investigation.

Use of the Naval Office and Customs records assumes that the problem of dating and location may be made comparable. Since the Naval Office records are daily entries (the Customs are yearly entries), the process may eventually involve adjusting the daily entries of the Naval Office records to the annual Customs entries.

In order to complete the data bank for the study of the British Empire in the eighteenth century it is necessary to transfer the following Customs materials from microfilm to machine-readable form:

Customs   3   (C.3)   Ledgers of imports and exports of England and Wales from 1697–1780.

Customs 17 (C.17) Reports on the state of navigation, commerce, and revenues for the years 1772 onward. These documents comprise the extension of the Customs 3 to the end of the 18th century.

Customs 14 (C.14) Ledgers of imports and exports — Scotland, 1755–1827

Customs 15 (C.15) Ledgers of imports and exports — Ireland, 1698–1829

It might be noted that in the eighteenth century, a major source of revenue to the Crown (as well as the method of controlling trade and economic development), was the *customs duty* imposed on *commodities* imported into England or Wales, or Scotland, or Ireland. Furthermore, there was a rebate of the customs duty on imports, subsequently reexported. In any event, the process of collecting and of rebating the *duty* or *customs duty* (money) involved keeping track of the commodities themselves. These Customs ledgers noted above take their names from the Commissioners of Custom who were charged with keeping track of the revenue collected or rebated. The ledgers are primarily valuable, however, for their detail of commodity movements.

Analysis by computer

The historian may then examine the effectiveness of the Navigation Acts in controlling commodity trade under the English mercantile system during the eighteenth century. In order to carry out such a study it is necessary to refine the basis upon which man may communicate with the computer regarding the data bank:

1. Specialized search and retrieval may be accomplished — i.e., for a particular commodity.

2. Conversion of given commodity weights and measures to a standard weight or measure. For instance, wine is recorded in casks, tierces, pipes, etc., each of which has a specific gallon value. One must convert all movements of wine to a gallon value.

The navigation acts

Study could then examine the effectiveness of the Navigation Acts in controlling commodity trade and economic development of the American plantations under the English mercantile system in the 18th century.[9] Mercantilism had four well-defined objectives (for England):

1. To encourage domestic shipping by the Navigation Acts.
2. To protect domestic grain growers.
3. To protect domestic (English) industries and to foster new ones.
4. To amass and to keep a large amount of hard money in domestic (English) public or private hands (favorable balance of trade).

These four objectives were related to the overall purpose of making the nation a strong military and naval power. The currency objective was the most important and embraced the other three.

These ideas were applied in English law up to the early nineteenth century at which point "laissez-faire" succeeded as the dominant philosophy in controlling national economic policy.

Parliament began enacting mercantile legislation in the seventeenth century and continued to add to the legislation (Navigation Acts) until approximately 1750. The application of mercantile ideas to all overseas colonies was undertaken through these series of acts. This kind of trade regulation has been called the "Old Colonial System."

The investigation itself, then, would consist of posing a series of hypotheses or questions that would be answered by reference to the computer-accessible data bank.

1. The law stated that only the following items could be exported from the American and Caribbean plantations to England: sugar, tobacco, cotton, ginger, dyewoods.
   Was the law obeyed?
   a. Did the American or Caribbean plantation export each commodity only to England?
   b. Did the American or Caribbean plantations import any of the commodity from any other port, or from any other country, or from any other plantation?
   c. Did England import each commodity only from the English plantations?
   d. Did England use all the commodity imported from its plantations, or did England reexport part thereof (for gold)?
   (Since the data bank would include the necessary data for the American plantations, the Caribbean plantations, and the total trade of Great Britain (including England and Wales, Ireland, and Scotland) the effectiveness of the legislation may be measured.)
2. A second question that could be answered at the same time as Question No. 1, above, is that concerning the economic structure of the plantations insofar as net commodity imports and net commodity exports are concerned.
3. The third question that could be asked concerns whether or not the plantations traded solely with England.

[9]Comparison of the Customs and Naval Office records assumes that the two data sets may be made comparable as to dating and location.

   a. The Staple Acts of 1663 provided that all goods from Europe or from European ports could be shipped to the Colonies only through English ports.

       Did all European goods (or the goods from European countries or ports) imported to the plantations come from England only?

   b. If the American and Caribbean plantations imported goods from countries other than England, which countries and which commodites were involved?

   What portion of the imported goods to the plantations came from these other areas?

4. Other questions that could be posed are:

   a. Smuggling has been a recurrent problem for students of the Old Colonial System. This problem could be at least partially resolved by comparing the Customs data with the Naval Office data, on a commodity by commodity, country by country basis.

   b. In 1699, the Woolen Act was passed. This act prohibited the export of, or intercolonial trade in, wool. The effectiveness of this act has been questioned and could be tested by evaluating the woolen trade between England and the plantations and among the plantations. This would involve testing the trade in wool or wool products against the data found in the Customs and in the Naval Office records.

   c. The effectiveness of the laws regulating trade has often focused upon the enumerated commodities. The commodities on this enumerated list were supposed to travel in prescribed methods, unique for each commodity: copper, fur, tobacco, cotton, wool, sugar, rice, indigo, molasses, naval stores. In addition, cereals, salt, food, and other provisions were barred from England. The Iron Act of 1750 encouraged the manufacture of bar iron and pig iron, but prohibited the making of finished products from iron except for kettles, salt pans, and cannon in the colonies.

       Each of these commodities would, in fact, form the subject for a testable hypothesis with regard to the effectiveness of the Navigation Acts.

The process of testing these questions or hypotheses against the data bank would be the first step. The evaluation of the answers against the existing qualitative evidence on the subject would be the second step. The final evaluation would involve the necessary adjustment of conventional historical generalizations in the light of the factual positions developed.

Anglo-Scots-Irish economic development and change

A second research project could examine the significance of the mercantile system in the economic development of England, Scotland, and Ireland.

1. The new historian may measure the growth and changes in the English economy by investigating the following questions (as example):

   a. How effective was the Staple Act in controlling the trade of the plantations?

   b. How effective was the Staple Act in directing the trade of the plantations through England, rather than through Scotland and Ireland?

    c.   How effective were the lists of enumerated commodities in controlling the trade of the plantations through England rather than through Scotland and Ireland?

    d.   What percentage of all goods, and which goods (by commodity) were imported into England for use internally and which goods were reexported?

    e.   What was the growth in the trade volume (by commodity and by total) of England during this period, of Ireland during this period, of Scotland during this period?

    f.   What change in the structure of English trade (by commodity, by volume, and by port of origin or destination) is seen in the eighteenth century? What does the trade structure indicate concerning the English economy in this period?

(Clearly, each one of these questions would have to be broken down into rather more specific questions, susceptible to computer analysis on the basis of one commodity, a year at a time, for each country involved. Trade volume, on some suitable basis, would need to be aggregated from the commodity level.)

2.   The historian could examine the nature of Scottish trade during this period and its implications:

    a.   What was the nature of the Scottish economy?

    b.   What was the development of Scottish trade as a portion of the overall Anglo-Scottish trade?

    c.   What commodities were traded between Scotland and England over time? To what extent did it affect the English trade with the plantations?

    d.   What was the change of the position of the Scottish trade as a part of the Empire trade in the eighteenth century?

    e.   To what extent did Scotland act as market for:
       i.   Plantation goods?
      ii.   European goods?

    f.   What, if any, were the significant reexports from Scotland? Where did they come from? What was their destination?

3.   The growth of the Irish economy in this period, might well be reflected in the Customs trade records:

    a.   What was the change in the total value of the export and import commodity trade of Ireland between 1700 and 1800?

    b.   What was the change in the structure of the Irish economy, measured by the type and quantity of commodities imported, exported, and reexported?

    c.   To what extent did Ireland act as a market for:
       i.   Plantation goods?
      ii.   European goods?

    d.   To what extent was Ireland a significant factor in the plantation trade in:
       i.   Woolens?
      ii.   Linen?
     iii.   Livestock or meat products?

4.   What was Ireland's role (and Scotland's role) as a supplier of commodities to England and as a market for English goods in the eighteenth century?

    a.   What commodities were supplied by England to Ireland (Scotland), by commodity, by volume?
       i.   At the beginning of the century?
      ii.   At the end of the century?
     iii.   At select points between?

  b. What was Ireland's (Scotland's) importance to England as a market for its products, by commodity?
      i. At the beginning of the century?
      ii. At the end of the century?
  c. How did the position change over time?
  d. What is the significance of the change?
  e. What does the change imply for the structure of the Irish (Scottish) economy?
  f. What was Ireland's (Scotland's) importance to England as supplier of products, by commodity?
      i. At the beginning of the century?
      ii. At the end of the century?
  g. How did the position change over time?
  h. What is the significance of the change?
  i. What does the change imply for the structure of the Irish (Scottish) economy?

CONCLUSION

The availability of computer technology to scholars makes possible for the first time a new approach to economic history. Specifically, the computer makes possible studies of economic growth and development in terms of the vast economic data presently available in raw form, but heretofore unusable. The traditional approach to the study of economic growth and development has, of necessity, been based on statutes, contemporary economic theory, contemporary polemic literature (usually accompanied by fragmentary selections of statistics), legislative debates, commercial correspondence and reports. It was simply not feasible to utilize the available raw data in a comprehensive manner prior to the development and refinement of the computer equipment and computer technology.

13

Data Conversion and Economic Model Building: Economic Growth and Development in Colonial America

ECONOMIC MODELS

Models and data

It is not too general to note that most models of economic growth and development are based upon relatively sophisticated data, such as the domestic census information. Furthermore, most of the models are "income" or flow-account models — that is, models whose significant variables are income — e.g., personal income, national income, and the like. Most of these present-day economic models are of limited usefulness when it comes to evaluating underdeveloped areas. One of the major problems is that the kind of data available in underdeveloped areas is neither in the proper form nor of the proper kind to be used as input for economic models.

Present-day underdeveloped areas, just as in colonial America, do have significant and available sources of data that may be used in economic model building. However, the data must be transformed; and the model must be modified to accept the available data before steps may be made in the area of underdeveloped areas — present or past. The approach suggested here may be relevant for handling the problem of analysis of growth and development in underdeveloped areas.

One of the practical problems that one confronts in the process of economic model building is the data problem. Economists have made considerable progress in the development of sophisticated models.[1] These models are theoretically capable of answering nearly every conceivable question that the economist needs to know about the economy of a country. The problem remains, however, that a model is only as good as its data. Here the economist confronts two kinds of problems, a conceptual problem and a practical problem.

Let us assume that we wish to use a model in evaluating some question of an economy and its growth. Let us also assume that this model uses personal income as one of its major variables. Certain questions arise concerning the definition to be given to personal income. Should one include imputed income for personal services?

[1]See: Jan Tinbergen & H. C. Bos, *Mathematical Models of Economic Growth* (New York, McGraw-Hill, 1962). Also: R. G. D. Allen, *Macro-Economic Theory — A Mathematical Treatment* (Toronto, Macmillan, 1967).

Should unilateral transfers be included or excluded? The results that a model will give are only as good as the data input. The data input depends on the definitions that guide the accumulation and preparation of the data.

The second problem of data input for model analysis is that of data conversion. In many instances the data available as input for a model is not in a form that is usable by the model. It is necessary, therefore, to convert the data from its given form to a suitable form. At this point the link is first made between economic model analysis and computer use.

Wealth and structure of the colonial American economy

Little quantitative evidence has appeared concerning the development process of the colonial period of our country. How the structure of the colonial economy changed from the time of its inception to that of the Revolution is vitally important in analyzing the impact of the American Revolution upon our new nation. Although a military conquest was won, it would have been only a matter of time for the colonies to succumb to the economic pressures of Great Britain had not economic independence been established some time before the Revolution. History bears us out when we say that the colonies had a good deal of economic independence at the time of the Revolution as is shown by their subsequent ability to sustain themselves during the period immediately following the war.

It is often claimed that the economic causes of the rebellion of 1776 were found in the North. The Northern economy — i.e., the economies of the Northern and Middle States — did not fit "well" within the mercantile system. The Northern colonies somehow developed in such a way as to be relatively independent of England in the economic sphere — i.e., as contrasted to the Southern one-crop (tobacco) shipments to England.

We may test this hypothesis on two levels:
1) by an examination of the development of the Northern economy from 1641–1776, using as our guide, Essex County, Massachusetts;
2) by an examination of the degree of reliance of the Northern colonies upon foreign trade.

In this study the important issue is how and why the structure of the colonial economy changed to be virtually independent (economically) of England by the end of the eighteenth century. This question can only be answered by looking at the development process of the colonies and the influence and impact of foreign trade on the colonial economy. Since the dependence upon Great Britain was decreasing during this period, the structural changes that took place in the colonial economy are worth investigation.

The preliminary conclusions developed from the first test of this question of economic growth suggests the familiar. There had been a relative increase in commercial capital relative to agricultural capital. The prices of British goods were relatively high compared with both domestic colonial alternatives and with colonial ability to pay. There appeared to be a definite substitution of domestic capital for British capital. A familiar illustrative example is the substitution of domestic wooden pegs for British nails. This substitution was found not only in building and woodwork but in agricultural implements — e.g., the harrow. Here was suggested, by the initial study, a significant range of substitution of colonial products for British imports.

A second aspect of substitution appeared broader. It appears that the colonial economy adopted patterns of growth that did not require British capital. This seemed to involve the development of trade goods and marketable products that could be produced in the colonies that required no British goods in the production process. Considerably more work is needed in order to clarify more precisely what happened. Insufficient work has yet been done to permit any conclusion on the degree of reliance of the Northern colonies on foreign trade.[2]

THE ECONOMY OF ESSEX COUNTY

Why Essex County?

With all the possible choices available, why did we choose Essex County as our trial county? There were several reasons, and it may be well to indicate what they were. It seemed that there were two basic data sets that we would need in one way or another before we were through. The first would be the records of estate inventory values. The second would be vital statistics. Essex County has a complete and continuous probate court estate series from 1641 and a complete vital statistic series. The present study considers the period 1641–1700. Our plans are to continue the Essex study up to 1790. Other areas such as Providence, Rhode Island, have comparable series, but they are not as extensive, nor are they as inclusive.

Suffolk County may well have a comparable probate court record series, as well as a vital statistics series; however, the size of the Suffolk County records (Boston) precluded work with them. Boston represented a potentially logical area for consideration if it would be possible to integrate the materials on the internal economy (probate court records and vital statistics) with the Naval Office records of Boston trade. However, there has been such a significant loss and/or destruction of the Boston trade records that they are extremely fragmentary. Thus, the absence of the suitable Naval Office records of maritime trade plus the size of the Boston materials made it necessary to work with a more manipulable record set.

There are certain advantages to the use of Salem in attempting to gain insight into the colonial economy. Compared with Boston, the Essex County area is undoubtedly more representative of the overall colonial development. Salem did not reach its peak as a maritime port until after 1790. Certainly Essex County represents the ubiquitous agricultural-extractive type of activity that is characteristic of the American colonial period.

The data sources

Essex County Estate Inventories

One of the common problems for the historian and the economic historian — and, in fact, for any social scientist dealing with the attempt to recreate past efforts of human development — is the dearth of *usable measurable data*. This problem often resolves itself into one of two serious limitations. There may be too little data available so that the evidence is highly fragmentary. Obvious instances are in the area of historical anthropology. The attempts to recreate the political and social structure of the Egyptian and Sumerian empires are greatly limited. The basic

[2]William I. Davisson and Dennis J. Dugan, "Growth and Wealth in The Colonial Economy: 1641–1682," *8th Annual Econometric History Institute, Paper* (West Lafayette, Indiana, Purdue University, February, 1968).

trouble here is that there is simply not enough documentary or other evidence to sufficiently close the gaps in knowledge to present a coherent and comprehensive picture.

The other possible limitation is that concerning the early or colonial period of American history where in certain areas such as trade, shipping, and distribution, the information available is so voluminous that it cannot easily be handled. In this situation what usually happens is that rather unscientific (not statistically accurate) samples are used or the data are ignored altogether. The result is that the research centers on rather vaguely defined samples or ignores the larger field entirely. Narrow specialists arise who handle limited aspects of the problem.

In American history, it is nearly 1800 before useful census data series begin to appear consistently. The basic question remains for the colonial period — roughly defined here as from 1630–1790 — whether some consistent and usable data series might exist that would provide a useful series of price and wealth trends.

The New England forefathers were extremely methodical in many things, including many areas of economic endeavor. Two of the areas bear directly upon the present problems, the methods of prior survey and subsequent settlement on the land, and the probate of estates preparatory to distribution of the property to a beneficiary.

The probate court records found in the Quarterly Courts of Essex County are marvels of statistical detail. The first Quarterly Courts were established on March 3, 1636, and apparently the first records of probate began just after 1640. The completed study, from 1641–1700, will involve detailed examination of approximately 1,700 separate estate inventories contained on approximately 130,000 Hollerith (IBM) cards.[3] The ubiquitous element of colonial society was land. It was the basis of economic, political, and social activity, eventually outlasting church influence. The study of the history of the county and the township records indicates that a major purpose of the recording of deeds and of the probate was to maintain control of land and land ownership. Estates of negligible value, and of sizeable but negative value (debts greater than assets) are all included in the probate records. The probate records clearly comprehend all landowners in Essex County regardless of location or wealth (size of estate). They constitute a remarkably valuable, accurate, and comprehensive data source.

Table 13-1 indicates a copy of the probate of the estate for one John Huchison who died August 2, 1676. His estate was appraised for probate on November 8, 1676. The important thing to note is that the estate inventory is a listing of the things that he owned and owed, with the count and the values associated.

The purpose of the Essex County study was to attempt, if possible, to utilize the computer to develop answers from the data bank to the following types of questions:

1. What was the progress of prices of individual commodities and of consumer and trade goods (wholesale) commodities, during the period 1640–1682?
2. What impact, if any, did the establishment of the Massachusetts mint of 1653 have on these price trends?

[3]For earlier and preliminary studies see: William I. Davisson "Essex County Price Trends: Money and Markets in 17th-Century Massachusetts" (April, 1967), and "Essex County Wealth Trends: Wealth and Economic Growth in 17th-Century Massachusetts" (October, 1967) *Essex Institute Historical Collections.* See also: Willaim I. Davisson and Dennis J. Dugan, "Growth and Wealth in the Colonial Economy: 1641–1682," *8th Annual Econometric History Institute,* Paper, Purdue University, West Lafayette, Indiana, February, 1968.

TABLE 13-1.   Essex County Quarterly Court Records (November, 1676, pp. 230–231).
Estate of John Huchison (died Aug. 2, 1676).

Inventory of the estate of John Huchison, who deceased about Aug. 2, 1676, taken Nov. 8, 1676, by Nathaniel Ingersoll and Joshua Rea, and allowed, 29:9:1676, in Salem court; waring apparrell, 61i. 10s.; foure oxen, 181i.; five cowes, 15l.; two three years old, 51i.; tow yearling, 31i.10s; tenn sheep, 31i.10s; five horskind, 5l.; one horse, 41i.10s.; two calfes, 11i.10s; five hogges, 31i.; sevenn pigges, 11i.15s.; two hundred achres of land & medow & orcharde, one house & Barne, ————; in iron, 12s.; one fring pann, liron pott, 13s.; two axes & other tooles, 13s.; three parre sheettes, 31i.; one wheell, two pare pillowberes, 10s. 6d.; napkins, table cloth, 11i.2s.; bassen & putter, 17s.; wooden ware, cheste 9s.; one fether bed, 31i. 10s.; wollen yarne & woole, 21i.; rug, blanketts new cloath, 21i. 5s.,; tow gunnes 21i. 15s.; yokes, chaine, sheer, coulter, 11i.; cleves & pinn, foure pillowes, 11i. 3s.; engling corn and hay, 61. 10s.; money, 7s.; 100 akers of land with halfe the houseing in present possesion 7 100 akers of land, Revertion as appeareth by deed of giffte, 1301i. Debts due to the estate, 71i. 14s.; 250 akers of land, 401i.; debts due from the estate, 151i. 10s.; total 3731i. 5s. 6d.

3.   Would it be possible to develop a wheat or grain price trend for Essex County that would permit comparison with the Eton College (London) price trends for wheat during the period 1640–1682?

4.   Would it be possible to develop, at least initially, a satisfactory consumer and producer goods (trade goods) price trend?

5.   Would it be possible to develop an analysis of wealth trends (personal wealth) for the period in question by type of property, by year, and by size of estate?

6.   Using the assumption that the given data constituted 90 percent of the original records, what would a deflated price series tell us about the nature of economic growth and development in Essex County during the period in question?

It is quite clear that in order to examine the data to develop the answers to the questions suggested above, the data bank must be established so that each appraised item appears separately with the relevant related information including date, quantity, value. Therefore, the first step was to establish a regular or standardized Hollerith card layout for keypunching. The table below indicates how the data were keypunched. (It was also clear that certain pieces of information had to appear on each data card in order to facilitate the computer processing of the data.)

1.   It was necessary to provide certain information so that the computer could control the data cards (or tape) in carrying out the program instructions. The coding was provided by keypunching on each card:
     a.   name of the decendent
     b.   date of estate inventory
     c.   property type

2.   The name and description of the property had to appear on each card, descriptive of the chattel, property, or other asset being inventoried.

3.   Some coding was necessary in order to insure that all the cards in a given estate were present and to keep the cards of the various estates in the proper order.

4.   It was necessary to devise a classifications scheme to distinguish those inventoried items that had both a value and a quantity from those that had only a value:
     a.   In developing a price series for commodities or asset items, both a total value and a quantity figure is necessary in order to calculate a value per unit.
     b.   In developing wealth series by broad classification of assets, only a value is necessary.

In this last problem, the inventoried items were found to fall into these classifications:

1. Those items that had *both* a value and a quantity specified for each commodity or asset shown. These items were designated with a "1" (Column 59).
2. Those items that had neither a value nor a quantity or those items that had only a quantity. These items were specified or designated with a "0" (Column 59).
3. Those items that had a value (and sometimes a quantity) where the value shown was for more than one type of item or asset were designated with a "J." For instance, about two-thirds of the way through the inventory in Table 13-1 is the entry, ". . . yokes, chaine, sheer, coulter, 11i." This would be translated (oxen) yokes, chain, (plow) share, and a (plow) coulter valued at £1/00/00 (1 pound in Massachusetts money). This refers to four separate items with an aggregate value of £1/00/00. Four Hollerith cards were punched: one for yokes, one for chains, and one for sheer, each designated with a "0" designating neither a quantity shown nor a value. (These cards would not be useful in constructing a price series since a value per unit could not be calculated.) The item coulter would be shown with a value of £1/00/00, designated with a "J" indicating that the value shown is for the item on the card with the "J" and for the immediately preceding "0" cards. While this commodity would not be useful for calculating a price series, it could be used in property classification for a wealth investigation since all the items are farm implements, tools or equipment.

The data were keypunched as indicated in Table 13-2.

As the final part of this chapter, let us take each field and determine why it was included to be keypunched in the card. First, the card was laid out as it was because, according to the keypunch operators, the layout shown was about the easiest to keypunch. Since it makes little difference to the programmer and the computer, this always an advisable step. A keypunch layout devised inappropriately can cause a significant unanticipated increase in the cost. Since it will cost approximately 10 cents per card punched, this can become a real factor and should always be considered.

Field No. 1 shows the name of the person deceased. Since the analysis here did not involve dealing with individual estate values in the calculations, why punch on the name of the deceased? The obvious reason is that it facilitates verifying or checking the accuracy of the keypunching, and it facilitates controlling the cards to determine whether any cards are missing from the estate. Field 1 together with Field 4, the card sequence number, permit this. Field 4 simply represents a numbering system where each item in each estate is given a number. If there were 65 items in a given estate, there would be 65 sequence numbers for that estate, 1–65. Once the sequence numbers are in, it is easy to check the accuracy of keypunching each estate, relatively easy to verify any given item, and relatively easy to determine when any card of a given estate is lost. Thus, Fields 1 and 4 were primarily verification and control fields. Field 2 was for the property type code and Field 3 was a control punch.

Field 4, Columns 22–24 on the Hollerith card, represented the sequence number for card control. Field 5 is the name of the asset or property item exactly as found in the original estate record. Field 6 is the item control. It contains either:

1) a **1** (number 1),
2) an **0** (zero),
3) a **J** (letter J).

TABLE 13-2. Estate of J. Turner: Salem, Mass., Nov. 15, 1680[a]

Name 1	2 3 4	Asset Item	5	6 7 8 9 101112 13
	b c			d e f g h i j
TURNER J	11C001GOODS	SUNDRY		0 1511680
TURNER J	21C002MERCHANDIZE			J000000284309111511680
TURNER J	11C003STUFF	HOUSEHOULD		0 1511680
TURNER J	11C004BAGGS			J000000129508001511680
TURNER J	03C005HOUSEING			0 1511680
TURNER J	03C006LAND			0 1511680
TURNER J	03C007HOUSE	DWELLING		0001000000000001511680
TURNER J	03C008LAND			0 1511680
TURNER J	03C009HOUSEING	OUT		0 1511680
TURNER J	03C010WAREHOUSES			0002000000000001511680
TURNER J	03C011WHARFE			J001000050000001511680
TURNER J	11C012HOUSE			0001000000000001511680
TURNER J	11C013STUFF	HOUSEHOULD		0 1511680
TURNER J	08C014STOCK	AT BAKERS ISLD		J000000005000001511680
TURNER J	01C015LAND	AT CASTLE HILL		1000000007000001511680
TURNER J	01C016LAND	PARCELL		1002000004000001511680
TURNER J	03C017WAREHOUSE			1001000001200001511680
TURNER J	03C018HOUSE			0001000000000001511680
TURNER J	03C019LAND			J000000014000001511680
TURNER J	03C020WAREHOUSE	NOT YET BUILT		1001000002500001511680
TURNER J	01C021LAND			1000000004000001511680
TURNER J	22C022VESSELLS	KEATCH BLOSOME		1001000017000001511680
TURNER J	22C023VESSELLS	KEATCH PROSPEROUS		1001000012000001511680
TURNER J	22C024VESSELLS	KEATCH JNO./THOMAS		1001000010000001511680
TURNER J	22C025VESSELLS	KEATCH WILLING MIND		1001000009000001511680
TURNER J	22C026VESSELLS	KEATCH		1000500019000001511680
TURNER J	22C027VESSELLS	PINK SPEEDWELL		1000500010000001511680
TURNER J	22C028VESSELLS	KEATCH SOCIETY		1000380015000001511680
TURNER J	22C029VESSELLS	KEATCH WM./JNO.		1000380010000001511680
TURNER J	22C030VESSELLS	KEATCH FRIENDSHIP		1000250006500001511680
TURNER J	22C031VESSELLS	KEATCH FRATERNYTY		1000130004000001511680
TURNER J	22C032SHALLOP			1001000005000001511680
TURNER J	22C033SLOOP			1000250004000001511680
TURNER J	15C034BOOTE	PLEASURE		1001000000800001511680
TURNER J	22C035SHIPP	WM/JOHN		1000340050000001511680

a Salem Quarterly Court Records, November, 1680, page fifty-seven.

b property type code — 22 is a vessel. 15 indicates a personal accessory or personal asset not elsewhere classified.

c sequence code.

d quantity: a = whole number units; b = decimal or fractional part — e.g., 50 in area "b" is one-half.

e Massachusetts value in pounds — £.

f shillings

g pence

h day

i month

j year to three digits: 680 = 1680.

This code is clearly vital in programming to determine when and how the property listed on the card may be included in either a price or a wealth series. Field 7 shows the quantity of the item as shown on the estate — e.g., *five* cows, *four* slaves, *fifty-five* bushels of grain, etc. The field is actually divided into two separate parts, a units field and a decimal field. The first three columns of the field are for the units —

225 acres of land. The last two digits or columns of the field are for a decimal value. For instance, 22525 would mean 225.25 acres of land. The decimal point is not needed because a field may be set up into two or more segments; or, even more simply, the one field could be broken into two separate fields. In the present study, it was desired to include whole units and decimal values in a single field.

Field 8, Field 9, and Field 10 are taken together. Values in colonial Massachusetts were shown in pounds (sterling), shillings, and pence — where a pound was equal to 20 shillings, and a shilling was equal to 12 pence. The usual designation is 20/12/06. This would be translated as 20 pounds, 12 shillings, and 6 pence. Field 8, to five digits, shows the pounds sterling value; Field 9, the shillings; and Field 10, the pence.

Fields 11, 12, and 13 are also taken together. Field 11 represents the day; Field 12, the month; and Field 13, the year in which the estate was inventoried. The date of the inventory is the more important figure here since we are not concerned with individual estates, but with prices and wealth figures as of a given date; hence, the date of the estate inventory is used. The day is shown as a two-digit number between 1 and 31. The month is shown as a two-digit decimal number between 1 and 12. The year is shown as a three-digit decimal number. The maximum extent of these series would be from 1640 through 1800. Beginning with 1800, relatively reliable price series are provided through research organizations; hence there would not be the need to continue. It is not necessary to identify all four numbers of the year, only three: the year 1676 becomes 676.

Essex County Vital Records
The basic data source for developing mortality statistics in Essex County is the township vital record statistics. These are available for each town (township) in the county and cover the period from the establishment of a town to 1850. From work presently being done with these records, it will be possible to develop the necessary mortality statistics.

Until this work is completed it is generally necessary to rely upon related studies such as the following:

John Demos, "Notes on Life in Plymouth Colony," *William and Mary Quarterly*, 3s, **XXII** (April, 1965), pp. 284–286.

Philip J. Grevan Jr., "Family Structure in Seventeenth-Century Andover, Massachusetts," *William and Mary Quarterly*, 3s, **XXIII**, (April, 1966), pp. 234–256.

David J. Rothman, "A Note on the Study of the Colonial Family," *William and Mary Quarterly*, 3s, **XXIII** (October, 1966), pp. 627–634.

With the exception of the Grevan Study most of the work is from outside Essex County; however, these studies will suffice until more exhaustive work is completed.

DATA CONVERSION AND MODEL ANALYSIS

Very often, the process of model analysis may be handled by the computer. This generally falls into two separate kinds of operation:

1) converting data from its existent form to a form that may be utilized in the model,
2) using an existing standardized program procedure (canned program) in performing the statistical manipulation demanded by the model.

One of the common standardized procedures available that is often used in economic model analysis is the multiple-regression analysis. The following discussion is closely related to the last section of Chapter 9 on multiple regression.

The first problem is that of converting the data from its existing form as inventory records to a form suitable for the regression analysis. A regression model operates by examining the direction of change and the dependency of one variable on another. A regression-model analysis is performed for one or more independent variables and one dependent variable. The dependent variable is assumed to be dependent upon or to depend upon the independent variables. The latter are assumed to be affected by forces outside of the range of the model. Changes in the independent variable or variables are hypothesized to cause changes in the dependent variable. The results of the regression analysis measure the significance of these supposed effects. The multiple-regression analysis here indicates direction (of change) and dependency of one variable on another. If a shift occurs from one factor or variable to another, that shift will be noted.

A preliminary hypothesis to be tested by our regression analysis for Essex County might suggest that there existed a shift in the nature of economic activity from the (less advantageous) agricultural activity to the (more advantageous) commercial activity. It is supposed that this will be shown by the increase in the (relative) volume of commercial capital over the forty-year period, by the increase in the (relative) value of commercial capital, and by the increase in the amount of credit, debts and cash. At the same time it is suggested that there would be a decrease in the (relative) value and volume of agricultural capital. It is also decided that a regression analysis may most effectively test these hypotheses.

The analysis considers *commercial capital, agricultural capital, money, credits,* and *debts* as the separate relevant variables. Each Hollerith card represented one asset item and was coded to represent any *one* of the *twenty-four* possible property-type codes shown in Table 13-3 below. Therefore, the first problem of data conversion is to develop a program that will change the data from approximately 26,000 individual asset items into six categories, as shown below:

Category	Codes
1. Commercial Capital	22,23
2. Agricultural Capital	1,2,3,4,5,6,7,8,9,10
3. Money	19
4. Credits	20
5. Debts	24
6. Other (not used)	

These variables were aggregated annually for all years. The regressions were run on *yearly averages* and on *aggregates* for agricultural capital, commercial capital, money, and credits. Therefore, the Essex conversion program had to supply the researcher with the averages and aggregates of capital in each of the noted areas for each year in the period. Other aspects of the conversion are to fit the data into the format required by the regression program used and to (perhaps) convert the data to the required logarithm form.

One other factor of the conversion is that it is necessary to get all data into comparable values. For instance, one item may be valued in dollars, another item in shillings, another in pounds sterling, another in cents. The problem of conversion, therefore, is to get all variables expressed in the same value measure.

Most regression routines are *closed-format* programs — that is, the data must be presented to the program in a given order and in a given form on each input

TABLE 13-3. Essex County data: Property type structure

The data input cards for each estate will be ordered by asset type code (not by item code number). In the following program sequence, only the type code summaries are shown (with desired spacing).

Type Code	Description of Asset
1	Land
2	Land and Real Property
3	Real Property Only
4	Farm Equipment
5	Farm Implements
6	Harness
7	Tools
8	Livestock
9	Food
10	Farm, N.E.C. (Not Elsewhere Classified)
11	Household Ware
12	Bed and Bedding
13	Dishes and Dishware
14	Household, N.E.C.
15	Clothing
16	Weapons
17	(Personal) Accessories
18	Personal, N.E.C.
19	Money
20	Credit Assets
21	Other Assets, N.E.C.
22	Ships or vessels
23	Other off-site tangible assets
24 less	Debts, Assets Owed

record. In the instant case the data are to be presented to the program in fields, each of which is 10-columns wide, with appropriate control cards as shown in Figure 9-6 in Chapter 9 (p. 101). The program will provide the various tests of significance as indicated.

CONCLUSION

The accumulation of wealth is a process that generates growth and development in a given country or region. Such accumulation produces higher standards of living through increases in per capita income. Although this process of accumulation plays a vital role in traditional economic growth theory, the main emphasis of such growth theory has been on the growth of output per capita. The accumulation of wealth, despite its pertinent role in traditional analysis, has never received the publicity and the attention that public policy makers have heaped upon the growth rate of product and income. Perhaps the ready availability of national income accounts in economically advanced countries have tipped the scales in favor of income growth studies. Probably the singular use of models in the advanced countries has built the assumptions of such advanced economies into the models. A model, after all, implies its own assumptions. Finally, the lack of available and suitable income data has been a real hindrance in the analysis of underdeveloped areas.

The analysis, and the approach, noted above has centered upon the accumulation of wealth in the American colonial economy *as an underdeveloped economy*. From a pragmatic point of view, wealth and its accumulation must be an indicator of economic development. In the empirical work noted, the constraint exists because of data limitations.

On the other hand, investigation of the process of accumulation of wealth during this period can yield an explanation of the structural change that took place within the colonial American economy prior to the American Revolution. A look at the components of wealth and its determinants will surely increase our knowledge of the accumulation process of the period and of the structural changes that took place. The general results of this approach may be helpful in analyzing the development process in underdeveloped areas in the modern world. To this end the computer and the economic data bank will become increasingly important.

14

The Use of Computers in Psychological Research: A Complex Case Study in Cross-Cultural Research[1]

COMPUTERS AND THE RESEARCH PSYCHOLOGIST

Utilization of computers has infiltrated psychological research from the initia planning stages to the final stages of data analysis. Through computer technology the psychologist has an increased potential for developing new and improved research methods resulting in a broader yet more precise study of human and animal behavior.

The most extensive use of the computer by the psychologist has been for data analysis. The computer is capable of accomplishing in minutes, or even seconds, analyses which would have previously required weeks of computational drudgery. Indeed, many research projects, including the one to be presented in this chapter, would not have been attempted prior to the computer age because of the sheer bulk of data involved.

The use of the computer by the psychologist other than for data analysis has been both varied and extensive. Trends for future psychological laboratories have been determined because of the capability of the computer to control stimulus presentation and to record and process the responses given by subjects. This automation of stimulus presentation and response recording can be so arranged that several subjects can be tested simultaneously through a series of remote stations. When the computer is programmed to control stimuli, record responses, to feed information back to the subject regarding the accuracy of the response; the computer serves as a teaching machine. The computer, as a teaching machine, has the capability to vary the stimulus presentation as a function of the subject's responses. Thus, the computer is programmed so that each subject or student may proceed at his own rate. The subject is first given stimulus items which are not difficult and if the subject's responses are correct, more difficult stimulus items are given. If the subject's responses are incorrect, he is presented with easier stimulus items. Pro-

[1] Written by Dr. B. J. Farrow, Assistant Chairman of the Department of Psychology, University of Notre Dame.

grammed learning has much to recommend itself and is becoming widely accepted in various forms at all levels of education.

Stimulus materials have been generated by the computer. Perhaps one of the more impressive usages of the computer for this purpose was by Julesz (1968)[2], who studied depth perception through computer-generated dot patterns. Since each stimulus pattern consisted of thousands of dots which have been specifically manipulated and located, it would be virtually impossible to create the same stimuli without the computer. Computers have also been used to generate more conventional kinds of stimuli such as nonsense syllables, random forms, random numbers, and so forth. For visual presentations the computer is generally connected to a cathode ray television) tube or to a printer or computer typewriter. For auditory presentations, complex tonal patterns have been used.

When psychological theories can be stated explicitly and are mathematically complex and/or have many variables, the researcher can efficiently employ the computer to serve as subjects in simulated experiments.[3] Since the results from successful and unsuccessful trials can be stored in memory, the computer can be programmed "to learn from experience" (Marzocco and Bartram, 1962). Further, it can be programmed to simulate concept formation (Vossler and Uhr, 1962), problem solving (Gyr, Thatcher, and Allen, 1962; Hovland, 1960), pattern recognition (Newell, Shaw, and Simon, 1958; Selfridge and Neisser, 1960), intellectual functioning (Hovland, 1960), and artificial intelligence (Hunt, 1968). This use of the computer, however, does not negate the necessity of hypothesis testing with either human or animal subjects; indeed, the computer behavior in the simulated experiments must be compared with behavior of living, intact organisms.

The computer has provided an important service through its capabilities of information retrieval. The future developments for information storage and retrieval systems will be of tremendous importance for the researcher and the scholar.[4] The general goal of information retrieval is to locate all the information available on a given subject. The computer can be programmed to provide automatic search of specified information. This service can represent a tremendous time saving for the researcher. Otherwise, countless hours of searching the literature for information related to the immediate research problem would be required.

The overview of the use of the computer by the research psychologist is very short of a complete compilation, but does suggest the nature of activities that have been attempted. Even with all of the magical capabilities indicated by its usage it is well to remember that the computer is nothing more than a machine that is very fast and very accurate in obeying instructions. These instructions are absolutely critical; the machine will do only what the programmer tells it to do. As a tool for the researcher, then, the genius of the computer is dependent on the genius of the programmer.

A CASE STUDY IN CROSS-CULTURAL RESEARCH

The present chapter has as its focus the use of computer technology in the data analyses of a cross-cultural research project. First a brief description of the rationale

---

[2]See bibliography at end of chapter.
[3]See Chapter 2, discussion of Simulation, also Hunt (1968).
[4]This problem is not unlike that noted in Chapter 12, on Data Banks. The most advanced development of this phase of computer work has been done by IBM.

and the research methodology of the study will be presented. Following this, a detailed examination of the use of the computer in the data processing specific to the cross-cultural project will be presented.

The cross-cultural research project to be presented here is under the direction of John F. Santos (principal investigator) with close collaboration of B. J. Farrow and J. M. Farrow. This research project, involving Brazil, Mexico, and North America, is ongoing, with only the data collection from Brazil completed.

The rationale of the study

The theoretical rationale for the ongoing study of the perceptual, cognitive, and personality characteristics of Brazilians, Mexicans and North Americans stems directly from previous formulations of J. F. Santos (1966, 1967). Professor Santos has suggested that perceptual[5] and cognitive[6] processes are not only influenced by learning and motivational variables, but also by cultural variables — i.e., by social forces, familial dynamics, value systems, sociocultural premises (Diaz-Guerreo, 1963), etc. These cultural variables are also effective in molding the perceptual, cognitive, and personality characteristics of individuals. Ample evidence exists that bolsters these notions. For example, Solley and Murphy, in their book *Development of the Perceptual World* (1960), reviewed numerous studies which illustrated the role that learning and motivational variables play in perception, memory, and thinking. Indeed the learning experiences, the content of learning, and the reinforcing agents and stimuli may differ extensively across cultural groups. Sherif (1936), among others, has demonstrated that the judgement of perceived events can be influenced by social pressures. Furthermore, Gardner Murphy (1947), a pioneer in experimental social psychology, recognized the importance of cultural factors in shaping the cognitive processes; he has pointed out that group pressures can effectively modify the individual's habits of perceiving, recalling, and reasoning. Further, Bagby (1957) has rather dramatically demonstrated cultural influences on the selectivity of perception. Using a modified stereoscope, Bagby simultaneously presented culturally relevant and irrelevant stimuli in two independent visual fields. A comparison of a matched sample of Mexicans and North Americans indicated that subjects reported seeing the culturally relevant stimuli often to the exclusion of the culturally non-relevant stimuli.

Research methodology

Research strategy

The basic research strategy was to test individuals from Brazil, Mexico, and North America in a variety of perceptual, cognitive, and personality test instruments.[7] The different cultural groups are being equated as carefully as possible for

---

[5]Refers to perceiving—i.e., interpretation of the sensory information.

[6]Refers to thinking—i.e., memory, thinking, etc.

[7]The present investigation benefitted from the preliminary Brazilian studies of Santos in 1962 which served to provide normative data on several perceptual and cognitive tests. Following the preliminary investigations, an attempt was made to screen, develop, and modify a variety of psychological test instruments and procedures in order to obtain a relatively culture "fair" test battery designed to assess perceptual and cognitive processes and personality characteristics.

age, sex, socioeconomic status, educational level, and urban locale. Statistical comparisons of the means and variances of the various tests will be made in order to identify similarities and differences among the three cultural groups at each level of measurement — i.e., perceptual, cognitive, and personality levels of measurement. These comparisons will allow tests of specific hypotheses that were made prior to the data collection.

Factor analytic techniques will be applied to the test scores at each of the three levels of measurement for each cultural group. Comparisons of the similarities and differences in factors and factor loadings for the various tests within levels of measurement will be made among the three cultural groups. Furthermore, factor analytic techniques will be applied across the levels of measurement within each cultural group; that is, factor analytic techniques will be used to identify the clusters or patterns of relationships among the perceptual, cognitive, and personality variables.

The factor analytic approach to be employed following the completion of data collection is partially conceived to be hypothesis testing as well as descriptive; that is, the researchers have made a *priori* predictions concerning the relationships among certain sets of variables and about the ways in which these relationships may differ among the three cultural groups.

The sample test battery: Brazil

Since only one portion of the project has been completed, only the research activities of Brazil will be briefly described. The Brazilian samples were taken from Rio de Janeiro and Sao Paulo, Brazil, and were restricted to males and females between the ages of 25–40 from upper-middle to upper socioeconomic classes. The investigation in Brazil was divided into phases. The first phase, the pilot study, was geared to evaluate the various test instruments, instructions, and procedures of the test battery. In this phase the proficiency of the experimenters who had previously undergone extensive training was evaluated. The subjects, 15 males and 15 females from Rio, and 15 males and 15 females from Sao Paulo, were given the following tests: Questionnaire on Family Change; Minnesota Multiphasic Personality Inventory (MMPI); a modified form of the Holtzman Inkblot Test (HIT); the Autokinetic Perception Test; the Mooney Closure Test; the Porteus Mazes; Harvey's "This I Believe" Test (TIB); and Kagen's Conceptual Styles Test (CST).[8]

Following a few refinements in the procedures and instructions, the second phase (Study I) was initiated. There was a total of 40 subjects from Rio and 84 from Sao Paulo, with each sample represented by an equal number of males and females. All subjects were tested in two sessions since completion of the test battery required approximately four hours. The test battery for this phase consisted of Haiman's Open-Mindedness Scale, Penney's Reactive Curiosity Scale (RCS), the multiple choice form of Harvey's "This I Believe" Test (TIB/mc), in addition to the tests previously employed in the pilot study.

The third phase (Study III) employed 73 male and 73 female subjects from Rio de Janeiro. Deleted from the test battery used in Study II were the MMPI, the modified HIT, Porteus Mazes and the Autokinetic Test. Added to the test battery were the California Personality Inventory (CPI) and Luchin's Einstellung Test. The different test batteries in the three studies provided information on both the consistency of measurements across the samples and the relationships available from a wider variety of tests. In addition to the three studies mentioned, additional studies were conducted which involved college, high school, and elementary school students

---

[8]See Appendix 14-1, this chapter, for a brief description of the tests used in the various studies.

as well as children from the slum areas (the *favelas*) and nonslum children of the same age.

Although extensive data have been obtained from the Brazilian samples, comparable data from the North American and Mexican samples are incomplete at this stage and the proposed analyses will have to await completion of the data collection from these culture groups. However, various comparisons between test scores of the Brazilian and norms of these test scores from comparable American samples have been made. Keeping in mind that only preliminary analyses of the data are presently available, the results have been encouraging.

Correlation and factor analysis

Correlational and factor analytic procedures are the necessary statistical tools to answer many of the questions posed by the investigators.[9] Correlation refers to the relationship or association between variables expressed as a numerical index ranging from -1.00 to $+1.00$. The probability of the chance occurrence of a correlation coefficient between two sets of observations can be determined. The researcher is interested only in those relationships (correlation coefficients) that are very unlikely to occur as a function of chance. A correlation coefficient is determined for each pair of variables; thus, if the researcher had tested subjects over four variables, A, B, C, and D, correlation coefficients for the following variable pairs could be obtained: AB, AC, AD, BC, BD and CD. It is easily seen that as the number of variables are increased the number of variable pairs increase rapidly — i.e., 10 variables give 45 paired combinations, 100 give 4,950 paired combinations.

Since a large number of variables were used in the present study — e.g., 83 in Study I — the computer was employed to expedite these calculations. With 83 variables, giving 3,403 variable pairs, the desk calculator computations would have required virtually months of work; whereas, the computer (Univac 1107) required less than two minutes.

The output from correlation programs are usually in the form of a correlation matrix. The correlation matrix (elaborated in Chapter 15) gives the correlation coefficient for every combination of the variable pairs. Additional information from correlational programs are means and standard deviations.

The interpretation of the number of correlation coefficients yielded in a correlation matrix with as many variables as employed in the present study is at best unwieldy. However, factor analysis can serve to effectively organize these relationships into a more manageable form. Through factor analyses, the large number of relationships obtained in the correlation matrix are analyzed to give a new set of dimensions (factors) which were defined in terms of their communalities of the original variables. These dimensions or factors are thought of as constructs underlying tests and test performance.

Perhaps an example is warranted in order to illustrate the use of factor analysis in the present study to compare the test performance of subjects from Rio de Janeiro and Sao Paulo, Brazil. A comparison between these two cities was of interest since they represent quite different physical and social environments. Sao Paulo is inland, relatively flat, and is an industrial center whose social environment is much less relaxed than that of Rio. Rio de Janeiro, on the other hand, is a beautiful, coastal, mountainous city which is an entertainment and resort center.

Forty test variables employed in Study I were selected (based on various predictions of the experimenters) to differentiate subjects from the two cities. A

---

[9]For a simplified presentation of correlation analysis and factor analysis, see Chapter 15.

40 × 40 correlation matrix was obtained for each city, and identical factor analyses were then applied to each set of data.

A comparison of the two sets of factor analyses was made by inspection of the similarity of the two subject groups on the factor loadings of the specific variables (on the various factors). The factor structures may then be compared statistically (Veldman 1967, Program RELATE).

The results presented below are from the factor analyses applied to the data from Rio and Sao Paulo. For simplicity, the factor loadings for 20 variables on two factors are shown. Listed beside each variable are the factor loadings (correlation coefficient between variable and the factor) for Factor I and Factor II for each set of subjects. An examination of these results indicates that Factor I is identified by Variables 1 through 8, and that the factor structures and factor loadings associated with each city are very similar.

TABLE 14-1.   Rio and Sao Paulo: Factor analysis results.

	Factor I		Factor II	
Variable	Rio	Sao Paulo	Rio	Sao Paulo
1 RCS	0.864	0.943	0.049	0.072
2 Openmindedness	0.764	0.918	—0.047	0.164
3 Openmindedness	0.889	0.959	0.040	0.075
4 TIB Scale 1	0.858	0.845	—0.157	—0.075
5 TIB Scale 2	0.903	0.921	—0.095	0.026
6 TIB Scale 3	0.938	0.955	—0.124	0.067
7 TIB Scale 4	0.915	0.967	—0.188	0.052
8 TIB Scale 5	0.901	0.963	—0.208	0.051
9 HIT—Location	—0.050	0.031	0.165	0.821
10 HIT—Color	—0.100	0.107	—0.206	0.651
11 HIT—Shading	—0.021	0.016	—0.118	0.942
12 HIT—Pathognomic Verbalization	—0.111	0.019	—0.133	0.845
13 HIT—Human	—0.100	0.082	0.114	0.918
14 HIT—Animal	—0.190	0.081	0.231	0.946
15 HIT—FA	—0.040	0.031	0.371	0.970
16 MMPI—MA Scale	—0.017	0.011	0.787	0.559
17 MMPI—D Scale	0.028	0.027	0.739	0.189
18 MMPI—PT Scale	—0.065	0.168	0.718	0.114
19 MMPI—SI Scale	—0.279	—0.036	0.813	0.674
20 CST—IC Scale	—0.240	0.029	0.744	0.821

The similarity between the factor structure for the two cities is not as evident in Factor II. While Variable Nos. 16, 19, and 20 have similar factor loadings, pronounced differences are evident between the factor loadings for other variables. Several of the variables from the HIT load heavy on Factor II for Sao Paulo but not for Rio. Since factors are defined by the variables which have high-factor loadings, a common factor, perhaps could be described on Factor I for both Rio and Sao Paulo — but not for Factor II for the two cities. To elaborate, the tests which load on Factor I — i.e., the various scales of the TIB, the RCS, and the Open-Mindedness Scale — are individuals who tend to be flexible, open-minded, curious, and low on authoritarian or dogmatic characteristics. Subjects from Rio and Sao Paulo appear to be similar in these characteristics and their interrelationships. However, since the factor loadings for the various tests on Factor II differs considerably between the two samples, such a common dimension cannot be posited. Rather, the factors of each group must be considered separately. As such, the results suggest different kinds of interrelationship among the perceptual, cognitive, and personality characteristics which may, in turn, be used to map out differences between the psychological functioning of the two groups.

Comparison of factor structures — although presented superficially here — will be used extensively in the data analyses among the national cultural groups. The specific statistical technique for comparison of factor structures that will be employed was developed by Kaiser (1960), and has been programmed by Veldman (1967).

USE OF THE COMPUTER IN THE PRESENT STUDY

Now that the overview of the cross-cultural study of the perceptual, cognitive, and personality characteristics of Brazilians, Mexicans, and North Americans has been briefly presented, an examination of the application of computer technology is warranted. The researchers, attempting such a project which would involve hundreds of subjects and a large number of psychological tests (with each test having several sets of scores), planned to use the computer to its fullest advantage in terms of data scoring and data analysis.

The computer allowed the researchers to incorporate considerably more background data for each subject than would have been feasible using hand methods. The computer was used extensively in evaluating test data in an attempt to obtain culturally "fair" tests; item analyses were applied to existing tests as well as to newly developed tests in order to evaluate their appropriateness for a particular culture. The computer was also employed in establishing norms for several of the tests. Furthermore, the computer was essential in determining the intercorrelations between the response measures of the various dependent variables, and was further used in computing a series of factor analyses for both descriptive and hypothesis testing purposes.

For purposes of illustrating the role of the computer and its auxiliary equipment, we shall assume that the data collection in the cross-cultural research project has been completed. The investigators now have a half-ton of unanalyzed data which, with only clerical help and the desk calculator, would possibly require several years of work to complete the test evaluations and statistical analyses. Tracing what happens to the raw data down to the final statistical analyses will perhaps illustrate some of the various applications of the computer and the auxiliary equipment.

Several of the tests employed in the present study required hand scoring by trained personnel while other tests were such that the scoring could be automated by computer equipment. Figure 14-1 below indicates the differences in treatment of the raw data depending on whether hand scoring was required or automated scoring was feasible.

Obviously, when tests could be scored by the computer or by the auxiliary equipment, considerable time and energy can be saved. However, some information of interest to the investigators could not be ascertained through tests where scoring could be automated. For example, the Porteus Maze Test, CST, Mooney Closure Test, Autokinetic Test, and the Einstellung Test required hand scoring by trained personnel. As noted on the flowchart, the interscorer reliability (an index of consistency between scorers) must be determined for each test. In order to determine the interscorer reliability, all scorers were asked to score the same test protocols; and, in turn, correlation coefficients were determined between every pair of scorers. If

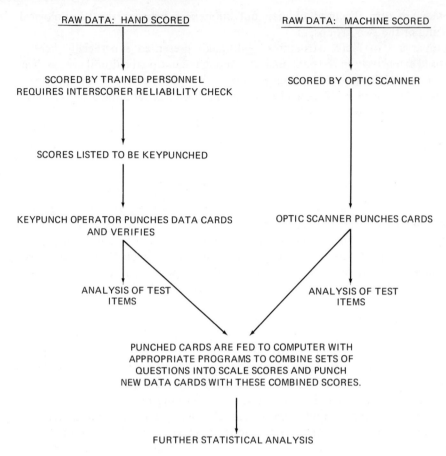

FIGURE 14-1.   Flowchart: Raw data to punched cards.

the interscorer correlation coefficients between scorers were low, further training was given to the scorers; or, perhaps, an individual was not allowed to serve as a scorer. As the raw data were scored, the trained scorer assigned a coded number or sets of numbers that had meanings specific to each test to each response given by the subject. These scores were listed on data sheets so that the keypunch operator could readily punch the data cards in the same format as the scores were listed. The data cards were then verified (by the keypunch operator) in order to locate mistakes that might have occurred from the transfer of the listed scores to the punched data cards. The punched data cards were used in two distinct ways: 1) for the analyses of the test items, and 2) to obtain combined scores that were employed in further statistical analyses.

Since the data cards at this stage contained specific scores for each test item, an item analysis could be applied to evaluate the extent to which each item was related to the total test score, and the intercorrelations among the various items. The results from the item analyses on each test were important in identifying various problems within each test for any given cultural group. For example, certain test items may not be relevant or meaningful to one cultural group but are relevant to the other cultural groups. The experimenters must make some decision (deletion, modification, or no change) about the value and treatment of those test items. Indeed, the item analyses were especially important in the pilot phase, since the tests used in the following studies could be modified in an attempt to approach a culturally "fair" test battery.

The second use of the data cards listing the scores of the specific test item scores required a program that would combine the scores in specified ways to give either total scores or scale scores. A given scale may consist of the combined score of several test items which purport to measure the same attribute or characteristic. Having several test items assessing an attribute rather than a single item serves to increase the power and the reliability of the measurement. These combined scores (the scale scores) can be readily obtained through a simple program instructing the computer to perform the appropriate summations of the responses to specified test items and, in turn, punch a new data deck containing these combined scores for each subject. The new data deck is then used for further statistical analyses.

The raw data that was machine scored required fewer steps, less time, and less opportunity for error. On those tests whose raw data consisted of true/false answers (MMPI, CPI, and RCS) or multiple-choice answers (Questionnaire on Family Change, Open-Mindedness Scale, and the TIB/mc), the subjects recorded their responses on IBM answer-sheet forms that could be processed through an optic scanner. The optic scanner is capable of transforming the subject's responses from the IBM answer sheet onto punched cards (or tape). These cards were then used to obtain item analyses and then used to obtain the combined scores that were used in subsequent statistical analyses.

An examination of the contents of the data cards is warranted, at this point. The initial columns contained background information about the subject. The test scores were located on the remaining columns. The kind of information contained on a given card is illustrated below:

Col. 1	Study No.
Col. 2	Location of the Study
Col. 3, 4, 5	Subject Identification Number
Col. 6	Sex
Col. 7, 8	Age
Col. 9	Marital Status
Col. 10	Number of Children
Col. 11	Birth Order of the Subject
Col. 12	Number of Persons Living in Household
Col. 13	Educational Level
Col. 14	Occupational Classification
Col. 15	Presently Working
Col. 16	Year of Testing
Col. 17, 18	Month of Testing
Col. 19	Experimenter
Col. 20	Card No. (used when each subject has more than one card in the data deck)
Col. 21	Response to Test Item #1
Col. 22	Response to Test Item #2
Col. 23	Response to Test Item #3
Col. 80	Response to Test Item #60

As illustrated above, the data cards contained considerably more information on each subject than the test scores, *per se*. This additional information was coded by numbers that had specific reference to certain facts about the subject. A code scheme was developed so that these numbers could be interpreted. The following examples illustrate such coding:

Col. 1	0 = Pilot Study
	1 = Study I
	2 = Study II

| Col. 2 | 0 = Rio de Janeiro |
| | 1 = Sao Paulo |

| Col. 6 | 0 = Female |
| | 1 = Male |

Col. 13	0 = No Formal Education
	1 = Elementary Education
	2 = Secondary Education
	3 = College Education
	4 = Post-Graduate Training

The background information on each subject contained in Columns 6 through 19 was correlated with the various test scores and also enabled the researcher to subdivide the data decks in a variety of ways for further analyses. With respect to the latter point, the data deck may be passed through a card sorter and sorted on the relevant column. It is then categorized into separate decks which are in accordance with the categories defined by the relevant column. For example, if the researcher was interested in separating the data deck by levels of education, the sort would be made on Column 13, giving five stacks of cards with each stack representing a different educational level. The data are now organized so that further analyses can be applied to the data to evaluate the differences or similarities of the test performance between subjects of the five educational levels.

The data cards containing the combined test scores are quite similar to those containing responses to each test item. The identical background information was contained in the initial columns followed by the scale scores from several tests which were placed on the same card for a given subject.

Separate data decks containing the scale and total scores were made for each study and city combination. For example, the Brazilian data were subdivided into five decks:

1. Pilot Study—Rio
2. Pilot Study—Sao Paulo
3. Study I—Rio
4. Study I—Sao Paulo
5. Study II—Rio

These data decks were used for subsequent statistical analyses using the computer. The first analysis involved a correlation program which provided the following output: means, standard deviations, and a correlation matrix. The correlation matrix provides a coefficient of relationship of the scores on each variable with scores on every other variable. This coefficient of relationship can be evaluated on a probabilistic bases — i.e., on the determinable probability that the observed coefficient of relationship is a function of chance occurrence.

CONCLUSION

Although the psychologist has called on computer technology to perform a variety of roles, the most common use is that of data analysis. The increased proficiency and efficiency of the computer frees the researcher from the more tedious and time-consuming involvements in data processing. Studies of the scope of the cross-cultural study described in this chapter would never be conceived if the computer were not available. The desk calculator and clerical help would be kept at hard labor for years to complete the data analyses required, while the total computer time for the same analyses will be less than five hours. The computer enables the researcher to evaluate data with considerably more sophisticated statistical procedures than previously possible. The sophisticated statistical procedures — i.e., factor analysis, multivariate statistics, etc. — frequently engender a better understanding of the research data.

The results of the study described are far from conclusive but serve to identify similarities and differences between cultural groups and provide a rich source for hypotheses for future testing. The working assumption of the researchers is that the characteristic manner in which individuals perceive, organize, interpret and react to the world about them is largely determined by the individual's conditioned modes of behavior, memories, expectations, values, affects, beliefs, etc. If this assumption is valid, a perceptual cognitive personality approach to cross-cultural research should provide information that is eminently important to a better understanding between and among people from various cultural groups. If more is known about the similarities and the differences between cultural groups in terms of basic perceptual experiences, cognitive processes, and personality characteristics, perhaps the origins of misunderstandings and conflicts could be better identified and more readily alleviated. Furthermore, this knowledge may well be useful, if not essential, for implementing new programs that involve change in underdeveloped countries.

appendix 14-1

A Brief Description of Tests

1. *Autokinetic Perception:* Perception of illusory movement of a stationary light. Test performance has been related to personality characteristics and psychopathology.
2. *California Personality Inventory:* A standardized personality test similar to the MMPI but containing different scales.
3. *Conceptual Styles Test* (*Kagen*): This test purports to categorize individual characteristic style of conceptualization — relational, analytic, or categorical inferential styles.
4. *Harvey's "This I Believe" Test:* Attempts to measure the conceptual functioning, varying from concreteness to abstractness — also related to authoritarianism and dogmatism.
5. *Holtzman Inkblot Test:* A standardized inkblot perception test that can be effectively employed as a projective test instrument; these test scores have been related to basic perceptual, cognitive, and personality characteristics.
6. *Luchin's Einstellung Test:* Better known as the *Water Jug* — problems which attempt to measure rigidity in a problem solving situation.
7. *Minnesota Multiphasic Personality Inventory:* A standardized personality test used extensively for research and clinical purposes.
8. *Mooney Closure Test:* Test consists of incomplete figures; the test measures the extent to which subjects can provide closure on partial information; related to perceptual flexibility and rigidity.
9. *Open-Mindedness Scale:* As the name implies, measures open-mindedness; this scale was derived from the *Authoritarian Scale* and the *Dogmatism Scale*.
10. *Porteus Mazes:* Only the qualitative measures were employed which purports to assess impulsivity, compulsivity, and rigidity.

11. *Reactive Curiosity Scale:* Purports to measure curiosity behavior.
12. *Questionnaire on Family Change:* Attempts to measure potentiality for family change as reflected in attitude toward education, birth control, younger generation, sex, religion, family authority, extended nuclear family structure, etc.

BIBLIOGRAPHY

Bagby, J. A., "A Cross-Cultural Study of Perceptual Predominance in Binocular Rivalry," *Journal of Abnormal Social Psychology*, Vol. **54** (1957), pp. 331–334.

Diaz Guerro, R. "Socio-Cultural Premises, Attitudes and Cross-Cultural Research", paper presented at the International Congress of Psychology (Washington, 1963).

Doyle, W., "Recognition of Sloppy Hand-printed Characters," Proceedings of the Western Joint Computer Conference (1960), pp. 133–143.

Gyr, J., Thatcher, J., and Allen, G., "Computer Simulation of a Model of Cognitive Organization," *Behavioral Science*, **7** no. 1, (1962), pp. 111–116.

Hovland, C., "Computer Simulation of Thinking," *American Psychology*, **15**, (1960), pp. 687–693.

Hunt, E., "Computer Simulation: Artificial Intelligence Studies and Their Relevance to Psychology," *Annual Review of Psychology*, **19**, (1968), pp. 135–168.

Julesz, B., "Experiment in Perception," *Psychology Today*, **2**, (1968), pp. 16–23.

Kaiser, H. F., "Relating Factors Between Studies Based on Different Individuals," unpublished manuscript (University of Illinois, 1960).

Marzocco, F. N., and Bartram, P. R., "Statistical Learning Models for Behavior of an Artificial Organism," in E. E. Bernard and M. R. Kare (eds.), *Biological Prototypes and Synthetic Systems*, (New York, Plenum, 1962).

Murphy, G., *Personality: A Bio-Social Approach to Origins and Structure*, (New York, Harper, 1947).

Newell, A., Shaw, J. C., and Simon, H. A., "Elements of a Theory of Human Problem Solving," *Psychology Review*, **65**, (1958), pp. 151–166.

Santos, J. F., "Personal Values and Psychological Characteristics in Latin America," paper presented at the Fourth National Conference of the Catholic InterAmerican Cooperation Programs (Boston, Mass., 1967).

Santos, J. F., "A Psychologist Reflects on Brazil and Brazilians," *New Perspectives of Brazil* (Vanderbilt University Press, 1966), Chap. 9.

Selfridge, O. G., and Neisser, V., "Pattern Recognition by Machine," *Scientific American*, Vol. 203, No. 2 (1960), pp. 60–68.

Solley, C. M., and Murphy, G., *Development of the Perceptual World* (Basic Books, New York, 1960).

Veldman, D. J., *Fortran Programming for the Behavioral Sciences*, (Holt, Rinehart, and Winston, New York, 1967).

Vossler, C., and Uhr, L., "A Computer Simulation of Pattern Perception and Concept Formation," in E. E. Bernard and M. R. Kare (eds.), *Biological Prototypes and Synthetic Systems*, (New York, Plenum, 1962).

15

Art, Politics, and Sex

The study

The results of a recent study at the University of Notre Dame indicate that artistic perception may be a more complex phenomenon than has been previously suspected. Current studies of artwork as psychological tools are continuing. Most of these current studies still employ expert judgments and/or accepted ranking procedures to categorize art on a given dimension. These procedures result in a unitary concept being employed to account for all the differences between the works of art — i.e., it is either aesthetically pleasing or it is not pleasing. The Notre Dame study analyzed the preferences expressed by college students for a wide variety of modern art. These preferences were analyzed into a series of independent subscales; that is, the standard "like" or "do not like" groups were broken into defined subgroups using a standardized computer program procedure. Thus the availability of the computer and computer technology makes possible a more complex and perhaps more realistic description.

It would appear from the Notre Dame study that the identified dimensions do not offer clear divisions between paintings as logically categorized by style, or by artist. Apparently, however, there is an interaction of style, content, color, and clarity to define each dimension. Previous studies have been able to identify only a single bipolar category or dichotomous reaction to the paintings. This study, through computer analysis, has been able to identify five groups that are, in essence, breakdowns of the previous dichotomous reactions. The five identifiable groups are labeled, for convenience, as follows:

1. *Structured realism:* highly representational paintings and photographic-type art.
2. *Primitive-analytic cubism:* paintings that severely tax a person's ability to identify the original theme of the painting.
3. *Synthetic cubism:* the use of angular marks to create an appearance of a person or an object.

---

[1]Dr. Eugene J. Loveless, Queensborough Community College, New York. This study is taken from: *"The Dimensions of Preference for Modern Art,"* Proceedings, 76th Meeting of the American Psychological Association, 1968.

4. *Surrealism:* an amorphous fluid-type of distortion which permits specific details to become exaggerated.
5. *Expressionism:* the accentuation of one particular color, modality, form, or other facet, to obtain a desired effect.

Thus, the implication clearly appears to be in support of a more complex concept of artistic perception than is currently available even when a relatively small number of works of art (160) and artists (3) are studied.

The identification of the components of artistic preferences is made clear by the specification of the underlying characteristics that contribute to these judgments. These characteristics are complexly interwoven into each picture so that classifying art on a single dimension makes it difficult to deduce psychologically meaningful implications from these works. The computer analysis has helped to isolate each dimension so that pure forms may be identified and applied in psychological research.

The approach

Studies which seek to employ works of art as measures of individual variation require a few statistical control procedures. These are relatively easy to master and to administer. The computer programs necessary to successfully complete such work are also available.[2] The first question that comes to mind concerns the method of response. The University of Notre Dame study illustrated here used the "like" or "do not like" dimension. This simple dichotomy of responses is the broadest and most comprehensive category that may be employed in studies which use artistic materials as data. On the Hollerith card the data would appear as 1 for like, and an 0 for dislike. Conceptually each card column would represent a picture, with the individual's response to each picture coded into the appropriate column as a 1 or an 0. The usual method for this is to have the answer written or inserted into a pre-printed form, with the data subsequently keypunched onto the Hollerith card.

The reason for recording each response is twofold. In the first place, it is important, for the psychologist's work, to know how frequently the general public likes or does not like a given work of art. This constitutes the "level of endorsement" for a work. After a given picture or group of pictures have been seen by a large number of subjects, the endorsement level will be measured by the percentage of the total that do like the picture. This endorsement level is usually obtained by a frequency-count computer program, normally available as a standardized program procedure.[3]

The second reason for recording and analyzing the data is that it becomes important to sort the artwork into different categories, based on style, content, author, or whatever characteristics are implied from a clear-cut objective and empirical basis. These objective categories are revealed by the application of factor analysis to the responses of people who like and dislike the pictures.

While it is not necessary to explain in detail this second phase or to explain how a factor analysis program operates, the following sentences may be useful in indicating something of the nature of factor analysis. It is sufficient to add that without the

---

[2]The most general program group would be the BMD group, cited in Chapter 9. See also: Hallworth and Brebner, *A System of Computer Programs* (British Psychological Society, London, England, 1967).

[3]See Chapter 9 for a discussion of the standardized program procedure for single-column frequency count.

computer this kind of analysis (even on the small number of pictures and artists), would not be practicable.

Factor analysis is a statistical technique for breaking down an intercorrelation matrix (table) among the major abilities, dimensions, or components which contribute to each correlation coefficient. In the case of the art, the like or dislike responses showed systematic relations among the five groups of pictures (realistic, surrealistic, etc.). The relative clarity or purity of each style was represented as a coefficient between each picture and the factor representing that style. These coefficients are referred to as factor loadings and are considered to be meaningful when they are greater than 0.30 (as a rule of thumb). Each factor then reflects a linear description of the most representative pictures (based on the empirical analysis), in the order of the saturation of each picture on that factor.

In order to understand the idea of factor analysis, one must first consider correlation. Basically, the correlation between two variables is an index of the degree to which they are associated. For example, the degree of correlation between two pictures from the study is an index of the extent to which people who like one picture also like the other. If all the people who like one picture also like the other, the correlation between the pictures is perfect and the value is 1.00. If none of the people who like the one picture like the other, the correlation is zero.

The basic material for factor analysis is a correlation matrix as shown in Figure 15-1, below. In the correlation matrix the correlation (association) between each picture (or variable) and every other picture (or every other variable) is represented. The matrix illustrated below is a hypothetical matrix for illustration.

The diagonal (Cells 1,1; 2,2; 3,3; 4,4; 5,5) contains the correlation coefficients between each picture and itself; thus, all the diagonal values equal 1.00. Since the matrix is a square, all the information above the diagonal is repeated below the diagonal. A correlation matrix contains a series of values, and each value relates to only two of the variables (in this study, pictures), involved. If the matrix is a large

PICTURES

PICTURES	1	2	3	4	5
1	1.00	.90	.15	.09	.95
2	.90	1.00	.25	.10	.85
3	.15	.25	1.00	.80	.17
4	.09	.10	.80	1.00	.21
5	.95	.85	.17	.21	1.00

FIGURE 15-1. Intercorrelation matrix.

one — e.g., 160 by 160 — it may be very difficult to interpret the matrix by inspection.

An early attempt at a sort of factor analysis consisted of analyzing a correlation matrix into a set of *clusters*. A cluster is defined, for our purposes, as a set of variables (pictures) which are highly correlated with each other, and which tend not to be correlated with other variables (with variables in other clusters). If it is possible to analyze a matrix containing, for example, 100 variables into a set of 10 clusters, it is reasonable to assume that the relationships expressed in the matrix are due to no more than 10 basic and relatively independent influences or factors. The nature of each factor can be determined, roughly, by examining the variables that comprise the cluster.

The matrix shown in Figure 15-1 contains two clusters. Note that the correlation between Pictures 1 and 2 is 0.90, the correlation between 1 and 5 is 0.95, and the correlation between 2 and 5 is 0.85. Since these pictures are correlated with each other and not highly correlated with other pictures, they comprise a cluster as defined above. The other cluster consists of Pictures 3 and 4, since they are highly correlated with each other and not with Pictures 1, 2, and 5.

Factor analysis is much more sophisticated than cluster analysis, but the results of a factor analysis can be interpreted in a similar manner. The results of a factor analysis are typically presented as a factor matrix in which the rows represent variables, and the columns represent factors. The entries in the cells of the factor matrix are called loadings, and a given loading can be seen as representing the correlation between a factor and a variable. Thus the nature of a factor can be determined by examining the variables that have high loadings on that factor.

Table 15-1 is illustrative of the two tests used in evaluating the reactions to the pictures. The table shows 25 of the 160 pictures as an illustration. As suggested in the table, the number of artists represented was small in order to minimize the effect of personal stylistic variables. Picasso was the basic artist because of his range of styles. Mondrian pictures were included in the structured realism group. Van Gogh pictures were included in the expressionist group. Each artist was included on an *a priori* basis because they appeared to represent psychologically meaningful dimensions of art. In consultation with a resident artist the pictures were grouped into sixteen groups. These sixteen groups included the five shown above but were more detailed. The factor analysis program reflected only the five factors or groupings, perhaps reflecting the differences when professionals and laymen regard artworks.

Table 15-1 shows the title and the painter for each of the pictures. The Factor No. (I, II, III, IV, or V) indicates the factor into which this picture was classified by the factor analysis program. Loading is defined as the amount of commonality between/among items in one factor with some trait in common and identifiable from other factors or groupings in the same matrix. In looking at the column *loading*, any value over 30 represents a commonly accepted standard for inclusion within a factor and uniqueness of that factor as compared with other factors. The final column simply shows the percent of total viewers that liked each picture — i.e., the level of endorsement.

The data set

The pictures were projected from color slides before two separate groups and were presented to 30 to 35 viewers at a time. The first subgroup viewing the pictures represented 600 students at several colleges throughout the United States. These

TABLE 15-1. Paintings, factor loadings, and preference levels for artworks

Title	Painter	Factor	Loading	% Liked
Figure (1910)	Picasso	I	61	51
Girl with Mandolin (1910)	Picasso	I	60	40
The Kitchen (1948)	Picasso	I	55	45
Road with Cypresses	Van Gogh	I	54	60
The Loom (1884)	Van Gogh	I	52	62
Harlequin Leaning (1909)	Picasso	II	70	23
New York City (1924)	Mondrian	II	66	63
Fruit and Wineglass (1908)	Picasso	II	63	38
Self-Portrait with Pipe	Van Gogh	II	62	28
The Sower	Van Gogh	II	59	56
Young Girl at Mirror (1932)	Picasso	III	72	78
Circus Family (1905)	Picasso	III	72	51
Bull and Horse (1934)	Picasso	III	70	26
Nude (1932)	Picasso	III	67	59
Woman at Mirror (1937)	Picasso	III	64	34
Man Smoking (1914)	Picasso	IV	69	57
Three Musicians (1921)	Picasso	IV	69	54
Bather Seated (1929)	Picasso	IV	58	51
Green Still life (1914)	Picasso	IV	55	49
Unidentifed	unidentified	IV	41	76
Still life with Antique Head (1925)	Picasso	V	78	39
The Schoolgirl (1919)	Picasso	V	73	30
Woman in Blue	Picasso	V	69	39
Still life with Glass (1942)	Picasso	V	65	56
Still life with Guitar (1937)	Picasso	V	59	22

Eugene J. Loveless, "Dimensions of Preference for Modern Art," *Proceedings of the 76th Annual Convention of the American Psychological Association*, **3** (1968), pp. 445–446, reproduced by permission.

students were primarily from psychology and education departments. The students responded on optical scan sheets for each picture. The scan sheets were converted to Hollerith cards for analysis. Use of a single-column frequency-count program provided the information for Column 5 of Table 15-1.

A second subgroup represented students from a private nonsectarian college in a major metropolitan area who were taking their first psychology course. This group constituted 193 viewers. These persons responded as did the first group, and the resulting cards were subjected to the BMD factor analysis program (Chapter 9). The results of the analysis are shown in columns 3 and 4 of Table 15-1.

Conclusions

Whatever method of external validation is to be used, the materials originally selected *a priori* have now been established to have constituent subgroups or subscales. These represent empirically established dimensions of artistic preference. The pruning and selection of the most potent and independent representatives of each subscale provides rapid and dependable materials for further application and validation procedures on any equivalent population.

PREDICTING ELECTIONS

One of the more widely used phases of computer application is in data prediction. Computers and computer programs are used to predict anything from company sales and profits to football game winners and elections. Until one sits down to figure out what is involved, it may all sound quite mysterious. Let us take the problem of predicting elections and examine it briefly.[4]

What is the point of predicting an election result? The answer seems to be that someone wants to know who will win the election before all the votes are finally counted.[5] The key here, therefore, is *when* will the outcome of the election be predicted. There are two logical times: 1.) Before the day of the election. 2.) After most or all the voting polls have closed, but before the entire count has been tabulated.

If election prediction is to be done *before election day*, the prediction must be based on an "attitude." This involves, normally, a sampling technique. Research organizations must determine, a) the attitude of the voters insofar as the voters favor one candidate or issue over another, b) assuming the voters favor one candidate or issue today and were to vote accordingly today, whether they would vote that way *on the day of the election*.

The outcome of the *future* election is then predicted on the basis of today's attitude. If, over time, voters have been switching from one candidate or issue to another, that also may be a factor to be considered.

In current elections, it is desired to know who will probably win before the votes are completely counted, but after the people have voted and the polls have closed. This has a different dimension. However, national election prediction is sometimes based on the *attitude survey* (discussed above) plus the vote pattern analysis. The vote pattern analysis works as discussed below. The presentation shown below is simplified for pedagogical purposes.

The point of being able to predict an election is that the concern is with the *registered voters who vote*. In order to be able to predict any election on any issue, it is essentially necessary to build a descriptive simulation model of the voting area. This involves the following variables:

1. The no. of registered voters of all concerned parties.
2. The no. of precincts and names.
3. The no. of larger areas — city, township, county, state, etc.
4. The names and denominations of all candidates.
5. The inclusive precincts and/or larger areas for each candidate in each area. (For instance, a candidate or an issue may be voted on in an area coincident with a county line or not. Some precincts may be counted in electing one candidate, but not be counted in electing another candidate in the same election. The problem is then to provide for the proper allocation of each precinct for each candidate and each issue in each election.)

In a given county (including cities):

1. All precincts may vote on gubernatorial candidates.

---

[4]c. f. Franz Lalt, Morris Rubinoff (eds.), *"Advances in Computers,"* Vol. 5 (New York, Academic Press 1964), "The Role of Computers in Election Night Broadcasting," by Jack Moshman, pp. 1–21.

[5]In predicting a firm's sales, the predicted sales can be a valuable guide in coordinating purchasing and production. Since there is a lag between production and sales, the value of sales prediction is almost self-evident.

2. All precincts may vote on county officials.
3. Some of the precincts may vote on localized county improvement projects (assessed on a local basis within the county, district by district).
4. No precincts outside cities may vote on city elections, etc.

Once the precincts are properly allocated for each race and for each candidate it is necessary to prepare the input data which is grouped into two categories:

1. *Data needed before the election night:*
   a. names of each candidate or issue, the number and names of precincts for each office or issue, and the party affiliation of each candidate.
   b. the total registered vote for each precinct by party. (This datum is questioned by many who note that much more important is the voting pattern of the registered voters who vote. Necessary weights here may include: crossover vote, percentages of registered voters who vote, and the actual voting trend in one election compared with past elections.)
2. *Data needed on election night.* This constitutes the vote by candidate and by race or issue from each voting machine or precinct.

The program should provide at least three different types of output: 1) Cumulative vote totals per race, per candidate, or per issue. 2) Percentage of vote for each race, candidate, or otherwise. 3) The *total vote* for each candidate when each precinct is counted, as it is counted — i.e., the prediction of the final outcome successively modified as additional precincts are counted. (This constitutes the prediction of the election outcome from the initial descriptive simulation model, successively modified.)

A simple and common technique for ascertaining this outcome of the election (predicting the outcome) is to use statistical correlation. Calculate the *correlation coefficient* (or percentage) of voter turnout to registered vote for each candidate (party), for each precinct or machine. Calculate the correlation coefficient for the party votes respectively of the total vote cast for each machine or precinct. The calculation of the voter turnout and the indication of the party voting trend for each candidate will permit an extrapolation to ascertain the total vote outcome; *that is, prediction of the final outcome is based on the number (percent) of voters voting by party voting most heavily by precincts.* An assumption is made that little cross-party voting will be done. In a race that is likely to find considerable cross-party voting, this must be considered by the program (if possible). In the national election, some quantified or weighted factor provision is made to include relation of actual vote patterns, registered vote patterns to the attitude surveys, etc.

Basically, the program stores data in core storage either as an array (column vector) or as a matrix. A pointer is used when it is necessary to select from that array or matrix particular data.

The example shown below illustrates one use of a pointer. The basic data-storage array is ICTOTL. This array contains, in each cell of the array, the vote for a candidate running for *any elected office* (race) in the election. The votes are stored in the array according to a sequence (ICODE). In the example shown, if there were 150 candidates, each candidate's cumulative vote total would be stored in ICTOTL. Since each candidate runs for a particular office, we need a pointer to show which candidate votes are competitive for each office or race.

There might be 50 elected offices to be filled — hence, 50 races. Each of the 150 candidates would belong to a given race. Thus, the ICTOTL would look as follows:

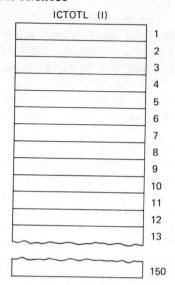

ICTOTL (I)

Each cell of the array — e.g., ICTOTL(1), ICTOTL(2), ICTOTL(3) through to ICTOTL(150) — contains the cumulative vote total for one of the 150 candidates.

It is necessary, however, to group the candidates by *race*, for purposes of performing the various vote predictions:

1. Who has the most votes at any given time or point in a race.
2. Who will win the race (prediction) based on votes cast and party eligibles.

It is, therefore, necessary to group the votes in ICTOTL by race. This is done by establishing two arrays — IR1ST and IRLAST. Each array has as many cells as there are races — i.e., in this case, 50. With 50 races and 150 candidates, there would *average* 3 candidates per race.

The values of the array IR1ST and IRLAST indicate the *first* and *last* candidate for each race. The value of Cell 1 in IR1ST is the cell number in ICTOTL containing the first candidate of RACE 1. The value of Cell 1 of IRLAST is the cell number in ICTOTL containing the last candidate of RACE 1.

For instance, there are 150 numbered candidates for all races. We shall assume that there are 50 races, and that each race is numbered from 1–50. There are from 1–10 candidates in each race. The representative models of IR1ST and IRLAST is below:

Race No.	Race
1	Governor
2	Attorney General
...	....
50	Dogcatcher

IRIST

1	1
2	4
3	7
...	...
50	149

IRLAST

1	3
2	6
3	7
...	...
50	150

In short, Candidates 1, 2, and 3 are competing in Race 1 for Governor. Candidates 4, 5, and 6 are competing in the second race, etc.

The program shown on Table 15-2 is extremely limited for expository reasons. However, as should be clear by now, the essence of predicting elections from vote data is to be found in the tabular or *table structure* of the data. If the data on candidate and party names and races, registered votes, and actual vote are properly coded and stored in computer core storage, the development of cumulative vote totals, percentage vote, correlation coefficients, etc., becomes a rather elementary matter. *Basically, the programming problem for predicting elections involves table structure and organization.*

TABLE 15-2. Election program.

```
      FOR      ,MAIN
      COMMON/PARTYD/NP,NAMEP(2,10),NAMEPS(10),IPTOTL(10)
      COMMON/RACED/NR,NAMER(4,50),IR1ST(50),IRLAST(50)
      COMMON/CANDD/NC,NAMEC(4,150),ICPRTY(150),ICTOTL(150)
      NP=0
      NR=0
      NC=0
      CALL INPRTY
      CALL INRACE
      CALL INVOTE
      CALL OUTSUM
      STOP
      END


      FOR      ,INPRTY
      SUBROUTINE INPRTY
      COMMON/PARTYD/NP,NAMEP(2,10),NAMEPS(10),IPTOTL(10)
      COMMON/RACED/NR,NAMER(4,50),IR1ST(50),IRLAST(50)
      COMMON/CANDD/NC,NAMEC(4,150),ICPRTY(150),ICTOTL(150)
      DIMENSION NAME(2)
      DATA IRACE/5HRACE
   90 FORMAT (A5,1X,2A6)
C
C     ***   READ END-CODE OR SHORT NAME, FOLLOWED BY LONG NAME   ***
C
   10 READ 90, ICODE, (NAME(I), I = 1,2)
      IF (ICODE.EQ.IRACE) RETURN
C
C     ***   MAKE AN ENTRY FOR ANOTHER PARTY   ***
C
      NP=NP+1
      DO 20 I=1,2
   20 NAMEP(I,NP)=NAME(I)
      NAMEPS(NP)=ICODE
      GO TO 10
      END


      FOR      ,INRACE
      SUBROUTINE INRACE
      COMMON/PARTYD/NP,NAMEP(2,10),NAMEPS(10),IPTOTL(10)
      COMMON/RACED/NR,NAMER(4,50),IR1ST(50),IRLAST(50)
      COMMON/CANDD/NC,NAMEC(4,150),ICPRTY(150),ICTOTL(150)
      DIMENSION NAME(4)
      DATA IDATA/5HDATA  /IBLANK/5H
```

TABLE 15-2. Election program. (Continued)

```
 90 FORMAT(A5,1X,4A6)
 91 FORMAT(43H THIS CARD, IS MISPUNCHED OR OUT OF SEQUENCE   ,A5,1X4A6)
C
C    ***   READ END-CODE, NEW-RACE, OR NEW CANDIDATE IN CURRENT RACE   ***
C
 10 READ 90,ICODE,(NAME(I),I=1,4)
    IF (ICODE.EQ.IDATA) RETURN
    IF(ICODE.NE.IBLANK) GO TO 30
C
C    ***   NEW RACE—NO CANDIDATES YET   ***
C
    NR=NR+1
    DO 20 I=1,4
 20 NAMER(I,NR)=NAME(I)
    IR1ST(NR)=NC+1
    IRLAST(NR)=NC
    GO TO 10
C
C    ***   NEW CANDIDATE—BUT FIRST MAKE SURE WE HAVE A RACE & PARTY   ***
C
 30 IF(NR.LE.0) GO TO 50
    DO 40 I=1,NP
 40 IF(ICODE.EQ.NAMEPS) GO TO 50
    GO TO 80
C
C    ***   NOW NEW ENTRY   ***
C
 50 NC=NC+1
    ICPRTY(NC)=I
    DO 60 I=1,4
 60 NAMEC(I,NC)=NAME(I)
C
C    ***   INITIALIZE TOTAL VOTES AND UPDATE POINTER IN RACE TABLE   ***
C
    IRLAST(NR)=NC
    ICTOTL(NC)=0
    GO TO 10
 80 PRINT 91,ICODE,(NAME(I),I=1,4)
    GO TO 10
    END


    FOR          ,INVOTE
    SUBROUTINE INVOTE
    COMMON/PARTYD/NP,NAMEP(2,10),NAMEPS(10),IPTOTL(10)
    COMMON/RACED/NR,NAMER(4,50),IR1ST(50),IRLAST(50)
    COMMON/CANDD/NC,NAMEC(4,150),ICPRTY(150),ICTOTL(150)
    DIMENSION IVOTE(150)
    DATA IDONE/5HDONE  /
 90 FORMAT(A5,15I5/(5X,15I5) )
 91 FORMAT(10H BAD DATA:,5X,A5,15I5,/(20X,15I5) )
C
C    ***   READ END-CARD OR VOTES—ONE PER CANDIDATE   ***
C
 10 READ 90,ICODE,(IVOTE(I),I=1,NC)
    IF(ICODE.EQ.IDONE) RETURN
C
C    ***   CHECK VOTES FOR REPORTING OR TRANSCRIBING ERRORS HERE   ***
C
    DO 20 I=1,NC
```

TABLE 15-2. Election program. (Continued)

```
   20 IF(IVOTE(I).LT.0) GO TO 80
C
C    ***   IF NO OBVIOUS ERRORS ON CARD, TOTAL VOTES FOR EACH CANDIDATE   ***
C
      DO 30 I=1,NC
   30 ICTOTL(I)=ICTOTL(I)+IVOTE(I)
      GO TO 10
C
C    ***   VOTE CARD IN ERROR   ***
C
   80 PRINT 91,ICODE,(IVOTE(I),I=1,NC)
      GO TO 10
      END


      FOR       ,OUTSUM
      SUBROUTINE OUTSUM
      COMMON/PARTYD/NP,NAMEP(2,10),NAMEPS(10),IPTOTL(10)
      COMMON/RACED/NR,NAMER(4,50),IR1ST(50),IRLAST(50)
      COMMON/CANDD/NC,NAMEC(4,150),ICPRTY(150),ICTOTL(150)
   90 FORMAT(1H1,57X,5HPARTY,10X,5HTOTAL/ /(50X,A1,5X,2A6,I10) )
   91 FORMAT(/ / / / /12X,4HRACE,23X,5HTOTAL/58X,5HPARTY,5X,9HCANDIDATE,18X,
     1 5HTOTAL/ /)
   92 FORMAT(/ /10X,4A6,I10)
   93 FORMAT(60X,A1,5X,4A6,I10)
C
C    ***   INITIALIZE PARTY TOTALS   ***
C
      DO 10 IP=1,NP
   10 IPTOTL(IP)=0
C
C    ***   SUM CANDIDATES' VOTES BY PARTY   ***
C
      DO 20 IC=1,NC
      IP=ICPRTY(IC)
   20 IPTOTL(IP)=IPTOTL(IP)+ICTOTL(IC)
C
C    ***   PRINT PARTY NAMES AND TOTALS   ***
C
      PRINT 90, NAMEPS(I),(NAMEP(J,I),J=1,2),(IPTOTL(I),I=1,NP)
      PRINT 91
      DO 50 IR=1,NR
      I1=IR1ST(IR)
      I2=IRLAST(IR)
      IF(I1.GT.I2)GOTO 50
C
C    ***   PRINT RACE NAME AND TOTAL   ***
C
      IRTOT=0
      DO 30 IC=I1,I2
   30 IRTOT=IRTOT + ITOTAL(IC)
      PRINT 92,(NAMER(J,IR),J=1,4),IRTOT
C
C    ***   PRINT CANDIDATE NAME AND TOTAL   ***
C
      DO 40 IC=I1,I2
      I3=ICPRTY(IC)
   40 PRINT 93,NAMEPS(I3),(NAMEC(J,IC),J=1,4),ICTOTL(IC)
   50 CONTINUE
      RETURN
      END
```

The program shown is divided into five parts: a main or calling program, and four subroutines. The main program simply defines the tables and places them in COMMON for subroutine use. It sets certain counters to 0, and defines the tables to be used in organizing and storing the input data.

Part II of the program is a subroutine, the function of which is to read the names of the parties into computer storage. Each input card is divided into two fields:

1. (Col. 1–5) — a short coded designation for the party, ICODE
2. (Col. 7–18) — the name of the party, NAME

The data in the card are stored in consecutive cells of the array:

Data	(in)	Card Field	(stored in)	Array
Party Name (short form)		ICODE		NAMEPS
Party Name		NAME		NAMEP

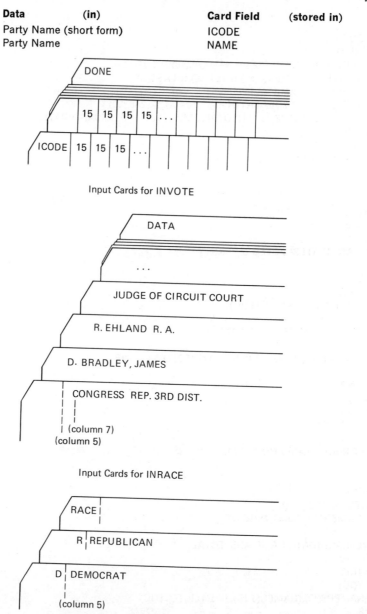

Input Cards for INVOTE

Input Cards for INRACE

Input Cards for INPRTY

FIGURE 15-2.   Input data.

When all party and candidate names have been stored, the program control returns to the main program. These data are usually prepared prior to the election night.

Part III of the program is a subroutine, the purpose of which is to read the names of the races and candidates into the computer, to store them in the noted tables, and to maintain control over the location of each race and the candidates in that race.

Part IV of the program is the subroutine that inputs the voting machine data on each candidate and stores that data in an array. The cumulative vote for each candidate is accumulated in an array. The location of each candidate's vote in that array is located in another array called a pointer. Thus, the candidate's vote is referenced through the pointer. Since the essence of an election prediction program is the establishment and maintenance of data stored in table form (array form), the use of a pointer is essential to minimize storage locations, and to maximize program and machine efficiency in dealing with the data. Thus, the two essential characteristics to an effective election prediction program are the establishment of storage in core, and the use of pointers to locate the data stored. This part of this chapter is concerned with data storage and pointers.

Part IV also makes an elementary check to determine whether there are any obvious keypunch errors. If no errors are detected, the vote data for each candidate

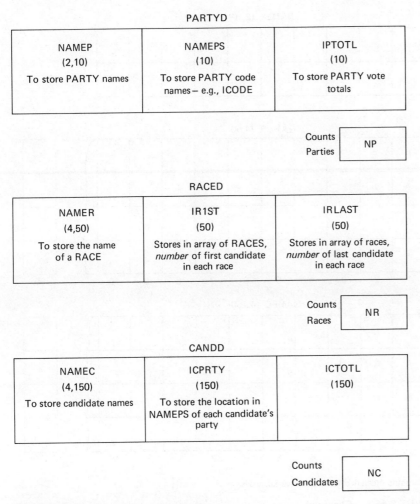

FIGURE 15-3.   Common area storage.

in each race from each voting machine are added into the existing vote totals, to arrive at a new updated vote total.

Part V of the program is a subroutine to accumulate vote totals by candidate and by party and to print out the vote totals.

If a more complex program were being considered, the development of vote projections — and the development of the various other data on party votes, etc. — would be done either in Part IV after updating vote totals, or in Part V.

Since the crux of any election prediction (or of a good many other) computer problems is in the storage of data, let us go into the program a little more thoroughly. The program is shown previously in Table 15-1. Figure 15-2 shows the input data form from the Hollerith cards, Figures 15-3 and 15-4 show the table structure, and Figure 15-5 shows the flowchart of the program.

There are four separate types of input:

1. Data on PARTY names — e.g., Democrat
2. Data on RACE names — e.g., Congressional Representative
3. Data on CANDIDATES — e.g., name of candidate
4. Vote data by machine or precinct.

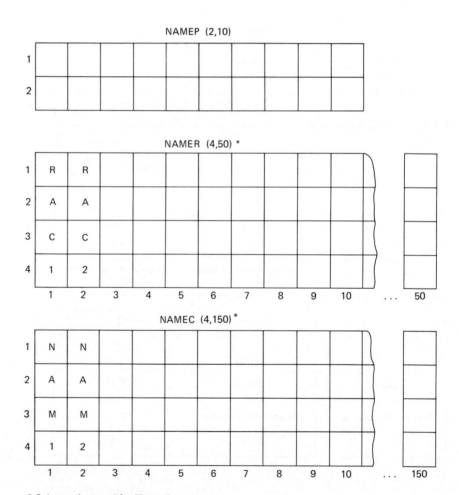

* Columns shortened for illustrative purposes.

FIGURE 15-4. Storage.

Data are organized (sorted) for input. A termination card follows each data series. The input data cards for the PARTY data are set up as follows:

A. (Columns 1–5), a code or short name designating the PARTY — stored in NAMEPS.
B. (Columns 7–18), the full name of the PARTY — stored in NAMEP. One party name and short name appears on each card.

NAME is used as an intermediate storage to read in data while tests are performed to see what has been read. The storage areas set up in the program are shown in Figure 15-4. The designation "RACE" appears in the first five columns of a card following the party name cards. This marks the end of the input data for INPRTY and the beginning of the input data for INRACE. The party names are stored in NAMEP and the party short names are stored in NAMEPS. The counter NP is incremented each time a new party (card) is read in. Thus NP controls the position of NAME in NAMEP, and of ICODE in NAMEPS.

The subroutine INRACE is executed after the subroutine INPRTY. INRACE contains:

1. A data card for each election race — e.g., for governor, mayor, or congress. The data cards for INRACE constitute race, office-seeker, or issue. The data cards are organized exactly as they appear on the voting machine. In this data subfile, the cards are blank on the first six columns, and the issue or race name begins in Column 7.
2. A candidate card for each candidate/issue in each race, ordered as on the voting machine or ballot, by race. Columns 1–5 of the candidate card contain the short name of the candidate's party. Columns 7–30 contain the name of the candidate.

In INRACE when ICODE (Columns 1–5) is blank, a new race is encountered. When ICODE equals "DATA," all the races and candidates/issues have been read in, and are stored in computer storage. INRACE has executed completely. All pre-election data are now in computer core. Three counters have been used:

1. NP counts the no. of parties.
2. NR counts the no. of races.
3. NC counts the no. of candidates.

These are used in properly setting the pointers:

NAMEP   an array containing the name of each party.
NAMEPS an array containing the short or coded name of each party.
NAMER   an array to store the name of each race.
NAMEC   an array to store the name of each candidate.
ICPRTY an array to store the location in NAMEPS of each candidate's party. (For instance, if there are 150 candidates and two parties, each location in ICPRTY would contain a "1" or a "2".)
IR1ST   an array of races where each location in IR1ST is a number of a race. (The value of each location is the *number* of the *first* candidate in *each* race.)
IRLAST an array of races where each location in IRLAST is the number of a race. (The value of each location is the number of the *last* candidate in each race.)

The data structure is now ready to receive the vote totals. The data presented for invote are ordered by voting precinct or vote machine. It is assumed that the voting record is presented on Hollerith cards, and that each card will identify the voting precinct or machine. The vote for each candidate or issue will be identified by its location on the Hollerith cards.

FIGURE 15-5. Flowchart.

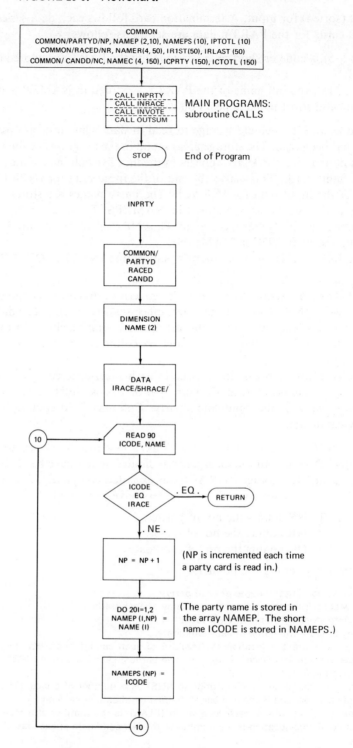

FIGURE 15-5. Flowchart. (Continued)

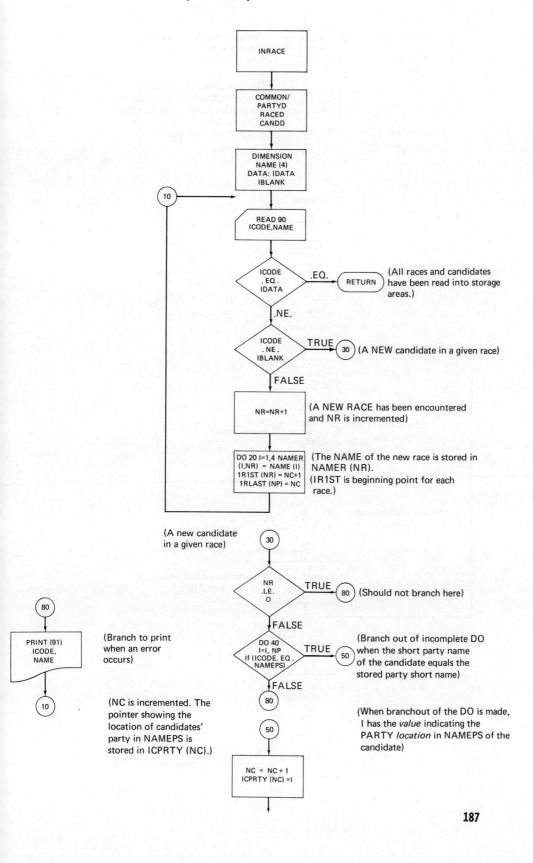

INRACE

COMMON/
PARTYD
RACED
CANDD

DIMENSION
NAME (4)
DATA: IDATA
IBLANK

10

READ 90
ICODE,NAME

ICODE
. EQ .
IDATA .EQ. RETURN (All races and candidates have been read into storage areas.)

.NE.

ICODE
. NE .
IBLANK TRUE 30 (A NEW candidate in a given race)

FALSE

NR=NR+1 (A NEW RACE has been encountered and NR is incremented)

DO 20 I=1,4 NAMER
(I,NR) = NAME (I)
1R1ST (NR) = NC+1
1RLAST (NP) = NC (The NAME of the new race is stored in NAMER (NR).
(IR1ST is beginning point for each race.)

(A new candidate in a given race) 30

NR
.LE.
0 TRUE 80 (Should not branch here)

80

FALSE

PRINT (91)
ICODE,
NAME (Branch to print when an error occurs)

DO 40
I=I, NP
If (ICODE. EQ.
NAMEPS) TRUE 50 (Branch out of incomplete DO when the short party name of the candidate equals the stored party short name)

FALSE

80

10

(NC is incremented. The pointer showing the location of candidates' party in NAMEPS is stored in ICPRTY (NC).)

50

(When branchout of the DO is made, I has the *value* indicating the PARTY *location* in NAMEPS of the candidate)

NC = NC + 1
ICPRTY (NC) =I

187

FIGURE 15-5. Flowchart. (Continued)

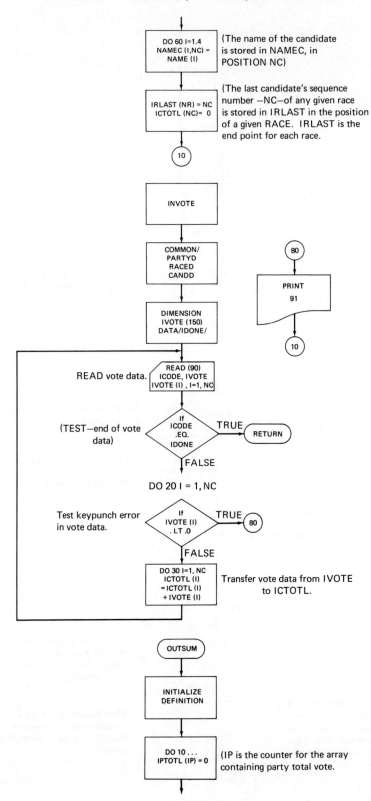

```
          DO 60 I=1.4          (The name of the candidate
          NAMEC (I,NC) =       is stored in NAMEC, in
             NAME (I)          POSITION NC)
```

```
                              (The last candidate's sequence
          IRLAST (NR) = NC    number —NC—of any given race
          ICTOTL (NC)= 0      is stored in IRLAST in the position
                              of a given RACE.  IRLAST is the
                              end point for each race.
```

(10)

INVOTE

```
          COMMON/              ( 80 )
          PARTYD
          RACED               PRINT
          CANDD                91
```

```
          DIMENSION
          IVOTE (150)          ( 10 )
          DATA/IDONE/
```

```
READ vote data.    READ (90)
                   ICODE, IVOTE
                   IVOTE (I) , I=1, NC
```

```
(TEST—end of vote         If           TRUE
    data)               ICODE              RETURN
                         .EQ.
                        IDONE
```

FALSE

DO 20 I = 1, NC

```
Test keypunch error       If           TRUE
in vote data.           IVOTE (I)            ( 80 )
                         . LT .0
```

FALSE

```
          DO 30 I=1, NC       Transfer vote data from IVOTE
          ICTOTL (I)               to ICTOTL.
          = ICTOTL (I)
          + IVOTE (I)
```

(OUTSUM)

```
          INITIALIZE
          DEFINITION
```

```
          DO 10 . . .          (IP is the counter for the array
          IPTOTL (IP) = 0      containing party total vote.
```

FIGURE 15-5. Flowchart. (Continued)

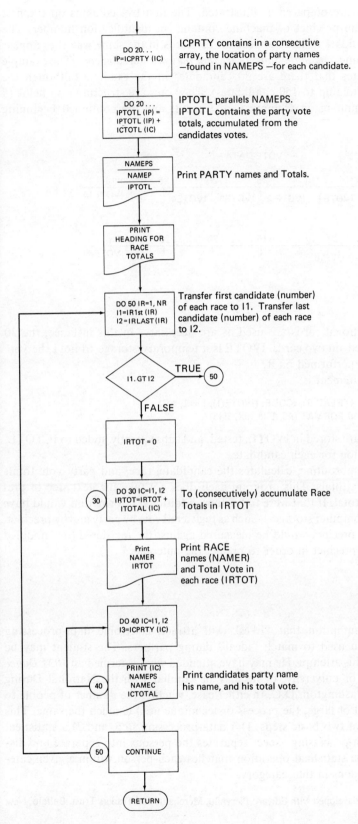

DO 20...
IP=ICPRTY (IC)

ICPRTY contains in a consecutive array, the location of party names —found in NAMEPS —for each candidate.

DO 20...
IPTOTL (IP) =
IPTOTL (IP) +
ICTOTL (IC)

IPTOTL parallels NAMEPS. IPTOTL contains the party vote totals, accumulated from the candidates votes.

NAMEPS
NAMEP
IPTOTL

Print PARTY names and Totals.

PRINT HEADING FOR RACE TOTALS

DO 50 IR=1, NR
I1=IR1st (IR)
I2=IRLAST (IR)

Transfer first candidate (number) of each race to I1. Transfer last candidate (number) of each race to I2.

I1. GT I2 — TRUE → **50**

FALSE

IRTOT = 0

DO 30 IC=I1, I2
IRTOT=IRTOT +
ITOTAL (IC)

To (consecutively) accumulate Race Totals in IRTOT

Print
NAMER
IRTOT

Print RACE names (NAMER) and Total Vote in each race (IRTOT)

DO 40 IC=I1, I2
I3=ICPRTY (IC)

PRINT (IC)
NAMEPS
NAMEC
ICTOTAL

Print candidates party name his name, and his total vote.

50 CONTINUE

RETURN

189

The vote data are prepared as illustrated. The first five columns on the first card for each voting precinct or machine contains an identification number. The votes for each candidate or issue appear on the cards in the same way they appear on the voting machine, *and in the same order that they are stored in core.* The example shown here indicates that there are 30 candidates in the example (although the program could handle up to 150 candidates). The votes are structured on fields (5 columns each) beginning on Column 6 of Card 1, and are continued beginning Column 6, Card 2:

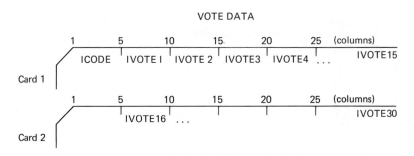

VOTE DATA

As many additional cards are used as are necessary. In this instance, the 30 candidates are stored on two cards. IVOTE is a temporary storage to hold the vote data while a test is performed on it.

The READ statement is:

```
READ 90, ICODE, (IVOTE(I), I = 1, NC)
90 FORMAT (A5, 15I5/(5X, 15I5)
```

The vote data are stored in IVOTE, tested, and subsequently added to ICTOTL, the vote accumulation for each candidate.

OUTSUM, a subroutine, calculates the candidate, race, and party vote totals and prints out these totals. This program itself does not take the next step in predicting an election total. If that were to be done, additional information would have been read into the computer storage — such as registered vote by party and by precinct. The actual vote by precinct would be measured against the registered (or modified registered) vote by precinct in order to predict the outcome.

THE MATCH GAME[6]

Under the assumption that "likes" will attract, electronic data-processing equipment has been used to match "ideal" dating partners. The student may be very familiar with this attempt. He may have attended what is termed an *IBM Dance* at his own college or university, or he may be familiar with the National Dating Game located in Washington, D.C. In either case, whether the number of people to be matched is small or large, the process or technique used is much the same. This technique consists of two basic steps, 1) a data-processing step, and 2) a statistical operation. The data-processing aspect separates the persons into separate and distinct categories. The statistical operation matches each person within a given category with other persons in that category.

[6]This segment was developed with Edward Piervallo, Merchants and Traders Trust, Buffalo, New York.

Data processing

There are certain characteristics which must be taken into account before any two people can be matched according to personality. Consider first the age of persons to be matched. It would be inappropriate to match a 21-year-old male with a 14-year-old female, although it may be perfectly satisfactory to match a 31-year-old male with a 24-year-old female. On a national level, it would be inappropriate to match a person living in Los Angeles with one living in New York. In addition, many match game techniques would not consider matching a 6-foot 6-inch male with a 4-foot 5-inch female, or vice versa. The necessary preliminary of categorization should be clear. The reader may wish to consider other items which would result in a more complex category-grouping.

The initial questions on a questionnaire to be used in a match game would generally consist of personal characteristics, location, and an individual's explicit preferences.[7] The data-processing section of a match program will then group and separate according to these initial questions contained on a questionnaire. Once all the males and females of a particular category are grouped, all remaining responses or answers which they give to personality questions are allocated to this category. To better understand this, note the program in Section B on the separation of candidates and parties, in a political election. Note that the separation in that case takes place according to party, candidate, and the office being sought. Also note that all the votes for each of these categories are allocated to the category concerned. The match game follows the same general procedure. We have a separation into categories according to specified answers given in a questionnaire. The remaining answers are further allocated to their respective respondents within each category.

The statistical technique

Upon completion of the data-processing section, we will have a set of categories containing both male and female respondents. Each category consists of those males and females who most frequently gave the same answers on the first part of the questionnaire. It is now the purpose of the dating game theory to match as closely as possible, those males and females contained within each category. To do this, the statistical technique of *correlation* is used.

The correlation coefficient as generated by the statistical technique of correlation measures the relationship between the two variables. This relationship must lie between 1 and −1. The closer the correlation coefficient is to +1, the higher is the relationship between the two variables or high positive correlation. If it is closer it is to −1, we say there is high correlation, however negative. If the correlation coefficient is close to 0, we say that there is no correlation, or no relationship, but rather independence between the two variables.

To apply this to the dating game theory: if we correlate the answers to the personality questions given by a male with the answers given by the female on the same questionnaire, we will find a relationship between those answers of the male and those of the female. Should the correlation coefficient generated by correlating this set of questions be very high (positive), it is possible that we have matched these two individuals. However, note that in each category, there are many other males and many other females. It is possible that one particular female or male will have

[7]The position of these questions in a particular questionnaire is of little significance. The important point is that they determine categorization.

a higher correlation coefficient with some other male or female. Therefore, each individual male or female must be correlated with every other male or female.

In the final analysis, we have a matrix of correlation coefficients. The first male with the first female, the first male with the second female, the first male with the third female, etc., and continuing throughout all combinations of males and females. Every combination of male and female must be taken into account.

Obviously, no two human beings are exactly alike (or exact opposites). Therefore, we would not expect to have correlation coefficients of $+1$. or -1. The problem, therefore, is how do we decide which male is to be matched with which female?

Assume that Girl 1 matches with Boy 10 of 0.98576, and Girl 1 matches with Boy 11 with 0.98501. (Note that Boys 10 and 11 have other correlation coefficients with every other girl.) The two described above happen to be the two highest. Girl 1 would be matched with Boy 10. Boy 11 must now be matched with another girl, who would have the next highest coefficient for Boy 11.

This involves a general process of taking correlation coefficients from highest to lowest. This disposes of the "match" problem for the programmer. However, this (may) result in serious mismatches for some of the participants. The mismatches are likely to occur at the two ends of the coefficient scale. This is a primary problem of the match game, but does not prevent the use of match game theory.

In general, most correlation programs are already set up to analyze every possible combination of data. Note that this will generate items in the correlation matrix which are meaningless. Males will be correlated with other males, females with other females, and the answers given by each respondent (whether male or female) will be correlated with themselves. These items, since they are irrelevant in matching respondents, must be deleted. This is accomplished in one of two ways: Method 1 would involve setting up the initial categories so as to permit the correlation program to distinguish relevant and irrelevant correlations; Method 1, therefore, requires that a correlation program be written which permits item deletion. The deleted items being those irrelevant combinations.[8]

Method 2 would involve using a correlation program which generates correlation coefficients for every possible combination. The deletion of irrelevant items would then be accomplished manually. For instance, by knowing whether a row or a column of the category matrix contains the data for a male or a female, we can know which items of the correlation output contain irrelevant correlations. Note the similarity of the two methods. In Method 1, we supplied our knowledge about the data in the category matrix to the correlation program (the correlation program having been set up to handle this information). In Method 2, the information about the category matrix is retained, and deletion is accomplished by hand.

An example of a dating game questionnaire (in abbreviated form) is shown in Table 15-3. Utilizing the basic form of this questionnaire, a class or group project should be set up to do the following:

1. Write up a sample questionnaire and have it filled out.
2. Write a categorization program to separate and group respondents according to personal characteristics and personal preferences.[9]

---

[8]Exercise: Explain in detail how a categorization program would have to be set up in order to permit efficient deletion of irrelevant items in the correlation program.

[9]The group or class should decide whether it is best:
    a) to arrange categorization so that it permits effective utilization (or writing) of a correlation program which incorporates item deletion (Deletion Method 1, above), or
    b) Use general correlation program and delete irrelevant items by hand (Deletion Method 2, above).

3. Write a correlation program to match as closely as possible those respondents contained in the respective categories.

(*Hint*: The politics program, which utilizes the pointer system, contained in Section B of this chapter carries out categorization according to party, candidate, and office sought. The basic algorithmic technique of this program can be efficiently utilized in the categorization of dating game respondents. Further, if the output of the contents of each category is arranged so as to fit within the limits of the closed-format multiple-regression program, it can be effectively used to match the respondents within each category. Note that part of the output of the multiple-regression program is a correlation matrix.[10])

TABLE 15-3. Questionnaire.

Personal Characteristics:

Name:

Sex: 1. Male 2. Female
Age: 1. 13 or under 2. 14 or 15 3. 16 or 17 4. 18 or over
Present Grade in School: 1. Junior High 2. Freshman 3. Sophomore 4. Junior 5. Senior
Height: 1. Under 5' 2. 5'–5'2" 3. 5'3"–5'5" 4. 5'6"–5'8" 5. 5'9"–5'11" 6. 6' and over
Weight in lbs: 1. 100-110 2. 111–120 3. 121–130 4. 131–140 5. 141–150 6. 151–160 7. 161–170
   8. 171 & over 9. Under 100

Questions:

Please circle the number of the response which is *most* appropriate for you (only one).

1. Do you feel it is proper for teenagers to go steady?
   1. Yes 2. No

2. On a first date, should a boy take a girl to a:
   1. Movie 2. Dance 3. Theatre performance 4. Athletic event 5. Bowling or pool, etc.
      6. Plan the evening on an "ad hoc" basis?

3. On what terms do you prefer to go out on a date?
   1. Very formal 2. Casual but polite 3. Very informal

4. What do you like to discuss on a date?
   1. Politics and current events 2. Religion and philosophy 3. Performing arts 4. Your
      own experiences and aspirations 5. Combination of the above 6. None of the above

5. Which extra curricular activity is most important to you?
   1. No extra curricular interests 2. Sports 3. Hiking 4. School sponsored clubs
      5. Sorority/Fraternity 6. Music 7. Art 8. Other

6. Which school subject is of greatest interest to you?
   1. Math 2. Biological Science 3. Physical Science 4. Foreign language 5. English
      6. Social Studies 7. Art 8. Music 9. Industrial Arts/Home Economics

7. Do you generally contribute to classroom discussions?
   1. Yes 2. No

8. Socially, do you feel that you are "hip" on what is going on in our society (dances, slang, clothes, styles of hair, general consensus of the time)?
   1. Yes, completely 2. For the most part, but not all 3. Some, but not very much 4. Very
      little 5. Not at all

9. Which of the following statements best describes you? (Circle one)
   1. One who looks for new things to do and likes to be on the go at all times.
   2. One who is very conservative on most subjects.
   3. One who is divided between the two.
   4. One who considers himself different from all others and can not be categorized in any way.

[10]If multiple regression is used, Deletion Method 2 must be incorporated.

appendices

appendices

A1

FORTRAN: Computer Language[1]

Computers operate directly with a special numeric code called machine language. All computers utilize their own special machine language. Unfortunately, this machine language is quite cumbersome and unique for each computer. In working with computers it is desirable to use a language that is easier to learn and which may be used on many different computers.

FORTRAN is such a language. FORTRAN is a problem-oriented language, independent of any given computer. A FORTRAN compiler, in a somewhat broader sense, is the name given to the computer programs that translate a program written in the FORTRAN language into machine language. A FORTRAN program is a series of statements written according to the rules (or grammar) of the language that, taken together, specify a solution to a problem. In order for the computer to carry out the solution to the problem, the various statements in the FORTRAN program must be translated into a set of instructions for the computer.

The program written in the FORTRAN language is called the *source program*,[2] or the *source code*. The machine language version of the source program (produced by the FORTRAN compiler) is called the *target code*, or *object code*. Thus, the process of solving a problem using a computer and FORTRAN can be described as follows:

1. The problem is formalized (stated).
2. A method of solving the problem is developed — algorithm, flowchart.
3. This method is translated into a FORTRAN program.
4. This program is processed by the FORTRAN compiler and translated into an equivalent program in actual machine instructions (object code).
5. The object code (object program) is loaded into the computer, supplied with the necessary data and run.

Various steps are performed in No. 4 alone. First the FORTRAN compiler is loaded into the computer. Then the source program, properly prepared, is processed

---

[1]For technical definitions of FORTRAN terminology, data, and procedures see the *ASA FORTRAN Standards Manual* or the *FORTRAN Manual* for your computer.
[2]See Glossary for operational definitions.

by the compiler. *The output from the compiler is the object code.* In other words, the source program is input to the compiler and the object program is output from the compiler.

The FORTRAN language is basically machine independent. Theoretically, a program written in the FORTRAN language can be compiled and executed on any computer that has a FORTRAN compiler. This is not always the case, however. There are two reasons for this: 1) there are basic differences among models of computers and the compiler for each computer; 2) there have been enhancements in the FORTRAN language to make it more usable. For example, since the first FOR-TRAN language (FORTRAN or FORTRAN I) was developed, FORTRAN II, FORTRAN IID, and FORTRAN IV, etc. versions have evolved. In each case the later version has included, in addition to the features of the preceding version, many new features.

The FORTRAN described in this text is FORTRAN IV. This version may differ in some details from the version of FORTRAN used on the computer available to the reader. In general, however, a program written in FORTRAN can be run with some modification on any computer having a FORTRAN compiler.

The FORTRAN compiler requires that the source program be prepared in a specific way. Each statement must be constructed according to the rules of FOR-TRAN. FORTRAN possesses both a grammar and an alphabet.

This alphabet is very restricted. It consists of 46 different alphanumeric characters.

1) The 26 letters of the alphabet.
2) Ten (10) decimal digits.
3) Ten (10) special characters.

The entire character set is shown below:

1) A B C D E F G H I J K L M N O P Q R S T U V W X Y Z
2) 0 1 2 3 4 5 6 7 8 9
3)   , . + − * / $ =

These are the only characters recognized in FORTRAN.

Just as the sentence is the basic unit of the English language, the statement is the basic unit of the FORTRAN language. The various FORTRAN statements fall into four general categories:

INPUT/OUTPUT: Statements which control the transfer of information into and out of the computer.

ARITHMETIC/LOGICAL: Statements which indicate the various calculations to be performed.

CONTROL: Statements that determine the sequence in which the programs will be executed.

SPECIFICATION: Statements which supply information to the compiler about the program. These might be called declarative statements.

FORTRAN statements are normally defined in relation to the 80 columns of a Hollerith card. For this purpose, the card is divided into various fields. These are:

Cols. 1–5:   Used for statement numbers or to include a comment.
Col. 6:   Used to indicate the continuation of a FORTRAN statement.
Cols. 7–72: Used for the FORTRAN statement.
Cols. 73–80: Ignored

The contents of Columns 73–80 are ignored by the *compiler* and thus may be used by the programmer in any manner that he desires. Most often, they are used to sequence number the cards in a program. This is useful in rearranging the program deck in case it gets out of order.

The actual FORTRAN statement is placed in Columns 7–72. Only one statement may appear on a card. Except in very rare instances, blank columns on a card are ignored. Thus, blanks may be used to improve readability. Statements too long to be contained in Columns 7–72 of a Hollerith card may be continued on a subsequent card by placing a character other than "0" in Column 6 of each subsequent card. The number of continuation cards depends on each individual FORTRAN compiler; that is, any one statement may comprise an initial line (Hollerith card, Columns 7–72), and additional continuation lines. Normally, programmers number continuation cards sequentially — e.g., 1, 2, 3, etc. — in Column 6.

Many FORTRAN statements refer to other statements in the program. Any statement which is referenced by another statement in the program must be assigned a unique numeric *statement number*. This statement number is punched in Columns 1–5 of the appropriate FORTRAN statement. It is not necessary to number all FORTRAN statements. Only those statements which are referenced by other statements in the program should be numbered.

Although statement numbers are composed of digits, they should not be considered as numeric quantities but simply as labels to identify particular statements. As such, they must be unique; that is, no two statements in the source program may have the same statement number. Since statement numbers are not considered as numeric quantities, no sequencing is implied by the values of the statement numbers.

The programmer may insert comments in the program to remind himself why he did something in a particular way. Comments may also be used to identify the program in the event that the programmer does not use it for a long period of time and then has to go back to it. A comment is inserted in the program by placing a C in Column 1 of the appropriate statement card. Any card with a C in Column 1 is ignored by the compiler. If a comment extends over more than one Hollerith card, a C must appear in Column 1 of each additional card. A comment may appear anywhere in the program.

The form in Figure A1-1 illustrates the usable columns available for program development. Each row or line in the figure represents one Hollerith card. As illustrated, Column 1 is for the C designation for a comment. Columns 1–5 may contain the statement number associated with the statement. Column 6 is used only when a continuation of a statement, begun on a preceding card, is needed. Columns 7–72 represent the portion of the card available for formulating the FORTRAN source program statements. This form is the form used for coding all FORTRAN programs. The Hollerith cards are keypunched from this form, using the indicated column layout.

CONSTANTS AND VARIABLE NAMES[3]

Two basic elements of the FORTRAN language are *constants* and *variables*. A constant is a quantity that represents itself. Most often, constants are numeric quantities. Examples of constants are:

$$3 \quad \text{or} \quad 8.7164 \quad \text{or} \quad 5197368$$

[3]For technical definitions of these and any other FORTRAN terminology, data, and procedures see the *ASA FORTRAN Standards* or the *FORTRAN Manual* for your computer. For operational definitions see Glossary.

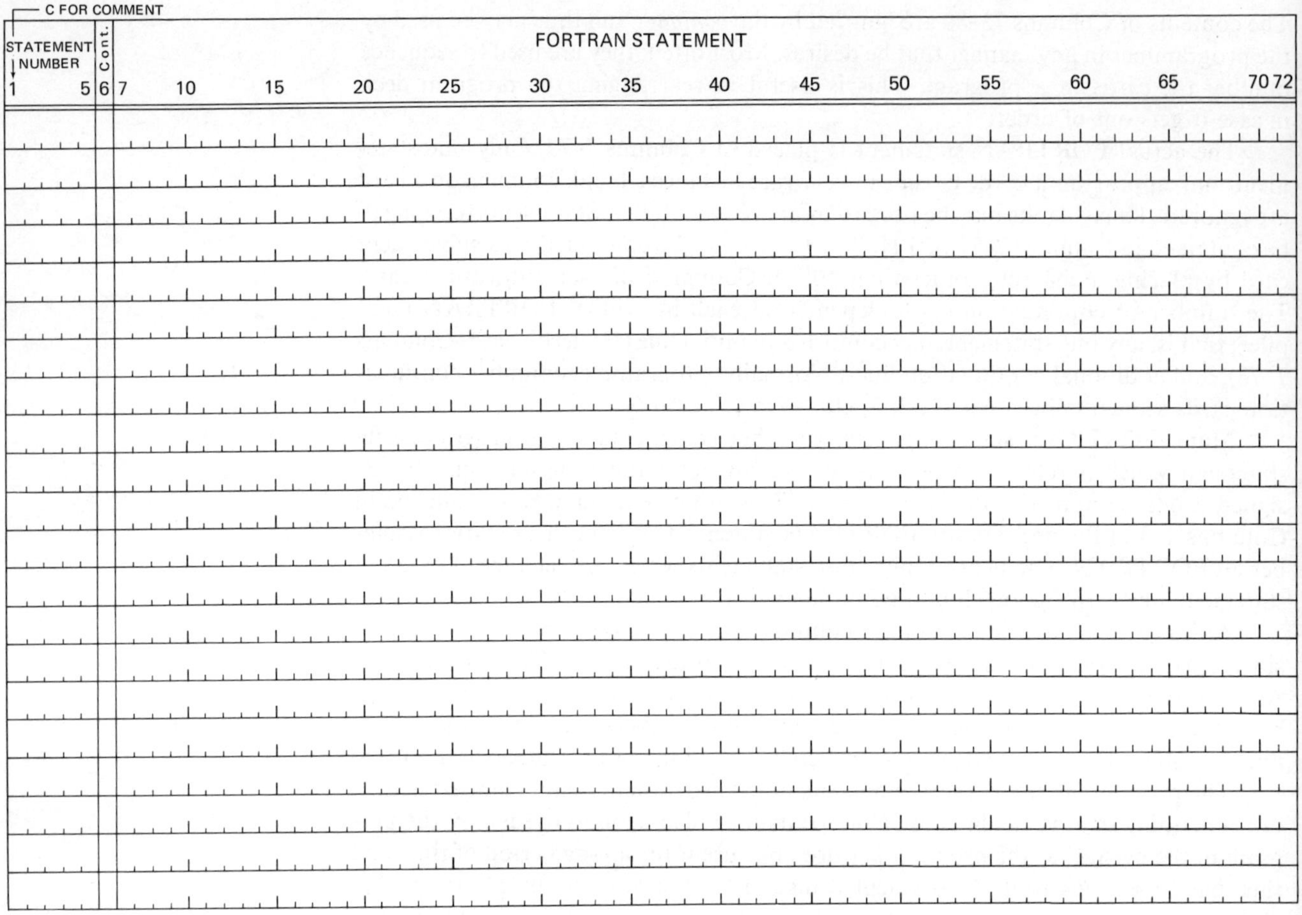

FIGURE A1-1. Fortran source program, statement lines (cards).

A variable is a label that represents a specific location in computer core storage. In machine-language programming, information is stored or regained by specifying the appropriate core-storage location address. In FORTRAN programming, information is stored or regained by specifying a *label* (called a *variable name*) representing the appropriate storage location address.

The use of a variable name (label) to represent something else is not unique to FORTRAN programming. For instance, the circumference of a circle may be calculated from the formula,

$$\text{Circumference} = 3.1416d$$

where "d" represents the diameter of a circle. In the formula, 3.1416 is a constant, while "d" is a variable name. The *value* of "d" depends on the size of the circle in question. Thus "d" is a label that is a variable name that represents other values.

Types of constants

A constant is a quantity that represents itself. Five different types of constants may be used in FORTRAN programs.

Integer constants

An integer constant is a signed or unsigned string[4] of digits. Examples of integer constants are:

```
                    999999999
                   −999999999
                    345
                   −367
                    0
                   −1
                    003
```

In general, FORTRAN integer constants may not exceed five digits; however, some FORTRAN compilers accept integer constants considerably larger. A negative sign must precede a negative integer constant. The plus sign is optional for a positive integer constant. An integer constant is said to be signed when it is immediately preceded by a + (optional) or a minus − sign.

A decimal point is never used with an integer constant. Integer constants are never used when it is necessary to utilize fractional values or when fractional values might be important. No other characters (such as commas) may appear in integer constants. Thus the following are not valid integer constants for most FORTRAN compilers:

Constant	Why Invalid
30,682	Special character in constant.
30.789	Special character in constant.
879568361	Constant too large (size of an integer constant depends on the individual FORTRAN compiler).

Any integer constant may have any number of digits written into the source program. However, the FORTRAN compiler will retain only the five leftmost significant digits. If the number 879568361 were included in a FORTRAN source program, the number would go into computer storage as 87956.

Real constants

A real constant is represented by a string of digits which contain a decimal point. The length of the datum thus formed, measured by the number of digits, is limited. Generally, a real constant may contain up to eight significant digits although this varies with each computer-compiler system. The magnitude of a real constant is also limited by the specific computer-compiler system.

Actually, any constant may have any number of digits written into the source program. However, the FORTRAN compiler will retain only the eight leftmost significant digits. If the number 1234567.89 were included in a FORTRAN source program, the number would be retained in computer storage as 1234567.8.

Examples of real constants that would be acceptable to most FORTRAN compilers are:

```
             0.
       1234567.
           −.1234567
          1234.567
          −0.1
```

Very large or very small real constants cannot be conveniently expressed in this form (as above); they must usually be written in exponential form.

---

[4]An operational definition for "string" is list or series. The term string is usually used with respect to digits — e.g., a string of digits is 12378.

An exponent is a number (integer number) written above and to the right of a constant indicating that the constant is to be multiplied by itself N-1 times where N is the number. For instance, 10^3 is another way of saying $10 \times 10 \times 10$. The number 10 is multiplied by itself twice. Thus, 2^{27} is a way of saying that 2 is to be multiplied by itself 26 times.

Computers will handle real constants in exponential forms. It is, in fact, a very convenient way to handle large numbers. The general method of writing an exponential number in a FORTRAN source statement is as follows: *Real number* followed by *E* followed by a $\pm$, followed by the *exponent*. Thus, $+4.0E+03$ actually means $4.0 \times 10^{+3}$. This is $4.0 \times (10 \times 10 \times 10)$ which is $4.0 \times 1,000$ which is 4,000.

A + sign following the E and before the exponent means that the decimal point is to be moved to the right; a minus sign means that the decimal point is moved to the left. The integer number following the sign indicates how many digits to the right or to the left the decimal point is to be moved. In the example shown above, the decimal point was moved three places to the right. The value of $+4.0E-03$, the number would be 0.004. The sign in front of the real number indicates whether the value is positive or negative. The sign following the E and preceding the exponent indicates which way the decimal point is to be moved in arriving at the true value of the exponential form.

Let us pursue this idea of exponential numbers somewhat further. Most FORTRAN compilers will accept this exponential form in more than one way. The following methods of writing the exponential form of a real constant in the FORTRAN source program (depending on the individual compiler) will all give the same value of 4,000:

$$+4.0E+03$$
$$4.0E3$$
$$4.0E+3$$

The first character of the *exponent* must be an E(ASA FORTRAN). The plus sign may be omitted. However, a *minus sign must appear, if a minus sign is meant to appear*.

If one desired to read a group of real numbers into the computer and wished to ensure that the decimal point came in the same place for all of the numbers, the following would accomplish this assuming that a real constant of seven significant digits is acceptable to the FORTRAN compiler:

123.678	or 0.123678E+03
0.123678	or 0.123678E+00
12367.8	or 0.123678E+05
123678.	or 0.123678E+06
.0000000123678	or 0.123678E−07

Logical constant

FORTRAN IV compilers recognize and accept a unique kind of nonnumeric constant called a *logical constant*. A logical constant is either TRUE or FALSE. The FORTRAN representation of logical constants is:

$$.TRUE.$$
$$.FALSE.$$

The periods are part of the logical constant and must be included.

Double-precision constant

The form and interpretation of a double-precision constant is exactly the same as is an exponential number, except that the E of the exponential form is replaced by a D. We have noted that the number of significant digits acceptable to *any* FORTRAN compiler is usually limited to eight.

Regardless of the number of significant digits that may be handled by a FORTRAN compiler, what if requirements of accuracy demand that more significant digits be utilized than your computer can handle in a single location of storage? The obvious answer is to put two consecutive storage locations together to contain the number.

The maximum real constant is assumed to be limited to seven significant digits, for example: 1216989. What would happen if it were desirable to manage the number 12169897843612 (fourteen significant digits)? At least one decimal digit should appear to the left of the decimal point. The following form would be acceptable to almost all FORTRAN compilers: 0.12169897843612D+00. In this instance, the D indicates that two consecutive storage positions are to be used to contain this number, and the decimal point is to be left where it is. In case the sign following the D is followed by an integer constant (either a positive or negative sign and the constant is not 0), the decimal point will be moved to the right (+) or to the left (−) as indicated. For instance, the number 0.12169897843612D+08 has the meaning:

$$12169897.843612$$

The fact that double precision is available to FORTRAN programmers in most FORTRAN compilers should not be ignored. Whenever any programmer cannot obtain enough significant digits using the real constant form, it is possible to double the number of significant digits available by using the double-precision notation. The real constant is often referred to as a single-precision real number because it is limited to a single core-storage location, and hence to the number of significant digits that may be contained therein. The double-precision real constant simply refers to a number that is large enough to require two consecutive core-storage locations.

Complex constants

There is one additional type of constant, the complex constant. A complex number consists of two parts, one part is real, and one part is imaginary. Complex numbers are not often used in statistical manipulation, but are common in mathematical work. The complex constant utilizes two consecutive positions of core storage, the real number part appearing in the first location, and the imaginary part appearing in the second location. A complex number, for example is $5 + 6i$ (the "i" designates imaginary). To the FORTRAN programmer, complex numbers are written as a pair of real constants, separated by a comma and encased within parentheses. The complex number $5 + 6i$ would be written:

$$(5.0, 6.0)$$

Variable names

Variable names refer to some designated core-storage location or sequence of locations. It is usually desirable to have the name reflect the contents that will be in the given storage location. The use of variable names to represent constants is referred to as use of the *mnemonic code*. When one desires to reference a value that is in some designated storage location, one does this by using the variable name that has been assigned to that particular (numbered) storage location — i.e., the variable name is, in fact, the label of the address of the storage location. If one were going to refer to storage location 10012 in computer storage in FORTRAN one must assign a name to the location and refer to this name alone.

The basic rule for establishing variable names to represent the storage locations of constants is to have the name indicate the nature of the constant. A variable name can be no more than six alphabetic or alphabetic and numeric characters in length. The variable name must always begin with an alphabetic character. No special characters may appear in a variable name.

Remember, the variable name is, in fact, a label assigned to an address in computer core storage. When one uses the variable name, the name references the contents of the storage location by referencing the address of the storage location. Assume the INTEGER number 10506 is stored in core-storage location 33651. If the name of that core-storage location is LABEL, then whenever the name LABEL appears in that FORTRAN source program, the reference is always to core-storage location 33651. The contents of LABEL will be made available to the source program as requested. If the INTEGER number 10506 is stored in LABEL, the *value* of LABEL is 10506. If the number 10506 has subsequently been replaced by another INTEGER number, the value of LABEL is accordingly changed.

Thus, we can now define precisely two terms that will continually be used in the text:

1. *Constant:* A quantity that may not be redefined — hence, a constant represents itself. There are six types of constants: INTEGER, REAL, EXPONENTIAL (E Notation), DOUBLE PRECISION, LOGICAL, COMPLEX.
2. *Variable:* A name that references a given core storage location — hence, *whose value is the contents of the core storage location.*

Just as there are six types of constants, there must also be six types of variable names. Whenever a value is being referenced by using a variable name, the type of variable name must agree with the type of value. For instance, only INTEGER variable names may be used with INTEGER values, etc.

If the variable name begins with I, J, K, L, M, or N (and is no longer than six alphanumeric characters with no special characters appearing in the name), then the FORTRAN compiler always accepts that variable name as an INTEGER variable. If the variable name begins with any other letter of the alphabet, then the FORTRAN compiler always accepts that variable name as a REAL variable name.

For example, if one were engaged in a time series analysis — following the change of a single-numeric sequence over time, such as the change in population of Massachusetts from 1640–1800 — the Hollerith card input series would contain two fields. The year — e.g., 1740 — *and* the population of Massachusetts in that year. One of the fields on the Hollerith card would contain the series of four digits representing the year. The year, 1740, would be shown as an integer number. The second field on the Hollerith card would contain a string of digits indicating the population.

If it were desired to reference a particular year in FORTRAN, the variable name IYEAR would serve nicely. The variable name IYEAR serves two purposes:

1. It identifies to the compiler that the number found in the location specified by IYEAR is an integer number.
2. The name IYEAR is a continual reminder to the programmer that he has set up a specific location that contains an integer number representing one of the years of the time series.

The points of the mnemonic code are that it identifies the type of data for the compiler and is a constant reminder to the programmer of the kind of data being stored in any given computer core-storage location. We have, however, indicated thus far the possibility of showing only two types of variable names: INTEGER and REAL. Since there are six types of constants, there must be six types of variable names. In order to illustrate the formation of the other types of variable names, we must note the so-called *default condition* of the Fortran compiler.

The default condition of the FORTRAN programming compiler is simply the *assumed behavior on the part of the compiler unless overridden by the programmer with a specification statement.* For instance, any variable name beginning with I, J, K, L, M, or N is automatically assumed by the compiler to be an INTEGER variable name indicating that INTEGER data will be stored in the named locations. Any variable name beginning with any other letter of the alphabet is assumed by the compiler to be a REAL variable name indicating that REAL data will be stored in the named location. However, it is possible to *override* these automatic assumptions on the part of the compiler with specification statements, the explicit type statements.

Let us assume that we have the following three variable names: SUM, CODE, and AVERAGE. Each variable name begins with a letter other than I, J, K, L, M, or N indicating that each separate storage location contains real value(s). Let us also assume, however, that for some reason, it is desired to have these variable names contain INTEGER data. This can be done by using an INTEGER type declaration statement. The general form for a type declaration statement is INTEGER, then the list of variable names separated by commas. For example, the statement,

INTEGER SUM, CODE, AVERAGE

causes the compiler to treat the variable names SUM, CODE, and AVERAGE as INTEGER variable names. Thus the information stored in the locations represented by these variable names must be in the INTEGER mode.

The type-specification statement must appear in the program before any reference is made to the variable names. Type-specification statements are available for each of the various types of numeric constants represented in FORTRAN. The exponential constant (E notation) is a REAL constant; hence, it is handled by a REAL variable name. For instance, in order to handle ICODE, IABLE, and KING as REAL variable names, or exponential variable names, the programmer would write:

REAL ICODE, IABLE, KING

The use of this type statement would cause these variable names to reference REAL constants. In this way, the EXPLICIT-TYPE statements may be used to override the compiler's normal operation to give any variable name the desired notation. The programmer must be careful to utilize the EXPLICIT-TYPE statement in the source program prior to any reference to the variable name. The EXPLICIT-TYPE statement is normally the first or second program card in a FORTRAN source program.

There are EXPLICIT-TYPE statements for six types of data values. They are illustrated as follows:

EXPLICIT-TYPE statement	used with
INTEGER list[5]	Integer constants

[5]A "list" is a set of separate identifiable elements each of which is set apart by a comma. An INTEGER type statement, followed by a list of variable names in a FORTRAN source program statement, is illustrated as follows: INTEGER ABLE, BAKER DATA1, DATA2 In such a list, no comma is placed following the final element of the list.

REAL list	Real constants
REAL list	Real, exponent[6]

[6]A constant with exponent.

DOUBLE PRECISION list	Double-precision constants[7]
COMPLEX list	Complex constants[7]
LOGICAL list	Logical constants

VARIABLE NAMES: ARRAYS AND TABLES

We have already defined a variable name as a name that specifies a given location of core storage. Whenever a variable name is found in a FORTRAN source program, the FORTRAN compiler *automatically assumes* that it is desired to associate *only one* numbered core-storage location with that variable name. However, should one desire to store more information under a *given variable name* than can be contained in a given single core-storage location, then one must override the compiler's default assumption with a DIMENSION statement.

The DIMENSION statement uses the following general form: DIMENSION followed by a list of variable names with a pair of parenthesis immediately following each separated by commas. The number inside the parentheses tells the FORTRAN compiler how many core locations to associate with the given name.

Let us say that we desired to establish IYEAR, XNUMBR, and CODE, as arrays with IYEAR and XNUMBR to contain ten data observations (10 words) and three core words associated with CODE. The appropriate form for the DIMENSION statement to override the default assumption of the compiler is:

DIMENSION IYEAR (10), XNUMBR (10), CODE (3)

The DIMENSION statement must appear before any reference is made to the dimensioned variable name. Usually, the DIMENSION statement will be the second statement in the FORTRAN source program, immediately following the EXPLICIT-TYPE statements.

Let us say that we are going to do a time series analysis, and we need to store ten data observations, each data observation to be in a separate core-storage word, but each of which is to be referred to by the same variable name. How can we store these data in computer core storage and get the correct data observation into each numbered location of the dimensioned array?

An array is regarded by the computer as a *column* of numbers. We have noted that we desire to store in the computer memory ten numbers, each of which is a real number. The first step is to establish the array under a given variable name, and to assign a given number of consecutive core-storage locations to that variable name. Let us call this array COLUMN. The DIMENSION statement to set up the array would be:

DIMENSION COLUMN (10)

[7]May be listed as a (number) constant, or in exponential form as discussed above.

Conceptually, this would establish a column of 10 sequentially numbered computer storage locations in core storage, under the general name of COLUMN, as illustrated below:

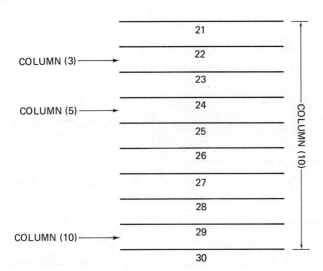

This simply illustrates that the DIMENSION statement has overridden the normal default assumption of the compiler. The DIMENSION statement instructs the compiler to assign ten consecutive core-storage locations to the given variable name. Each of the numbered core-storage locations in the array (under the variable name COLUMN) retains its own core-storage address. If one refers to COLUMN in the FORTRAN source program, one is actually referring to the entire array. If, however, in the FORTRAN source program (at some point after the DIMENSION statement), one refers to COLUMN (3), one is actually referring to the third storage word of the array or what would be storage location 23 above. If the programmer referred to COLUMN (5), reference is thereby made to the fifth position in the array, or to Location 25 above.

It is possible to address specifically any given location in an array. This is done simply by indicating the name of the array, and then the specific position in the array — e.g., COLUMN (10). The number appearing in the parentheses following the array name (must be an INTEGER) is a *subscript*. The default condition of the FORTRAN compiler will indicate an error in your FORTRAN program if you try to reference a specific location in an array, before a DIMENSION statement has established the array.

In programming, one must be careful not to use a subscript that is larger than the number of positions established for the array in the DIMENSION statement

Table look-up

An array having more than one DIMENSION limit is sometimes called a data matrix or table look-up. The DIMENSION statement,

DIMENSION DATA (10,3)

establishes a table, as shown in Figure A1-2, that consists of three columns, each column having ten consecutive storage locations. One uses subscripts to refer to

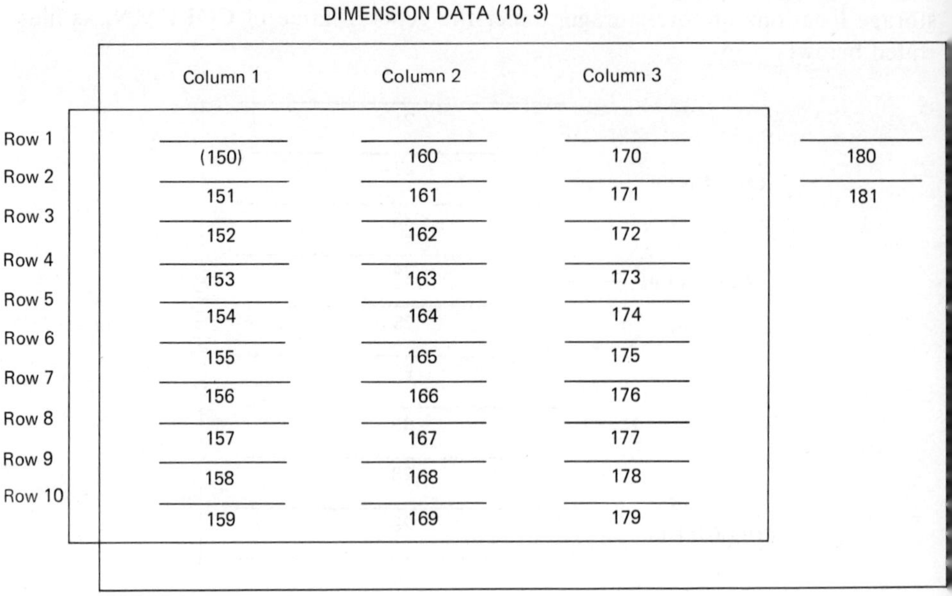

DIMENSION DATA (10, 3)

	Column 1	Column 2	Column 3	
Row 1	(150)	160	170	180
Row 2	151	161	171	181
Row 3	152	162	172	
Row 4	153	163	173	
Row 5	154	164	174	
Row 6	155	165	175	
Row 7	156	166	176	
Row 8	157	167	177	
Row 9	158	168	178	
Row 10	159	169	179	

DATA (1,1) would be computer word Location No. 150.
DATA (1,3) would be computer word Location No. 170.
DATA (8,2) would be computer word Location No. 167.
DATA (10,1) would be computer word Location No. 159.
DATA (11,3) would develop an error condition in the program, because you have gone outside of the defined table and messed up some other part of the program. You would have put something into computer word Location No. 180, which is outside the defined table data and in some other part of the program.

FIGURE A1-2. Data table.

particular locations in the table, just as one used subscripts to reference a particular location in an array. In the reference to the table, the first subscript always refers to the row in the column, the second subscript refers to the column.

Computers have varying capacity for multiple-dimensional arrays, and some medium-size computers can handle five or more dimensional arrays. A one-dimensional array is analogous to a column on a page in a book. A two-dimensional array is analogous to the page in the book which may include more than one column on each page. A three-dimensional array is analogous to a given row, on a given page, in a specified book. A four-dimensional array is analogous to a given row, on a given page, in a book of a given series.

There is always a limit to subscripts, and that limit varies with individual computer and compiler systems. However, in general terms, the most complex form of a subscript for dimensioned variable names is as follows:

ABLE(I∗J+M)
or
ABLEI(∗J—M)

The result or value of the expression (I∗J+M) or (I∗J—M) indicates the location desired in the dimensioned variable ABLE.

1. When is a "C" used in the first column of a FORTRAN source program statement? What, if anything, does a "C" indicate when it is found on a FORTRAN source program statement?
2. When are the last eight columns used in FORTRAN source program statements?
3. Shown are some variable names and constants. Cross out the invalid ones and identify the others with R indicating REAL, or with I indicating INTEGER.

LUCKY	10,000	3AB
.07E—8.0	WAR	X2
INVALID	PRICE $	C444D
$3.41	KOW	DEMONSTR
I/O	.—07E—891	FORMAT
SINE	BA	PK
IREAL	99.9E+4	

4. What is an explicit statement, and how is it used in a FORTRAN program?
5. Distinguish (define):

> Subscript
> Array
> Table look-up

6. What is a "data matrix"?
7. Why are the following DIMENSION statements wrong?

> a. DIMENSION, X(32), Y(32)
> b. DIMENSION (X932), Y(32)
> c. DIMENSION (X, (32), Y(32))

8. Give six real constants, each in three different forms.
9. Give six integer constants. May these constants appear in different forms?

10. Is a type statement necessary if:

> a. K2A is the name of an integer variable?
> b. M3 is the name of a real variable?
> c. A7J is the name of an integer variable?
> d. B6L is the name of a real variable?

11. Which of the following are valid INTEGER constants? For those that are not valid, give the probable reason.

a. 005	f. —44,444
b. 01234567891011	g. 329.0
c. —250	h. 3290
d. 465789012345	i. 12345
e. 5.5	

12. Which of the following are valid REAL constants? If any are not valid, give the reason why.

a. 3.54159738	g. 123.45678910
b. 0.147E—42	h. 16.E5
c. 17E02	i. 0.04E—3.0
d. 1.09E—29	j. 3.1415
e. 1,001E+17	k. 2.
f. 17	l. 6.0E65

13. Can any of the following variable names appear in a FORTRAN program? For those that are incorrect, tell why.

    a. X123567
    b. X1234
    c. 17A
    d. A17
    e. A17

    f. X*Y
    g. ABC
    h. ABLE
    i. ABLE123

14. None of the following are valid FORTRAN statements. Tell why not.

    a. REAL A32, B6XY, 13C, IJK
    b. INTEGER JACK, ABLE,
    c. LOGICAL P, Q, R(3*I+5)
    d. DIMENSION (X(15), Y(10), Z(8).

15. Which of the following are legitimate FORTRAN constants? Why are the invalid ones wrong?

    a. 1468
    b. 145698
    c. 145.0E+5

    d. 145.040
    e. 3.1415968961
    f. 1456789101112

16. Which of the following are legitimate FORTRAN subscripts. Give reasons for those which are wrong.

    a. ABLE (10000000)
    b. ABLE (−10)
    c. ABLE (10)

    d. ABLE (2+J)
    e. ABLE (60+5*J)
    f. ABLE (I+J*K−17)

FORTRAN Source Program: Input/Output

We noted in the previous chapter that a FORTRAN source program is a series of FORTRAN statements concerned with manipulating information. Whether one is working with mathematical concepts using complex values, testing some hypothesis statistically, or simply manipulating alphabetic data, the results of the computer analysis depend upon the values which constitute the raw data for the study.

There are three basic ways in which the data or the values may originate: 1.) Values may be data that are read into the computer and assigned as values to some predetermined variable name. 2.) Values may originate as constants, written in the FORTRAN source program. 3.) Values may be assigned to some variable name by an arithmetic assignment operation. The purpose of this chapter is to consider the basic ideas of FORTRAN input and output.

FORTRAN input

Data may be present when a FORTRAN source program is written and included in the program itself. FORTRAN constants may be written into the source program to be used in the information processing. However, the program may be written without the data being available to the program in some manner.

Perhaps the basic way of getting data assigned to some variable, named, storage location in the computer is by the FORTRAN input procedure. The FORTRAN READ statement causes information from some input device to be received into the computer system and assigned to named locations of core storage. The READ statement normally operates with a FORMAT statement that controls the nature and layout of the data being received from the input unit. In the FORMAT statement, the programmer specifies each field (length) and the type of data in the given field. The general form of the FORTRAN input or READ statement is:

READ (U,F) list of variable names

The word READ instructs that data indicated on some input unit is to be transferred into core storage under designated variable names. The parentheses always enclose two labels, which may be treated as INTEGER variable names or INTEGER constants whenever the computer has the capability of accepting data from more than one type of input device.[1] Each input device has a unique number for each computer system. The purpose of the U is to indicate which input unit contains the data to be received into the computer. Tradition has designated Unit 5 as the card reader and Unit 6 as the printer. Other numbers are used for card punches, magnetic tapes, magnetic drums, paper-tape readers, paper-tape punches.

The second number in parentheses — e.g., the F — represents a numeric label, which may be treated as an INTEGER constant or variable, that designates the statement number of the FORMAT statement that accompanies the given READ statement. This double position of the same label F — i.e., in the READ statement and as a statement number — ties the READ and the FORMAT statements together. The READ statement tells the FORTRAN compiler to accept data from a particular input device. The indicated FORMAT statement tells how the fields are grouped and the nature of the data in each field. Each field defined in the FORMAT statement is to be stored under the corresponding variable name in the READ statement.

The purpose of the FORMAT statement is to designate the length of each of the fields contained in the input record and to indicate the nature of the data in each field — alphabetic, integer, real, exponential, double-precision, logical, complex. For this purpose, the various data types are reported by alphabetic codes. For instance, the format specification to represent an integer value in a field 10 characters long is: I10. The general forms for FORMAT notation are:

Notation Code	Value
Iw	INTEGER
Fw.d	REAL
Ew.d	REAL with Exponent
Aw	Alphabetic (alphanumeric)
Dw.d	Double-precision
Lw	Logical
Fw.d, Fw.d	Complex[2]

The letter first appearing in the format code indicates the type of value:

I means INTEGER value
F means REAL value
E means REAL value with exponent
A means ALPHANUMERIC value
D means DOUBLE-PRECISION value
L means LOGICAL value

The w indicates the number of Hollerith-card columns *or* the number of characters — e.g., in magnetic-tape unit records — comprising the field. The d shows the positions to the right of the decimal point.

The existence of any number to the right of the decimal point indicates the number of digits to the right of the decimal point:

Number in Input Device	FORMAT Notation	REAL Value
56781400	F6.2	5678.14
12345678	F8.0	12345678.
12345678	F8.8	0.12345678
12345678	F8.4	1234.5678
00000001	F8.8	0.00000001
00000001	F8.0	1.

[1] Where the computer system has only one input device available to it, the normal form of the READ statement is: READ F, list.

[2] Complex FORMAT notation is shown as 2 REAL notation codes, the first associated with the real half of the complex number, the second with the imaginary half.

In REAL values, a decimal point need not appear in the input field. The decimal point may be properly placed in the FORMAT notation. If, however, a decimal point is placed in the *input field*, it overrides the decimal location specified by the FORMAT notation. It is necessary to remember that the double-precision value is simply a REAL value that has had the length of its significant digit capability extended by using an EXPLICIT-TYPE statement.

The various FORMAT notations for FORTRAN input data are as follows:

Nature of Data	Length of Field	FORMAT Notation
Integer	10 characters	I10
Real	8 characters (no fraction)	F8.0
Logical	7 positions or characters	L7
Real with exponent	8 positions	E8.0
Double-precision	14 characters	D14.0
Alphabetic	6 characters	A6

For alphabetic values, a field on an input unit record containing more than six characters[3] would require more than one storage location.

Assuming that an alphabetic field contained fifteen characters, three storage locations would be required, with six characters in each of the first two units and three characters in the third. A FORMAT notation to contain 15 alphabet characters would be: 2A6,A3. A READ and FORMAT combination to read a fifteen-character alphabet field (Columns 1–15) and a twenty-five-character alphabet field (columns 21–45) would be:

```
DIMENSION ANAME (3), DATA (5)
READ (INPUT, 14) ANAME, DATA
14 FORMAT (2A6,A3, 5X, 4A6,A1)
```

In addition to containing data specifications, FORMAT statements can contain various control specifications. For example, control specifications may be utilized to cause the READ statement to ignore part of a data unit record or to skip to the next read or write position, as illustrated below:

FORMAT Specification	What Happens
1X	Skip a column or character on the input or output device.
/	Skip a line on the printer or skip to the next unit record on the read device.

The position that a *particular field* occupies on a unit record — e.g., a Hollerith card on input — is not specified in the FORMAT statement. Instead, the position of the field is derived as a result of the various FORMAT specification codes. The first code specification identifies the columns included in the input record beginning with Column 1 of the input unit record. For example:

FORMAT Specification	Meaning
FORMAT (I5,I3)	Columns 1–5 of the input record contain an INTEGER value, and Columns 6–8 contain another INTEGER value.
FORMAT (5X, A5, F8.0)	Skip the first five columns; Columns 6–10 contain an alphanumeric value, and Columns 11–18 contain a REAL value.
FORMAT (5X, 6A6, /)	Skip the first five columns; Columns 6–41 contain an alphanumeric value (dimensioned); skip to the next input unit record.

---

[3]Actual number of characters would depend on the individual computer used—six characters are assumed here for illustrative purposes.

Let us take a very simple example of a READ instruction as found in a FOR-TRAN source program. The following sequence will serve:

READ (05,16) ABLE, CODE, INUMBR, DATA, ANAME
16 FORMAT (5X, A5, 2X, F5.0, I6, 2 (5X, A4))

The READ command alerts the FORTRAN compiler that information is to be presented to the computer through a card reader — e.g., 05.

The input unit record on a card reader is a Hollerith card, comprising eighty columns. FORMAT Statement 16 indicated that:

5X: The first 5 columns are to be skipped.
A5: An alphanumeric value is formed in Columns 6–10 that is to be stored in the computer under the name ABLE.
2X: Columns 11 and 12 are to be skipped.
F5.0: A REAL value is in Columns 13–17 that is to be stored in the computer under the name CODE.
I6: An INTEGER value is in Columns 18–23 that is to be stored in the computer under the name INUMBR.
2 (5X, A4): Columns 24–28 are to be skipped. An alphanumeric value is located in Columns 29–32 that is to be stored in the computer under the name DATA.
Columns 33–37 are to be skipped. An alphanumeric value is formed in Columns 38–41 that is to be stored in the computer under the name ANAME.

There must be only as many variable names as there are defined data fields. The *mode* of the variable name must agree precisely with the *mode* of the FORMAT notation. Once one has accounted for the last data field on a unit record input device, it is not necessary to account for the remaining columns on the card. For instance, in the situation shown above, we have accounted for 41 of 80 columns. The compiler simply ignores Columns 42–80. It is very important to remember that the order in which the variable names are listed on the READ statement must agree with the order in which the fields are shown in the FORMAT statement. Finally, it is not necessary that any particular spacing be utilized. As a general rule, spacing is used to indicate most clearly to the programmer the nature of the data. For instance, the following two READ statements are identical as far as the FORTRAN compiler is concerned:

READ(5,16)ABLE,CODE,INUMBR,DATA,ANAME
READ   (5, 16)   ABLE,   CODE,   INUMBR,   DATA,   ANAME

Normally, the rule is to write a FORTRAN source program statement so that you, the programmer, can most easily understand what has been done.

FORTRAN output

FORTRAN output commands are very similar to the FORTRAN input commands. The FORMAT statement is set up the same way. The only difference is that in FORTRAN output, the purpose is not to take data into the computer but to put it out in some manner. Common means of FORTRAN output are on a line printer or on to magnetic tape. The principle shown here is the same.[4]

---

[4]The discussion of the printing of formatted output records is, of course, subject to the constraint found in each computer-compiler system. (Please check the FORTRAN manual for your system.) However, the general rule found in the *ASA FORTRAN Standard Guide* will be useful to indicate here. The general rule is that the first character of any formatted record is not printed. The first character of a record determines vertical spacing:

In the instance of FORTRAN output, it is desired to take data that is stored in the computer core storage and write it on some kind of device — e.g., printer, magnetic tape, paper tape, etc. In this instance, the data to be printed is stored in the computer core storage under some variable name. The FORMAT statement indicates the spacing and nature of the data when written on the output device.

The WRITE statement is substituted for the READ statement. The WRITE statement to write data on some output device from the variable names ABLE, CODE, INUMBR, DATA and ANAME would be:

```
        WRITE (06, 17) ABLE, CODE, INUMBR, DATA,ANAME
     17 FORMAT (3X, A5, 3X, F7.0, 3X, I6, 2(3X, A4))
```

Those WRITE and FORMAT statements would take the values in computer storage under the indicated variable names and would write the information on a designated output unit — i.e., indicated here as unit 06 of a line printer. The information indicated would be printed with three spaces between each datum printed. There is one difference that should be noted. If the reader recalls, the value assigned to CODE (a REAL constant) was placed in the core-storage location named CODE, a decimal point was placed in the indicated location, and provision was made for a plus or minus sign at the head of the number. When that REAL value is subsequently read out of core storage and printed on some output device, it is necessary to allow for the decimal point and the + or − sign, even though only the minus sign would actually print out. Since the REAL value was read in under an F5.0, it is necessary to provide two additional columns when it becomes output. Therefore, a REAL value must provide an output for two additional columns and the number itself; that is, since the REAL number itself was five digits in length, the field must allow for seven columns — five for the number, one for the decimal point, and one for the sign — on output.

Let us now prepare a very short FORTRAN input/output program that will read some information from Hollerith cards into the computer, and print the data back out on a printer in a different form. The program to do this is shown in Table A2-1.

TABLE A2-1. Simplified FORTRAN program.

```
     DIMENSION ANAME (3), ANOUN (6)
     INTEGER ADAY, AMO, AYEAR
     READ (5, 10) ANAME, ITYCOD, ISEQ, ANOUN, EVALUE, XQUANT, XPOUND, XSHLNG,
    1XPENCE, ADAY, AMO, AYEAR
  10 FORMAT (3A6, I2, 1X, I3, 5A6,A4, A1, F5.2, F5.0, 2F2.0, 2I2, I3)
     WRITE (6, 20) ANAME, ADAY, AMO, AYEAR, ANOUN, XQUANT, XPOUND, XSHLNG,
    1XPENCE
*  20 FORMAT (3A6, 5X, 2(I2), I3, / 10X, 5A6, A4, 5X, F7.2, 5X, F7.0, 2 (2X, F4.0)/ /)
     STOP
     END
```

*Many of the FORTRAN compilers require that a 1X precede the first output format notation, as discussed in this chapter.

Character	Vertical Spacing Before Printing
Blank	One line
0	Two lines
1	To first line of next page
+	No advance

Thus, the following would cause the printer to move to the top of the following page and print a blank line as the first line on the top of the next page:

```
        WRITE (6, 10)
     10 FORMAT (1H1)
```

The data being read in and written out are the Essex County estate inventories discussed in Chapter 13.

Card Columns	Data Item	Mode
1–18	Decedent's name	Alphabet
19–20	Property code	INTEGER
21	Card code	Alphabet
22–24	Sequence number	INTEGER
25–58	Item inventoried	Alphabet
59	Value code	Alphabet
60–64	Quantity	REAL
65–69	Value (pounds sterling)	REAL
70–71	Value (shillings)	REAL
72–73	Value (pence)	REAL
74–80	Day, month, year	INTEGER

The program simply reads the basic data into the computer and stores each value in core storage under a designated name. It is clear, however, that two alphabetic fields are too large to be contained in a single designated core location. Therefore, the first statement in the program is to *dimension* an array of sufficient size to contain the alphabet names. The name of the decedent requires eighteen columns on the Hollerith card; therefore, three designated locations of core storage are needed. The name of the item inventoried in the estate requires thirty-four card columns; hence, the item takes six designated units of core storage.

We discussed the DIMENSION statement above as a way of containing a series of separate data values under a single variable name. This is the primary use of the DIMENSION statement. However, it is possible on input and output and core storage to use a DIMENSION statement to contain a single value under a single variable name, where the value requires more than one storage location. In the instance shown here, the section of the Hollerith card showing the decedent's name requires three core-storage locations, under a single name. This can be accomplished by using an array. In this instance, the DIMENSION statement sets up a three-word storage series under a single variable name. Each of the three core-storage locations contains one-third of the total Hollerith card field. The DIMENSION statement shown here establishes an array for the decedent's name amounting to three consecutive core-storage locations in length and an array for the estate item inventoried that is six consecutive core-storage locations in length.

The second statement of the program is the INTEGER statement. Here the point illustrated is that the names ADAY, AMO, and AYEAR — representing the day, month, and year of the date of the estate inventory — are considered as REAL variable names because their first letters begin with a letter other than I, J, K, L, M, or N. However, it is desired to have these variable names represent INTEGER values. This is done by the INTEGER statement, which defines ADAY, AMO, and AYEAR as INTEGER values. Normally, the default assumption of the FORTRAN compiler would be to establish ADAY, AMO, and AYEAR as REAL alphanumeric variable names because of their first letter. However, the default condition is overridden by the INTEGER statement.

The next statement of the program is the READ statement, which causes the computer to read from a card reader, designated as 5. Remember that in the parentheses following the READ statement, the designation of an input device may be by an INTEGER constant or an INTEGER variable name.

The READ statement then refers to the FORMAT statement that controls the field specifications of the input Hollerith card. Following the parentheses is a list of the variable names that designates the locations in core storage in which the fields will be stored. The following summary of the READ and FORMAT statements illustrates how the format notation identifies the fields on the unit input record which are then stored under variable names in the computer core storage:

Format Notation	Value	Hollerith Card Columns	Variable Name Used for Core Storage
3A6	Alphabet	1–18	ANAME[5]
I2	INTEGER	19–20	ITYCOD
1X	Skip	21	------
I3	INTEGER	22–24	ISEQ
5A6,A4	Alphabet	25–58	ANOUN
A1	Alphabet	59	EVALUE
F5.2	REAL	60–64	XQUANT
F5.0	REAL	65–69	XPOUND
2I2.0)	REAL	70–71	XSHLNG)
)	REAL	72–73	XPENCE)
2I2)	INTEGER	74–75	ADAY)
)	INTEGER	76–77	AMO)
I3	INTEGER	78–80	AYEAR

Each field that is needed is stored in a designated core location. The field on the card that is not needed is simply skipped using the X notation.

The information is now all located in the computer core storage. Let us assume that we desire to print the information out on a printer. We desire to print the name of the decedent, the day that the estate was inventoried, the name of the decedent, skip five spaces, and then print the date with three spaces between the various parts of the date. We then desire to have the printer skip to the next line and print the remainder of the data beginning with the item inventoried.

We have considered up to this point the situation where a FORMAT statement applies to (only) one input or output record — i.e., Hollerith card, etc. A FORMAT statement, however, may refer to more than one input or output record. This is done by using a slash mark — i.e., /. Basically, anytime that a slash mark is encountered in a FORMAT statement, a *new record* (Hollerith card or line) is indicated.

Situation A shown below is identical to Situation B. Both would cause two output records to be created. The first output record would contain ABLE, BAKER, and ABLE2. The second output record would contain BAKER2 and CHARLS.

```
A.    WRITE (6, 10) ABLE, BAKER, ABLE2
   10 FORMAT (1X, A6, F6.0, A5)
      WRITE (6, 11) BAKER2, CHARLS
   11 FORMAT (1X, A2, F3.2)

B.    WRITE (6, 10) ABLE, BAKER, ABLE2, BAKER2, CHARLS
   10 FORMAT (1X, A6, F6.0, A5/ 1X, A2, F3.2)
```

In the FORMAT statement shown in Situation B, the slash mark following the third output notation causes the remainder of the existing record to be skipped and the next output notation to start a new output record. The situation is the same for READ statements.

In Situation B, if one desired to have a *blank line* come between the two output records, the FORMAT statement would be as follows:

```
   ...
   10 FORMAT (1X, A6, F6.0, A5, / / 1X, A2, F3.2)
```

[5]Requires a previously defined DIMENSION statement.

In short, a slash mark in a FORMAT statement indicates that a record, either input or output, is to be skipped. In general, the following rules may be helpful to the programmer:[6]

1. A slash mark appearing at the beginning of a FORMAT statement causes all of the first record (card or line) to be skipped.
2. A slash mark in the middle of a FORMAT statement causes the remainder of the first record to be skipped.
3. A slash mark at the end of the first record causes the *next* record to be skipped.
4. If you wish one record unit to be skipped — e.g., a blank input or output record to appear — then you must usually provide the number of slash marks equal to the number of skipped records plus 1. If you wish to skip five blank lines on output between printed lines, you must provide six slash marks, etc.

ADDITIONAL PROGRAM STATEMENTS

We noted in the last program that following the final executable statement the word STOP appeared. This statement appears at the *logical end* of the program, when the program has been completely executed. The STOP statement causes execution of the program to cease. The card that appears as the *final card* in any program is the END card.[7]

HOLLERITH DATA

In many instances, it is desired to print out alphabetic information as heading for a table or to manipulate alphabetic information. The FORTRAN way of providing output titles or headings or other data is through the use of Hollerith constants.

The general form of Hollerith notation is: wH. The w refers to the number of alphanumeric characters in the Hollerith field. A Hollerith field may include letters, numeric digits, and special characters. The H identifies the field as a Hollerith field. A Hollerith field may,

a) assign a value to a variable name in core storage,
b) transmit data from a FORMAT statement to an output unit.

They may not be used in any other way. The primary use of a Hollerith field is to transmit data from a FORMAT statement to an output unit.

A FORMAT statement must always work with a WRITE (or READ) statement. The usual set-up for output of Hollerith data is:

```
WRITE (6, 14)
14 FORMAT (1X, 13HTABLE  HEADING)
```

---

[6]A record unit, as used above, is held to include the desired input or output record—e.g., 80 columns for a Hollerith card, etc.

[7]The reader should check the manual of his own computer FORTRAN system on the following statements: STOP, PAUSE, END, CALL EXIST, NAMELIST.

The WRITE statement controls FORMAT Statement No. 14. It is noted that no variable names follow the WRITE control designation. This is so because no values are being transferred from core storage to an output device. The FORMAT Hollerith notation indicates the number of alphanumeric characters in the field and identifies the field as a Hollerith field. The number appearing before the H — i.e., 13, in this case — must refer to the exact number of characters in the field, including blanks. After the field is completed, a comma or a right parenthesis must appear. If the number of characters including blanks in the field does not exactly equal the specified length of the field, an error will appear.

The indicated Hollerith field would cause the following heading on a printer:

TABLE HEADING

In the instance shown, the first letter of the Hollerith field would appear in Column 1 of the printed line.[8]

A second example of the use of a Hollerith field is shown below:

    DIAM = 52.36
    WRITE (6, 14) DIAM
14 FORMAT (5X, 36HTHE CIRCUMFERENCE OF THE CIRCLE IS   /, F6.2)

This would cause the following output line beginning in Column 6 of the printer output:

        THE CIRCUMFERENCE OF THE CIRCLE IS   52.36

Hollerith statements may be used in a number of ways for controlling or labelling output so that the output is clarified.

One other use of the Hollerith statement is in a DATA statement as a Hollerith constant. The general form of the DATA statement is:

        DATA NAME1, NAME2 . . . NAMEi / 6H   , 1HJ, . . . /

The DATA statement simply informs the compiler that the variable names appearing in the list immediately following the word DATA and before the first slash mark are variable names to be assigned in core storage. The Hollerith data fields appearing between the two slash marks are the data to be assigned to the respective variable names. As shown, the value assigned to NAME1 consists of blanks. The value assigned to NAME2 is "J." Whenever it is desired to use the assigned values elsewhere in the program, the variable name is used. The variable names in a DATA statement may be either single variable names or arrays. If the variable names are arrays, the array must have been previously dimensioned and the appropriate number of spaces provided.

QUESTIONS FOR DISCUSSION

1. What are the three ways of getting information into a computer? Discuss when each would most appropriately be used.
2. The general form for input or output of INTEGER constants is Iw.

[8]Normally, one does not use Column 1 on the printer. This is reserved for control purposes. To get a printer to skip a page, one writes:

            PRINT (5, 10)
          10 FORMAT (1H1)

      a. What does the I stand for?

      b. What does the w stand for?

      c. How does the compiler system handle terminal blanks? (Check the manual for your computer.)

      d. How does the system handle embedded blanks? What is an embedded blank? (Check the manual for your computer.)

3. In an output of INTEGER data, is the integer quantity "RIGHT" or "LEFT" justified? (Check the manual for your computer.)

4. In output of INTEGER data, what happens if your output notation is too small for the INTEGER quantity being output?

    INTEGER quantity 12345
    INTEGER notation I4

5. In considering INTEGER quantities, what does the notation 4(I6) mean?

6. Tell the length of the INTEGER quantities suggested by the following notation codes:

        I4   I11
        I2   2(I11)
        I6   2(2X, I4)

7. The general form for handling REAL mode quantities is Fw.d. Indicate what each of the elements signifies.

      a. What happens if a REAL quantity has no decimal point punched in the REAL quantity field?

      b. What happens if the REAL quantity has a decimal point?

      c. When a decimal point *and* a notation code (FORMAT) appear in a keypunched value, which dominates?

8. Given the REAL quantity 12345567 and the notation F7.3, how would the quantity go into core storage?

9. Given the REAL quantity 1234567 and the notation code F7.5, how would the quantity look in core storage?

10. Is a REAL quantity "LEFT" or "RIGHT" justified on output by your computer?

11. On output, what happens if the field length for a REAL value provided by the output notation is too small?

12. Why must the output (FORMAT notation) always be two positions larger than the input notation for a REAL quantity?

13. How would the following input numbers differ as REAL quantities:

$$0.123456E + 03$$
$$0.123456E - 03$$

14. In handling alphabetic information, if a data field is less than 6-characters long (check your own computer manual):

      a. Are the characters "left" or "right" justified (for both input and output)?

      b. What happens to the unused core areas?

15. In input and output of data, how are skipped areas indicated?

16. In producing output labels, how is the "H" or Hollerith statement utilized? Discuss.

17. What is the difference in the effect on input or output control if a slash (/) appears in the middle of a FORMAT record *or* at either the beginning or end of the FORMAT record?

    a. Beginning of a FORMAT statement.

    b. Middle of a FORMAT statement.

    c. End of a FORMAT statement.

18. What is a DATA statement and how is it used? Why is it used?

19. Write a FORTRAN READ-FORMAT statement series to input data according to Chapter 3, appendix 3-1.

    a. B-Card

    b. C-Card

    c. D-Card

20. Write a short program as suggested in this chapter to READ and WRITE data for the A-Card, New York Data, appendix 3-1.

FORTRAN Arithmetic

INTRODUCTION

Once data has been read into the computer core from a peripheral-storage device and has been assigned as a value to a named core location, the next step is to be able to manipulate the data or to form combinations of the data. We have already noted that each datum in a computer core storage is coded as a number. Therefore, all data manipulation and data combinations may be carried out by using FORTRAN arithmetic.

All values originate in one of three ways:

1. A value may appear as a constant written in a source program.
2. A value may be data, read into computer storage from a peripheral input device and assigned or placed into a given variable named core-storage location — e.g., using a READ statement.
3. A value may be assigned to a variable name using *FORTRAN* arithmetic.

We have discussed in Chapter A1 the writing of constants in FORTRAN source programs. Chapter A2 discussed the use of the READ statement to assign values to specifically named core locations. The purpose of this chapter is to discuss arithmetic operations.

FORTRAN OPERATORS AND EXPRESSIONS

Fortran operators

A FORTRAN *operator* is a symbol that indicates to the FORTRAN compiler that some kind of process is to be carried out with respect to stored data. The symbol may be a *special character* or a combination of *special characters and alphabet letters*. There are a total of fourteen different operators acceptable to FORTRAN IV. These include five arithmetic operators, six relational operators, and three logical operators as shown below.[1]

[1]Normally, only the arithmetic operators are acceptable to FORTRAN II.

FORTRAN Symbol	Process Performed (representing)
Arithmetic Operators	
+	addition
—	subtraction
*	multiplication
/	division[2]
**	exponentiation
Relational Operators	
.LT.	less than
.LE.	less than or equal to
.EQ.	equal to
.NE.	not equal to
.GT.	greater than
.GE.	greater than or equal to
Logical Operators	
.AND.	conjunction
.NOT.	negation
.OR.	alternative

Arithmetic expressions

The formula for defining the area of a circle is the expression:

$$3.1416 \times r^2$$

This expression consists of two terms combined into an expression using two arithmetic operators. In a FORTRAN source program the formula would be written:

$$3.1416*R**2$$

The value of *pi*, or 3.1416, is a REAL constant and a term. The term r is a variable name whose value is the radius of the circle. In short, the expression dictates that the value of the radius r is to be squared and this is to be multiplied times pi, or 3.1416.

This example is simply an arithmetic expression consisting of two constants, one variable, and two arithmetic operators. The point is that the expression has a value that can only be obtained by carrying out the processes indicated by the operators. When evaluated, any arithmetic expression has a value that is a number. That number is *less than zero*, *equal to zero*, or *greater than zero*. In this sense, then, any arithmetic expression may have one of three generalized values; it may be equal to zero, it may be less than zero, or it may be more than zero.

Logical expressions

The same kind of analysis is possible for logical expressions. Logical expressions are normally a sequence or combination of variables or constants connected by one or more relational or logical operators. Just as the arithmetic expression could be reduced to a value that was equal to zero, greater than zero, or less than zero, a logical expression may be reduced to a value that is either *true* or *false*. The result of

---

[2]The slash mark (/) as a FORTRAN operator appears only outside of a FORMAT statement. The division operator should not be confused with the slash mark in a FORMAT statement that causes the skipping of an input or output record.

the evaluation of any logical or relational expression is that the expression is either true or false. Thus, the value of any logical expression will be either true or false.

The following are examples of logical expressions consisting of variable names and relational operators:

ABLE .LE. BAKER
IABLE .LE. IBAKER
ABLE .LE. BAKER + 5.

An EXPLICIT-TYPE statement may be used to establish that the variables are integer in type. The first expression above indicates that the expression would be evaluated as true if the value of ABLE was *less than or equal to* the value assigned to BAKER. If the value assigned to ABLE is *greater than* the value of BAKER, then the expression would be evaluated as false.

The expression must be evaluated according to the logical or relational operators shown and the value assigned as true or false accordingly. The logical expression below indicates an expanded form of a logical expression using both logical and relational operators:

IABLE .EQ. IBAKER .OR. IABLE .GT. 156

This logical expression is divided into two parts, of which IABLE.EQ. IBAKER is the first. Here, there are two INTEGER variable names connected with a relational operator, this says that the value of IABLE is equal to the value of IBAKER. The second part of the expression says "IABLE.GT. 156.", which means that the value of IABLE is greater than the INTEGER constant 156. These two parts of the expression are connected by the logical operator.OR. .

If the value of IABLE is equal to the value of IBAKER, *or* if the value of IABLE is greater than 156, then the expression is true. Both relational and logical operators are *binary operators*. If the value of IABLE is not equal to the value of IBAKER, *or* if the value of IABLE is *not* greater than 156, then the value of the logical expression is false. A relational expression or a logical expression is evaluated to determine whether it is true or false.

The following are valid logical expressions if properly defined using EXPLICIT-TYPE statement:

ABLE
IABLE
IABLE .EQ. IBAKER

It is also possible on many FORTRAN compilers to mix arithmetic and logical or relational expressions. The following expressions are valid:

A + 20 .GT. B
ABLE − BAKER .EQ. CHARLES − 50

In short, expressions — whether arithmetic, relational, or logical — are combinations of constants, variables, and operators. *Arithmetic expressions* are evaluated into a single value — i.e., number — that is either less than zero, equal to zero, or greater than zero. *Relational expressions* consist of combinations of constants or variables connected by relational operators. If the values of the two constants or of the constant and the variable express or stand in the *relation* indicated by the *operator* — i.e., less than, greater than, etc. — then the value of the expression is true. Otherwise, the value of the relational expression is false. A *logical expression* is a combination of two logical constants, variables, or expressions connected with a logical operator.[3] A logical expression is true if the indicated relations and/or

---

[3]The logical operator .NOT. reverses the truth value of its modified expression or term.

true-false conditions exist. Otherwise the value of the expression is false. A relational or a logical expression when finally evaluated will have the value either true or false.[4]

FORTRAN ARITHMETIC

FORTRAN arithmetic operation symbols, or FORTRAN operators, designate the arithmetic operations that are to be performed on *terms*. The FORTRAN arithmetic operators are:

FORTRAN Symbol	Arithmetic Symbol	Definition
+	+	addition
−	−	subtraction
/	÷	division
*	×	multiplication
**	A^a	raise to power (of)

Evaluation is done according to certain rules (5 of them) for evaluating a FORTRAN expression:

1. A FORTRAN expression is always evaluated from left to right.
2. The terms inside a parentheses are always evaluated before any outside terms.
3. The exponents (raise to a power of) are evaluated.
4. The multiplication and division are evaluated.
5. The addition and subtraction are evaluated.

FORTRAN notation requires that the total expression be written on a single line. The expression above was written: $3.141R^2$. That is, the symbol representing that R was to be raised to a power was written above the line. In FORTRAN, that expression would be written: 3.1416*R**2, because all FORTRAN statements must appear on a single line or statement card. In that expression, the value representing R would be raised to a power, and that value would be multiplied times the constant 3.1416. *Parentheses are used whenever there is doubt about the order of operations.* For instance, the expression shown above could be written: 3.1416*(R**2).

We might say that the FORTRAN arithmetic is a multiple-pass arithmetic system. Whenever an arithmetic expression is encountered, FORTRAN makes one pass, from left to right, to determine whether there are any terms of the expression inside of parentheses. These are evaluated according to the rules for evaluating an expression. Then the expression is evaluated for any exponential operators. The expression is reread again from left to right and carries out any multiplication or division operations. Finally, the last pass is made that carries out any operations for addition and subtraction.

Before proceeding, let us be sure that we understand the basic rules of FORTRAN arithmetic. Let us assume that we have three variable names with the following assigned values as follows:

FIELD with a value of 10
DATA with a value of 5
DIFF with a value of 3

---

[4]We have noted that an expression may be evaluated to true or false. This is equally true of values that are numeric or alphabetic. Alphabetic characters are usually evaluated as INTEGER values, using an EXPLICIT-TYPE statement.

In the expression below:

FIELD+DATA*DIFF

the normal ordering rules — the default definitions of the FORTRAN compiler — should multiply DATA by DIFF, and then add the answer thus obtained to FIELD. The answer would be 25.

On the other hand, if it were desired to first add FIELD to DATA and then multiply that answer to DIFF, it is necessary to override the default definition of the FORTRAN compiler. *The normal default condition of the FORTRAN compiler always does the multiplication and division before it does the addition and subtraction. In order to override the default condition of the compiler, it is necessary to use parentheses, as shown below:*

(FIELD + DATA) * DIFF (Value is 45.)

In this instance, FIELD is first added to DATA (result is 15), and that is multiplied by DIFF. The value of the expression using the parentheses as shown is then 45.

The basic rule that is normally followed is that in the absence of specific overriding instructions, the FORTRAN compiler carries out the evaluation of a FORTRAN expression from left to right, following the ordering rules as indicated above. Any time that it is desired by the programmer to override the default conditions of the FORTRAN compiler, it is necessary to use parentheses.

Let us take another example. In the absence of any parentheses, "raising to a power" is the first operation carried out. Multiplication and division are carried out next — in the order encountered from left to right — and then addition and subtraction are carried out in order from left to right. The expression (in INTEGER form) below will illustrate the point:

$$5+10-15*20/4+100-2**2$$

This is an expression, made up of 8 terms connected by FORTRAN arithmetic operation symbols. Each operator, called a binary operator, connects two objects or terms.

The first operation carried out would be to raise the INTEGER 2 to the power of 2 — i.e., 2**2; thus, the value of this element of the expression becomes 4. The expression now looks as follows:

$$5+10-15*20/4+100-4$$

The second step then carries out multiplication and/or division in the order that these are encountered. In this instance, 15 is multiplied times 20, and *that result* is divided by 4:

15*20 becomes 300
300/4 becomes 75

The expression has now become:

$$5+10-75+100-4$$

The next step performs the addition and subtraction on connected *pairs* of constants, in the order that the binary operators are encountered. Four operations remain as follows:

5+10 becomes 15
15−75 becomes −60
−60+100 becomes 40
40−4 becomes 36

The value of the expression finally reduces to the single INTEGER value 36.

If the programmer intended something different, then parentheses could be used as follows:

$$5+10-15*(20/4+(100-2**2))$$

The value of this expression is — 1500.

The point is that the FORTRAN programmer must be extremely careful in setting up the FORTRAN arithmetic expressions. The parentheses should be used any time that it is necessary to overcome the default condition of the compiler in order to accomplish the desired result. The important thing is that the use of parentheses simply causes the program execution to evaluate the expression *beginning* with any terms inside parentheses before any terms outside of parentheses are evaluated. The innermost set of parentheses is always evaluated first in the event that there is more than one set of parentheses in an expression.

We can convert the expression to one using variable names. For instance, if INTEGER number values are as follows:

> ITEM has a value of 5
> JACK has a value of 10
> IDATA has a value of 15
> LOC has a value of 4
> LOC2 has a value of 100

then, ITEM+JACK—IDATA*(20/LOC+(LOC2—2**2)) as what value?

In writing arithmetic expression calculations, the FORTRAN programmer must not allow two operation symbols to be next to each other. The expression ABLE *—BAKER is incorrect. In this instance, a multiplication * and a subtraction — sign operator appear immediately next to each other. This expression would have to be written:

> ABLE*(—BAKER)

The "—BAKER" appearing as a single-signed variable name inside of parentheses as shown here is sometimes referred to as a *unary minus* quantity or value. This unary minus value — i.e., (—BAKER) or (—25.) — is always evaluted after the exponentiation and before any multiplication or division operations. The summary below is a review of the rules for calculation under FORTRAN compilers:

**	Exponentiation	(*first*)
—	Unary minus	(*second*)
*,/	Multiplication, division	(*third*)
+,—	Addition, subtraction	(*last*)

One point that ought to be kept in mind is that concerning INTEGER division — e.g., division of INTEGER numbers. In INTEGER division, the quotient (answer) will always develop to the nearest whole number.[5] For instance, if one were to divide the INTEGER number 5, by the INTEGER number 2, the result would be 2. If one divides the INTEGER number 5 by the INTEGER number 6, the result would be 0. In short, following any division of INTEGER numbers, the fractional value of the quotient will not be developed.

ASSIGNMENT STATEMENT

Once an arithmetic expression has been reduced to a single value, that value may be *assigned* to a variable name. The purpose of the arithmetic assignment statement

---

[5]The fractional part is not developed.

is to place a value — e.g., a number — into a designated named core location. The general form of the statement is: NAME = expression. NAME refers to any variable name. Expression refers to any arithmetic expression. Any arithmetic expression is: a) any single constant, b) any single defined variable name, or c) any combination of constants, variable names, and operation symbols. For instance, in the formula:

$$CIRCLE = 3.1416*RADIUS**2$$

the first thing that happens is that the expression "3.1416*RADIUS**2" is evaluated and a single value is obtained. Second, that value is assigned or placed in the computer core location named "CIRCLE."

In order for any expression to be evaluated, it is necessary to assign values to the variable names. This could be done through a READ statement or through an assignment statement. In the expression shown below, it is necessary to assign values to the variable names before the expression may finally be reduced to a single value:

$$ANSWR = ((A*(X**2))-((B*X)/2.)+5.$$

The computer must contain the values of A,B, and X. Depending on the values of A,B, and X, the expression may be evaluated and that value assigned to ANSWR. For instance, if:

$$A = 10.$$
$$B = 24.$$
$$X = 15.$$

then A,B, and X are the variable names indicating given storage locations, containing the values 10., 24., and 15., respectively. For instance, the value of A is 10. (a REAL number), etc. As the value 10. is placed into the designated core location, it replaces any previous value that may have been in that location.

This brings up an important point. If it is ever desired to utilize a core-storage location that contains a zero (0) it is extremely important to remember that the variable name must be preset to the desired value before using it. If a variable name is used in a FORTRAN source program without presetting it, the FORTRAN compiler will use the contents of that variable name location that *happen to be there*. *One of the major sources of error in FORTRAN programs is the attempt to utilize a variable name without setting it to the desired initial value.*

In the expression shown above, after the values A, B, and X have been set, the expression may be reduced to a single value, and that value will then be assigned to ANSWR.

QUESTIONS FOR DISCUSSION

1. Define each term and discuss — e.g., compare.
   a) INTEGER and REAL arithmetic
   b) FORTRAN and machine language.
   c) What is meant by:

   1. Instructions   3. Data
   2. Constants   4. Number
                5. Value

2. What are the five types of FORTRAN arithmetic operators?
3. What are the three types of FORTRAN logical operators?

4. What are the six types of FORTRAN relational operators?

5. How and why is a logical operator different in purpose from a relational operator?

6. What is a binary operator? Why are arithmetic, logical, and relational operators binary operators?

7. Evaluate the following expressions, (assuming: $I = 3$, $J = 4$, $K = 2$, $A = 3.0$, $B = 4.0$, $C = 2.0$):

    a. I*(J−(K+1))/K
    b. A*B/2.0**C
    c. K*I/3
    d. (A*B/2.0)**C

8. Write the following expressions correctly as FORTRAN expressions:

    a. $X+Y^3$

    b. $X^2+10X+Y^2$

    c. $A+\dfrac{B}{C-D}$

    d. $A^2+\left(\dfrac{B}{C+D}\right)^2+40D^2$

    e. $\left(\dfrac{X}{Y}\right)^G+1$

    f. $(1+X)^3$

9. For each of the following expressions, indicate whether the expression is correct or incorrect. If incorrect, what is wrong?

    a. I = J** −M
    b.   READ (10, 5) I
        10 FORMAT (I7)
    c. A + B = C
    d.   WRITE (5,20) I, C, B
        20 FORMAT (5I10)
    e. K1 = INCORRECT*LEFT
    f.   5 = (A + B) **I
    g.   WRITE (6,3) A
        30 FORMAT (1X, 10I)

10. What, if any, errors exist in the following FORTRAN statements? (there may be no errors):

    a. A*X + B*X + C + 5. = ICODE
    b. S = (B*3)1*E**3 (Mix mode)
    c. FORMAT (5 f 1 .2)
    d. FORMAT (I3, f6.7)

A4

FORTRAN Control

The discussion of FORTRAN up to this chapter has related only to a straight-line program. The FORTRAN program will be executed serially or sequentially in the order that the FORTRAN source program statements appear in the program, from the first instruction to the last. This is known as the default condition of FORTRAN program execution. In other words, in default of other specific and overriding instructions, the program will be executed serially from the first instruction to the last.

In most instances, it is desirable to modify this straight-line execution. There are two ways of modifying the program control. The first is by the establishment of a loop in the program. A loop is defined as a series of instructions executed more than once. The second way of modifying control is through a program decision which will direct that the next instruction shall be one of two, or more, possible statements.

UNCONDITIONAL TRANSFER OF CONTROL

An unlimited program loop is created by using the unconditional GO TO statement. The general form of the GO TO statement is:

GO TO N

The words GO TO appear in the FORTRAN source program. The N represents any statement number. We have noted previously that a statement number is not an INTEGER value; it is simply a *label* that in FORTRAN source programs happens to consist of numeric digits. For instance, execution of the statement:

GO TO 2

would cause Statement No. 2 to be executed next. In Chapter A2 we saw that a program was developed which directed that a card be read into the computer from a card input reader and that the data was printed out on an on-line printer in modified form. In that program, only *one card* was read into the computer and that card was printed on an output device. This illustrates the straight-line program, or the so-called default execution condition of FORTRAN program execution.

Using the unconditional GO TO statement, it is possible to rewrite the program to read and print card data with a single short program. Table A4-1 illustrates the use of the unconditional GO TO statement to create an unlimited loop.

TABLE A4-1. Source program loop: GO TO statement.

```
    DIMENSION RDCARD (14)
 10 FORMAT (13A6, A2)*
  1 READ (INPT, 10) RDCARD ◄──┐
    WRITE (INOUT, 10) RDCARD  │  RANGE
    GO TO 1 ◄─────────────────┘
    END
```

*Many of the FORTRAN compilers would require that IX precede the output format notation as discussed in Chapter A2.

The program shown on the table is representative only in that it shows the use of the GO TO statement to develop an unlimited program loop. Statement 1 marks the *beginning* of the loop. The GO TO statement marks the *end* of the loop. The *range* of the loop illustrates the statements included in the loop itself and is illustrated by the bracket. The FORMAT statement may either follow the READ and WRITE statements or be anywhere else in the program. Some programmers like to place the FORMAT statements immediately after the relevant READ and WRITE statements; others like to place them at the beginning or end of the program.

As long as there are cards in the input device (INPT), the program will continue. Each time the program has caused the information to be printed, the next instruction is the GO TO 1, which causes the next instruction executed to be Statement 1. The indicated program would terminate when there were no more cards in the card reader.

A second illustration of the GO TO statement may be helpful in indicating its use. Let us assume that we have a relatively large number of data cards with two fields of arithmetic data on each card. The data on the cards are INTEGER values and are in Columns 15–19 and in Columns 25–29. We desire to read the cards into the computer, add the two numbers together, print out the resultant total on Lines 5–9 of the printer, and go back and read another card. Let us assume that we desire to do this as long as there are cards in the read unit. The program that would accomplish this is shown in Table A4-2.

TABLE A4-2. GO TO statement.

```
 11 READ (INPT, 5) IDATA, IDATA2 ◄──(Beginning)──┐
  5 FORMAT (14X, I5, 5X, I5)                      │
    ISUM = IDATA + IDATA2                         │
    WRITE (INOUT, 6) ISUM                         │
  6 FORMAT (4X, I6)                               │
    GO TO 11 ◄──────(End)────────────────────────┘
    END
```

Let us note certain points about this program. The data being read into the computer is in INTEGER form. Therefore, the variable names IDATA, and IDATA2 begin with the appropriate letter (I,J,K,L,M,N for INTEGER variable names). The card is read into the computer with the INTEGER data in Columns 15–19 and placed in core storage under the variable name IDATA. The INTEGER data in card Columns 25–29 are placed in core storage under the variable name IDATA2. The remainder of the card columns are ignored by the FORMAT statement because they are not relevant for our use. The third statement of the program adds the numeric data in IDATA to the numeric data in IDATA2, and then places the result of the addition into the core location named ISUM. The act of placing the value (IDATA+IDATA2) into ISUM replaces any data that may have previously been located in ISUM. It is important to remember that in a FORTRAN source program an "=" symbol means *to replace* and does not mean an identity.

The WRITE statement writes or prints — on a printer device — on Columns 5–9 (indicated by the FORMAT statement) the numeric data contained in core storage under ISUM.[1] The next statement is GO TO 11. This causes the execution pattern (under the default condition) to be modified, and the next statement executed is No. 11.

The bracket indicates the range of the loop developed in this program. The range is simply the number of statements included in the loop — e.g., to be repeated. The *beginning* of the loop is the first statement of the loop, No. 11 in Table A4-2. The *end* of the loop is the GO TO 11 statement. As long as there were Hollerith cards in the reader or input device (INPT), the program would keep reading cards, adding the values together, and printing out the sum in the indicated location on the output device (INOUT).

CONDITIONAL TRANSFER OF CONTROL

Computed GO TO statement

The unconditional GO TO statement automatically transfers control to the indicated statement number each time that the GO TO statement is encountered. A slight modification of the GO TO statement makes it possible to transfer control *to any one of many numbered statements* in the source program. The general form of the computed GO TO statement is:

GO TO (N1, N2, N3, N4, . . . Nn), NAME

The words GO TO identify the statement as one which will transfer control from the GO TO statement to a designated statement. The list of numbers — N1, N2, N3, N4, . . . Nn — separated by commas inside the parentheses indicates the *possible statement numbers to which control may be transferred*. The list of statement numbers to which control may be transferred can be continued over more than one Hollerith card, using the *continuation statement form*. Following the parentheses is a comma and following that is an INTEGER variable name. The numeric value of the INTEGER variable name indicates a sequential position within the list. The statement number appearing in that position is the statement number to which control will be transferred.

The most important point to remember when using the computed GO TO statement is that within the parentheses each space separated by a comma is numbered sequentially — i.e., from 1. Illustratively, this is shown below:

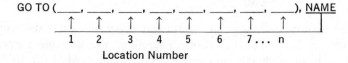

[1]Subject to the limitation specified in the *ASA Guide*.

The computed GO TO statement is rather like a combination of the unconditional GO TO statement plus an array — where the array fits between the parentheses following the GO TO. Each location of the array is numbered. The position immediately following the left parenthesis is always the *first* position, etc. The number of consecutive spaces that may appear in a computed GO TO statement is limited only by the number of continuation cards that may appear. The value of the INTEGER variable name appearing as the final item of the computed GO TO statement refers to a particular consecutively numbered location. The number appearing in each location is a statement number to which control may be transferred.

The form of the computed GO TO statement is as follows:

GO TO (45, 15, 1, 33, 166, 14), NAME

Examination of the computed GO TO statement indicates that there are a total of six positions provided as follows:

Computed GO TO Position No.	Statement No.
1	45
2	15
3	1
4	33
5	166
6	14

If the value of NAME is 1, then the next statement executed will be Statement No. 45 in the program. If the value of NAME is 2, then Statement 15 will be the next statement in the program that is executed. If the value of NAME is 5, then Statement 166 will be executed next.

The value of NAME must be greater than zero — it cannot be a negative number, and it cannot be zero; and its value cannot be greater than the number of positions provided. For instance, in the example given above, the value of NAME cannot be greater than 6. Furthermore, the execution of the program will terminate in an error condition or give the wrong result (depending on the individual computer) if the value of NAME is *less than 1 or greater than 6*.

Use of the computed GO TO statement

Assume that data are being read into the computer. The input record units contains data as well as a code. It is desired to group the data into summary storage areas according to the code that is associated with each data card.

Let us assume that each Hollerith input card is laid out as follows:

Card Col.	Information
1–4	Year
5–17	Import value
18–30	Export value
31–78	Blank
79–80	Code

We shall assume that the information shows the value of trade to the port of London between the years 1701–1800. The imports and exports are shown as sterling values. The code indicates where the merchandise came from or went to, in any given year. There are a total of 25 codes since there are 25 countries that London did business with in any given year.

There is, therefore, one card for each year for each country, or a total of 2,500 cards. It is desired to group each of the countries by region — i.e., a European port, an American colonial port, a Caribbean port, a Canadian port, and so forth. There are five regions consisting of 25 ports that traded with London. The point is to get each port associated with the proper region. For instance, as shown below, there were six separate ports in the region called "American Colonies".

ICODE	Port	Region
01	New England	
02	New York	
03	Philadelphia	AMERICAN COLONIES
04	Virginia	
05	Carolina	
12	Denmark/Norway	
14	East Country	NORTHERN EUROPE
11	France	
13	Germany	CENTRAL EUROPE
15	Netherlands	

In short, each country has a number code to identify it. New England is labeled as 01, New York as 02, etc. The computed GO TO is set up so that if ICODE is 01–05 — i.e., an American Colony — the next statement executed should be *Statement No. 10*. Statement 10 controls the aggregation of data for *each* American colonial port into a regional unit.

Therefore, the first 5 *locations* in the computed GO TO statement refer to the ICODES 01, 02, 03, 04, 05. If ICODE is either 01, or 02, or 03, or 04, or 05, the next statement executed is Statement 10, as shown below:

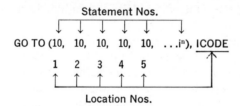

A segment of the program showing more completely the use of the computed GO TO is indicated below.

```
   READ (INPT, 5) IYEAR, AMPORT, EXPORT, ICODE
5 FORMAT (I4, F13.0, F13.0, 48X, I2)
   GO TO (10, 10, 10, 10, 10, 15, 15, 15, 15, 15, 20, 25, 20, 25, 120, 30, 30, 30, 30, 30, 15, 15, 15, 15, 30),
1CODE
10 ...
15 ...
20 ...
25 ...
30 ...

          ...
```

Immediately following the reading of a card into the computer, it is necessary to make disposition of that card — that is, to transfer the export and import data on the card to the proper area. It is noted that there were a total of 25 ports trading with London and that each port has a code beginning with 01 through 25. There are, therefore, 25 consecutive positions in the computed GO TO statement. Each location corresponds to a port code, specified by ICODE. The number appearing in that position is the statement number next executed if the value of ICODE corresponds to the sequential location of the computed GO TO statement. If ICODE has a value of 1, the next statement executed is Statement No. 10. If ICODE is 15, the next statement executed is Statement 20, etc. The various statement numbers (there are five possible transfers out of the computed GO TO statement) indicate transfer to a FORTRAN source program statement that designates an operation for a particular region.

The purpose of the computed GO TO statement shown above was simply to group data from 25 separate entries into five separate categories. This was done by transferring control from a READ statement to a specific location in the program that would then accomplish the desired grouping.

Assigned GO TO statement

The assigned GO TO statement is a combination of the computed GO TO statement and the arithmetic assignment statement discussed in the previous chapter. The general form of the assigned GO TO statement is:

GO TO INAME, (N1, N2, N3, . . .NN)

The variable name INAME is an INTEGER variable name reference. The list N1, N2, N3, . . .NN is a list of *statement numbers*. Each statement number is included in a list inside the parentheses. In order to utilize the assigned GO TO statement, a statement number must have been previously assigned to INAME, corresponding to one of the statement numbers inside the parentheses. For instance, the assigned GO TO statement might appear:

GO TO INAME, (50, 45, 13)

In this instance, INAME must have the statement number 50, or 45, or 13 assigned to it. There is a special assignment statement that places a statement label into a variable name which is used only in assigned GO TO statements, the ASSIGN statement. The general form of the ASSIGN statement is as follows:

ASSIGN I TO INAME

where I is a statement number. This statement places a *statement label* as the contents of INAME.

An ASSIGN statement must precede an assigned GO TO statement but must not necessarily immediately precede the GO TO statement. The usual form of an assigned GO TO statement is:

ASSIGN 45 TO NAME
. . .
GO TO NAME, (50, 45, 13)

In this instance, the branch would be to Statement 45. In the condition illustrated below, the branch would be to Statement 105:

ASSIGN 105 TO IABLE
. . .
GO TO IABLE, (45, 34, 105, 56, 78)

The assigned GO TO statement is another example of a conditional branch of program control. The branch depends on the condition specified. The difference between the computed GO TO and the assigned GO TO is that:

1. In the computed GO TO, the value of the INTEGER name refers to a specific location in the GO TO array. The statement number next executed appears in the given location of the array:

    GO TO (15, 14, 13, 78, 77, 66), ICODE

    If ICODE has a value of less than 1 or greater than 6, the program will fail in an error condition.[2] If ICODE has a value of 5, the next statement executed will be Statement 77. The value of ICODE (an INTEGER number) refers to a given location of the GO TO array.

2. In the assigned GO TO statement, the *statement number* must previously have been assigned to the variable name of an ASSIGN statement. An ASSIGN statement has no operational effect unless the program includes an assigned GO TO statement which is indexed by the variable name in the ASSIGN statement and where the assigned statement number appears in the GO TO list.

FORTRAN DECISION MAKING: IF STATEMENT

FORTRAN decision making may be defined as a test. Based on the outcome of the test, one or more alternative program paths may be chosen. The basic difference between the conditional branch statement discussed above and the IF statement is that the IF statement actually performs a test and branches according to the result of the outcome of the test. In the conditional GO TO statements discussed above a branch was made when a given condition was met; no actual test was performed.

The basic way of making a test in a FORTRAN source program is the use of the IF statement; which evaluates an expression and which — based on the outcome of the evaluation of the expression — can direct the program into two or more alternative paths.

The arithmetic IF statement

The general form of the arithmetic IF statement is:

IF (expression) N1, N2, N3

The word IF simply identifies that a test is to be made and that — based on the outcome of the test — a branch is to be made. The actual test in an arithmetic IF statement consists of the evaluation of an arithmetic expression. The nature of the test consists of two steps:

1. Evaluation of the expression.
2. Determination of whether the final single value of the expression is *less than zero*, *equal to zero*, or *greater than zero*.

If the value of the expression is less than zero, the next statement executed is that appearing in Position N1. If the value of the expression is exactly equal to zero,

[2]This depends on the software package of each individual computer (check your computer manual).

the next statement executed is N2. If the value of the expression is greater than zero, the next statement executed is N3. Basically, then, an arithmetic IF statement may make or develop a three-way branch as indicated; that is, following the IF test, one of three specified statements may be executed. An expression is either: 1) a single defined variable name, 2) a single defined constant (numeric or alphabetic), or 3) any valid sequence or combination of constants, defined variable names, and operation symbols.

An arithmetic expression, therefore, is either an alphanumeric term or a series of terms connected by arithmetic operators.[3] The simplest FORTRAN arithmetic expression would be an arithmetic (assume INTEGER) variable such as IVALUE.

An arithmetic IF statement (to use this simplest of all arithmetic expressions) would be:

IF (IVALUE) 10, 20, 30

If IVALUE were less than 0, the next statement executed following the IF statement would be Statement No. 10. If IVALUE were 0, Statement 20 would be executed next. If IVALUE were greater than 0, Statement 30 would be executed next. The value of the expression IVALUE shown above is assigned elsewhere in the program. In the IF statement shown below, the next statement executed would always be Statement 30 if IVALUE were 15.

IF (IVALUE) 10, 20, 30

We have discussed in Chapter A3 that each arithmetic expression is a combination of terms (either constants or variables) and arithmetic operators. Each expression, therefore, will be evaluated using the combinations of objects (terms) and operators. The result is a single value — this value of the expression controls the branch of the program.

An expression may consist of a single variable name.

IF (ABLE) 10, 20, 30

The value of "ABLE" determines the next statement executed. If the value of ABLE is read in through some input device, the value of ABLE will change.

Let us assume, in Table A4-3, that we are reading data into the computer and that as long as the data contained in Hollerith card field ABLE are positive, the program is to continue. If however, the data in field ABLE are either *negative* or equal to *zero*, we desire the program to stop operating. We shall also assume that there are three other data fields on the Hollerith card, which we shall call BAKER, DATA, and IDATA.

TABLE A4-3.   Program: IF test for END-OF-FILE.

```
 3 READ (INPT, 4) BAKER, DATA, IDATA, ABLE
 4 FORMAT (F6.0, F6.0, 10X, I9, 5X, F5.0)
   IF (ABLE) 10, 10, 11                          Range
                                                   of
11 WRITE (INOUT, 5) BAKER, DATA, IDATA, ABLE     Loop
 5 FORMAT (1X, F8.0, F8.0, 10X, I9, 5X, F7.0)
   GO TO 3
10 STOP
   END
```

[3]As discussed in the previous chapter, an arithmetic operator is: + meaning addition, — meaning subtraction, / meaning division, * meaning multiplication, or ** meaning exponentiation.

The IF statement as used in Table A4-3 is simply a test for the last card in the input card deck. The last card is identified because it contains either a *0* or any other *negative number* in Columns 37–41. Statement No. 10, the statement next executed if a zero or a negative number is detected in ABLE, is a STOP statement. This simply indicates that the program is completed, that all data have been processed, and that the computer should stop further operations on the program. If it were desired to have the program stop operations only if a negative number were detected in ABLE but to continue operating if a zero were in ABLE, the IF statement would be written as follows:

IF (ABLE) 10, 11, 11

The point noted above is that an IF statement is used to test a constant or a variable or an expression. Based on the outcome of the test, the program will branch to a designated statement. The important point to note is that the expression in the parentheses constituting the test is always evaluated first to determine a single numeric value for the expression.

Another instance of the use of the IF statement to determine the value of a field is shown below. Let us assume in Table A4-4 that the information is the same as in Table A4-3, except that the last card of the deck is to be indicated by five 9's in field ABLE. The IF test to determine the last card would be as is shown in the table.

TABLE A4-4.   Program: IF test, END-OF-FILE.

```
 3 READ (INPT, 4) BAKER, DATA, IDATA, ABLE
 4 FORMAT (F6.0, F6.0, 10X, I9, 5X, F5.0)
   IF (ABLE — 99999.) 11, 10, 11
11 WRITE (INOUT, 5) BAKER, DATA, IDATA, ABLE
 5 FORMAT (1X, F8.0, 10X, I9, 5X, F7.0)
   GO TO 3
10 STOP
   END
```

In processing data in many of the social sciences, the stored data are usually a combination of numeric and alphabetic fields. In many instances, it is necessary to test the alphabetic fields to determine whether the fields contain the same data, in order to make a program decision. What if one desired to determine whether one *alphabetic* constant assigned to one field ABLE were equal to a second alphabetic constant assigned to the field BAKER. This could be accomplished with the IF statement that follows:

IF (ABLE — BAKER) 15, 10, 15

In this instance, since the alphabetic constants are stored in the computer storage as numbers, the test (ABLE-BAKER) is, in fact, an arithmetic expression. If the alphabetic constants in ABLE and BAKER were equal, the result of the evaluation of the expression would be *zero*, and Statement 10 would be the next statement executed. If the alphabetic constant in ABLE were not equal to that in BAKER, the result of the evaluation of the expression would be other than zero, and the next statement executed would be Statement 15.[4]

[4]Depending on the individual computer, it is sometimes better to test alphabetic data as integer data, using an EXPLICIT-TYPE statement.

The logical IF statement

A second type of IF test available to most FORTRAN IV compilers or programs is the logical IF test. The general form of the logical IF test is: IF (logical expression) statement. The nature of the logical IF test is quite similar to the arithmetic IF test. Again, the word IF simply informs the compiler that a test is to be made. The nature of the test itself is found within the parentheses and is either a logical or a relational expression.[5] The logical expression is evaluated to determine whether it is true or false. If the logical expression is false, the next successive FORTRAN statement (following the logical IF) is executed. If the logical expression is evaluated as true, the statement following the parentheses in the logical test is executed. The statement may be any FORTRAN *executable* statement except a DO statement (discussed below) or another logical IF statement.

There are *two* — and only *two* — logical values (in FORTRAN) .TRUE. and .FALSE. An arithmetic expression is evaluated to be less than zero, zero, or greater than zero. A logical expression can be only .TRUE. or .FALSE. A logical constant is written into the source program as .TRUE. or .FALSE. (the periods are part of the value and must appear). Examples of logical values are shown below. The variable names must be defined as logical in an EXPLICIT TYPE statement and the logical value then assigned to the variable name:

```
LOGICAL ABLE, BAKER, ICODE
ABLE = .TRUE.
BAKER = .FALSE.
ICODE = .TRUE.
```

Logical expressions are normally a sequence or combination of variables or constants connected by one or more relational or logical operators. The logical and relational operators are binary in that each logical or relational operator must connect two objects or terms. The following are examples of *correct* logical expressions:

```
ABLE
ABLE .AND. BAKER
ABLE .OR. BAKER
ABLE .GT. BAKER
JCODE .GT. 36 .AND. JCODE .LT. 40
```

The following are examples of *incorrect* logical expressions:

```
ABLE AND BAKER (periods are part of the logical operator and must be included)
ABLE .OR BAKER(both periods must be included in the logical operator)
JCODE .LT. 36 .AND. 41 (logical and relational operators are binary; in this instance, they
                are being used incorrectly)
```

The third logical expression shown above is incorrectly written and illustrates the improper use of binary operators. If written correctly, the expression would read as follows:

```
JCODE .LT. 36 .AND. JCODE .LT. 41
```

The logical expression shown is a *compound logical expression* consisting of *two relational expressions* each of which acts as the object of the logical operator:

```
ICODE .LT. 36 .AND. ICODE .LT. 41
```

[5]See Chapter A3.

In short, each logical expression — whether simple or compound, whether using relational or logical operators — must include *two terms or objects for each relational and each logical operator*.[6]

Each logical or relational expression (constituting the logical test in a logical IF statement) is evaluated to determine whether it is .TRUE. or .FALSE. A logical expression of any kind may only be .TRUE. or .FALSE. Either of the following would define ABLE as a logical value:

A. LOGICAL ABLE
   ABLE = .TRUE.

B. READ (INPT, 6) ABLE
   6 FORMAT (L6)

The following is a relational expression consisting of two variable names connected with a relational operator:

IABLE .LE. IBAKER

The terms IABLE and IBAKER represent INTEGER variable names. The terms of the logical expression may be integer, real or alphanumeric. An EXPLICIT-TYPE statement may be used to establish that the variables are in the correct mode. The logical expression shown above indicates that the value of the variable IABLE is less than or equal to the value of the variable IBAKER. If the value of IABLE is less than or equal to the value of IBAKER, then the expression is true. If the value assigned to IBAKER is greater than the value assigned to IABLE, then the expression is false. Any logical expression must be evaluated according to the logical or relational operators to determine whether the expression is true or false.

The logical expression that forms the test in a logical IF statement is evaluated to determine whether it is true or false. If the value of the expression is TRUE, then the statement following the IF test is executed. If the expression is evaluated as FALSE, then the next statement following the logical IF statement is executed. The general form of the logical IF statement is (as noted above):

IF (LOGICAL EXPRESSION) statement

The object statement of the logical IF statement may be nearly any executable FORTRAN statement, although some are more common than others. However, there are certain statements that are never used as the object statement of a logical IF. These are:

DO statement (discussed below)
FORMAT statement
Another logical IF statement

The folowing logical IF statements are quite correct:

IF (LOGICAL EXPRESSION) GO TO 14
IF (LOGICAL EXPRESSION) ABLE = 445.
IF (LOGICAL EXPRESSION) ASSIGN 10 TO INDEX

IF (ABLE .EQ. BAKER) GO TO 13
GO TO 45

If the value assigned to ABLE is exactly equal to the value assigned to BAKER, then the next statement in the program executed is Statement 13. If the value of ABLE is not equal to the value of BAKER, then the FORTRAN program will next execute

---

[6]The exception is the logical operator .NOT.: (ABLE .LT. BAKER) has the same meaning as (.NOT. (ABLE .GE. BAKER)). .NOT. reverses the truth value of any expression that it modifies.

the statement following the logical IF statement. That next statement directs that the program GO TO 45, or to execute Statement 45 next.

The examples below indicate how IF statements may be used to control programs loops. Let us take some hypothetical college students and represent each student by a Hollerith card. The card indicates in the first 5 columns whether the student is male or female. We also know that at the end of all the student cards there is a card with 9's in the first 5 columns. We desire to write a program that will count the students, indicating how many of them are male, and how many are female. A male student is indicated by a 1 in Column 5 and a female student by a 2 in Column 5. The 99999 in Columns 1–5 indicates that all the student cards have been counted and is called an "end-of-file" card. A program that would accomplish the desired ends is shown in Table A4-5.

TABLE A4-5.   Use of the logical IF statement.

Program Statements	Explanation
ICTR = 0	Set counter to zero initially.
MEN = 0	
IWMN = 0	
5 READ (ININPT, 4) ISEX	Read the first 5 columns of the card
4 FORMAT (I5)	
IF (ISEX .EQ. 99999) GO TO 25	Test for last card.
ICTR = ICTR + 1	Count the students by adding to ICTR.
IF (ISEX .EQ. 1) MEN = MEN + 1	Add "1" to counter for male students if there is a 1 in Column 5.
IF (ISEX .EQ. 2) IWMN = IWMN + 1	Add "1" to counter for female students if there is a 2 in Column 5.
GO TO 5	
25 WRITE (INOUT, 6) ICTR, MEN, IWMN	After last card, branch is to Statement 25, which causes the values of ICTR, MEN, and IWMN to be written out as indicated.
6 FORMAT (5X, I5, 5X, I5, 5X, I5)	
STOP	
END	

Notice the loop in the program which is indicated with the arrows. The beginning of the loop is Statement 5. The end of the loop is the statement GO TO 5. After detecting the card with the five 9's in it, the program branches to Statement 25, which writes out the information on the printer as shown. The field ICTR is a counter indicating the number of students in the college, where one card represents a student. The ICTR also, however, represents a counter showing how many times the program executed the loop as indicated.

While this is a relatively simple program and one that would probably not be used in actual practice, it does indicate very simply two of the uses of the logical IF statement in executing and branching out of a loop.

As a final example of the use of the IF statement, let us examine how a controlled loop may be set up. Let us assume that we have 4,000 REAL values punched onto 4,000 cards. We need to write a program that will read the data into the computer, add each of the 4,000 pieces of information into an aggregate accumulator, and when all 4,000 cards have been read in, divide by 4,000 to obtain the *Mean* (average) value. We finally desire to print this value out on the printer. We shall also assume here that an end-of-file card may not be used. The program to do this would be as follows:

```
          CTR = 0.                              (set counter to 0)
          SUM = 0.
     ┌──▶ 4 READ (INPT, 6) DATA
     │                                          (read a card)
     │    6 FORMAT (F6.0)
     │      CTR = CTR + 1.                      (increment counter by 1)
 LOOP │      IF (CTR .EQ. 4001.) GO TO 45
     │      SUM = SUM + DATA                    (if CTR = 4001)
     │
     └──▶ GO TO 4
        45 AMEAN = SUM/(CTR − 1)                (branch out of loop to
                                                 Statement 45 when counter
          WRITE (INOUT, 11) AMEAN               equals 4001)
       11 FORMAT (1X, F8.0)
          STOP
          END
```

In this program, CTR acts as a means of counting the cards or values read into the computer and is also the basis on which the loop is broken. The branch is made out of the loop when CTR equals the test value of 4,001.

QUESTIONS
FOR DISCUSSION

1. Is STOP an unconditional control statement? What does STOP cause the computer to do?
2. What is the difference between the STOP and the END statements?
3. Ascertain the value of the following logical expressions (if M = 2, N = 5, I = 3):

   a. M+N.EQ.I+4.AND.N.LE.I+M   (.TRUE. or .FALSE.)
   b. I**2.GT.N*M.OR.I.LT.M.AND.M.NE.5   (.TRUE. or .FALSE.)
   c. .NOT. (M.LT.7.OR.N*I.GE.(N−M)*4)

4. What statements may not follow a logical IF?
5. A logical IF may compare two arithmetic expressions:
        (Arith. Expression *Relational Operator*   Arith. Expression)
   Illustrate (remembering the result of the comparison is a logical value).
6. In a logical IF statement, what is the general form of the test? Remember the basic form of the logical IF test is a comparison.
7. What is the general form of a computed GO TO statement? Explain each part.
8. Explain fully the following computed GO TO:

        GO TO (111, 6, 17), I

   The value of I may range from 1 to/and including 3. Why? What happens if I is greater than 3 or less than 1?
9. What is the general form of the unconditional GO TO statement? What occurs in program execution when the unconditional GO TO statement is encountered?
10. What is the general form of an assigned GO TO statement? Explain each part. What previous FORTRAN statement is needed to give an assigned GO TO statement operational effect?

A5

The Limited Loop

Up to this point we have indicated how a FORTRAN source program may carry out a straight-line program and a branch program in order to carry out certain operations a number of times. The next step is to show how a loop may be executed a given number of times; specifically, we desire to be able to instruct the compiler to count automatically. This automatic counting is performed by the DO statement. The general form for a DO statement is:

DO	INT	I	=	i,	limit,	increment
1	2	3		4	5	6

As indicated, a DO statement is divided into six parts. Part 1 is the word DO, which means "to carry out" or "to accomplish." The word DO is developed as the first word of a FORTRAN source program statement. A rather general interpretation of the DO statement would be, "DO the *following* loop."

Part 2 of the DO statement is the statement number marking the *end* of the loop, here called INT. The statement immediately following the DO statement marks the *beginning* of the loop. The statement number, immediately following the DO, is the statement number that marks the *end* of the loop. The statements between the beginning and the end of the loop inclusive constitute the *range* of the loop.

Part 3 of the DO statement is simply an (INTEGER) variable name, called the index variable or the counter of the DO statement. The index variable name is set to some determined value.

Part 4 of the DO statement, represented here by i, is the initial value of the index variable. This initial value may be an INTEGER constant (a number), or an INTEGER variable, whose value is determined elsewhere in the program.

Part 5 of the DO statement is an INTEGER constant or variable that marks the upper limit of the loop or indicates the maximum number of times that the loop is to be accomplished or done. If Parts 4, 5, and 6 of the DO statement are INTEGER variables, then the value must be established outside of the DO statement. Part 6 of the DO statement is also either an INTEGER constant or an INTEGER variable, that represents the increment to the index.

243

For instance, if one desired to establish a loop that would preset the initial value to 1 and *do the loop* 35 times, the DO statement would be written as follows:

DO 10 I = 1, 35, 1

This DO statement presets the variable name (counter) I to 1 and sets the maximum limit to 35. Further, the last part of the DO statement — i.e., 1 — states that each time the loop is accomplished, the counter, or the value of the index variable, is to be incremented by 1. The student should remember that there will be many times when it is desired to preset the counter to other than 1, and also many times when it is desired to increment the counter by other than 1 at a time.

The following is a valid DO statement:

DO 15 J = 1, 150

This DO statement establishes a loop whose beginning is the statement following the DO statement and whose end is Statement 15. The index variable (counter) is J, and the initial value of the counter is preset to 1. The loop will be done 150 times. In a DO statement, when the *increment* is not specified, it is assumed (default condition of the compiler) to be an increment of 1.

The following DO statement is also a valid statement:

DO 25 INDEX = IABLE, 27000, 3

This DO statement provides that the loop extends from the statement following the DO statement to (and including) Statement 25. The variable name given to the index variable is INDEX. The initial value of INDEX is set to the value of IABLE. The value assigned to IABLE would need to be set before the DO statement was encountered, such as:

IABLE = 3000
DO 25 INDEX = IABLE, 27000, 3

The increment to the DO counter would be by 3 — e.g., the *initial* value of INDEX is 3000, the second value (after the loop is accomplished once) is 3003, the third value is 3006, etc.

The DO statement illustrated on Table A5-1 is a proper statement, and the indicated loop would be executed seven times, as shown. The loop, as indicated, would be performed 7 times. The values of the index variable — i.e., INDEX — would be, successively, 1, 3, 5, 7, 9, 11, and 13. Upon completing the 7th loop, 2 would be added to the INDEX counter, and the counter would be 15 — which is greater than the maximum value allowable of 14. *The loop would be satisfied, and the statement following Statement 3 would be executed.* At the completion of each loop, the index variable is incremented by the indicated amount or by 1. If the value of the index variable is less than the maximum or upper limit, the loop will be performed another time. The loop will be performed once if the value of the index variable is just equal to the upper limit or test value.

TABLE A5-1. Use of a DO statement.

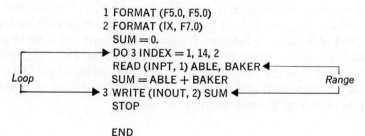

```
      1 FORMAT (F5.0, F5.0)
      2 FORMAT (IX, F7.0)
        SUM = 0.
        DO 3 INDEX = 1, 14, 2
        READ (INPT, 1) ABLE, BAKER
        SUM = ABLE + BAKER
      3 WRITE (INOUT, 2) SUM
        STOP

        END
```

Let us assume for the moment that we have 27,000 Hollerith data cards, and that we wish to read them from the card reader into the computer and print them out again. This can be done by using a DO statement as in Table A5-2. When the required number of cards have been read into the computer and printed out, the loop will terminate, and the program will stop.

TABLE A5-2. Use of a DO statement.

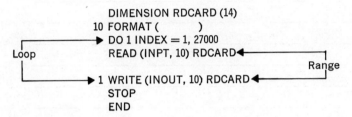

```
          DIMENSION RDCARD (14)
       10 FORMAT (       )
          DO 1 INDEX = 1, 27000
Loop      READ (INPT, 10) RDCARD
                                        Range
        1 WRITE (INOUT, 10) RDCARD
          STOP
          END
```

The range of the loop is indicated by the right-side bracket. The READ statement marks the beginning of the loop, and Statement 1 marks the end of the loop. Since it is generally a good idea only to write executable statements in a DO loop, the FORMAT statement appears in the program, but outside the loop. Having completed to Statement 1, the control loops back to the DO to increment. Then, the control tests the counter, INDEX against the test value. If the INDEX value is less than the maximum or test value, the range of the loop is again executed.

When the value of INDEX is just equal to the test value, the range of the loop is executed one more time, and control again loops back to the DO to satisfy the identity of the value of INDEX with the test value.

Having returned again to the DO, the value of INDEX is incremented and again tested. This time the value of INDEX would be greater than the test value, and the loop would terminate by having control branch to the STOP statement. The next statement executed would then be the one following the statement marking the end of the loop — i.e., Statement 1.

The CONTINUE statement is a dummy or nonoperative statement. Its primary use is as the end of a DO loop — the last statement of a DO must not transfer control. It is also used when an IF inside a DO LOOP is satisfied. Control may be transferred from the IF to the CONTINUE when the calculations in the DO are complete. A transfer within the DO cannot return to the DO itself unless one intends to start the DO again.

THE NESTED DO STATEMENT

Let us say that in the development of a FORTRAN program it is necessary to read some alphabetic names from Hollerith cards into the computer, store the data in a two-dimensional array — and be able to utilize the data elsewhere in the program. Let us further assume that there are 109 names and that each name requires 48 columns on a Hollerith card. Thus, we would have to envision a two-dimensional array that has 109 columns, each column with eight rows. We shall call the table ANAME. The table would be established with a DIMENSION statement as follows:

DIMENSION ANAME (8, 109)

Conceptually, the table would look as shown below:

ANAME   . . .

(ROW)

1   ____ ____ ____ ____ ____ ____ · · · ____

2   ____ ____ ____ ____ ____ ____ · · · ____

3   ____ ____ ____ ____ ____ ____ · · · ____

4   ____ ____ ____ ____ ____ ____ · · · ____

5   ____ ____ ____ ____ ____ ____ · · · ____

6   ____ ____ ____ ____ ____ ____ · · · ____

7   ____ ____ ____ ____ ____ ____ · · · ____

8   ____ ____ ____ ____ ____ ____ · · · ____

     (1)   (2)   (3)   (4)   (5)   (6)   (109)

COLUMNS

We have noted that each numbered core location in the computer is capable of handling 6 alphabet characters. Each name then requires eight sequential core locations. Therefore, in reading the names into the core table, it is necessary to store each name vertically in a given numbered column. Name 1 would go into Column 1, Name 2 would go into Column 2, Name 3 would go into Column 3, etc.

A DO loop to get the names into the proper location would be as shown below:

```
      DIMENSION ANAME (8, 109), RDCARD (8)
396   FORMAT (8A6)
      DO 1 J = 1, 109
      READ (INPT, 396) RDCARD
      DO 1 I = 1, 8
1     ANAME (I, J) = RDCARD (I)
```

First, the program dimensions the table ANAME — 109 columns with eight rows capable of containing 48 character positions in each column. Second, the DO statement is set up to go through a loop 109 times. The DO counter, named J, corresponds to the second dimensioned number in ANAME.[1] The next instruction following the DO statement is the READ instruction, which reads a card from an input unit (Hollerith card) and stores the data temporarily in the core array RDCARD. At this point in the loop, J has a value of 1; that is, reference is currently made to Column 1 of ANAME. However, both Column 1 of ANAME and RDCARD comprise eight storage locations. It is now necessary to get position 1 of RDCARD into Position 1 of Column 1 of ANAME, Position 2 of RDCARD into Position 2 of ANAME Column 1, etc. It would be possible to do this by a series of eight assignments:

```
      ANAME (1, J) = RDCARD (1)
      ANAME (2, J) = RDCARD (2)
      ANAME (3, J) = RDCARD (3)
      · · ·
      ANAME (8, J) — RDCARD (8)
```

[1]The general form of the table dimension ANAME is: ANAME (I, J).

We recall that J = 1 (Column 1 of ANAME). This value has been set by the initial value of J, when the first DO statement was encountered. At that point, J was set equal to 1, and there has been no occasion yet to change it.

The same thing, however, can be accomplished with a second DO statement as shown in the following example, which represents a second DO loop inside the first DO loop: DO 1 I = 1, 8. This permits all eight positions of RDCARD to be placed in the corresponding eight positions of ANAME (J) where J = 1. At this point, the end or lower limit of the first DO loop has been reached and control returns to the initial DO. The current value of J is incremented then checked against the J limit. If J is less than or equal to the J limit, the program loop is again executed. If J is greater than the J limit, the control next executes the statement following the lower limit of the loop.

It should be noted that the inside or second DO loop goes through eight cycles while the outer or first DO loop goes through one cycle. Can you properly note the range of both loops? The effect of these two DO loops is to properly place the data from the 109 Hollerith cards into the 109 columns of ANAME. If you understand this, you understand the function of the DO statement and the DO loop.

REVIEW AND CAUTION ON THE USE OF THE DO LOOP

The general form of the DO statement is:

DO n INDEX = M1, M2, M3

The n is the statement number marking the end of the loop. INDEX is the INTEGER variable name representing the index or counter. The value M1 represents the value to which INDEX is preset. The value M2 represents the upper limit — i.e., maximum value, or test value — of the counter. M3 is the value representing the amount of the increment to INDEX each time the loop is accomplished. It is important to correctly define the *range* of the loop. The range is from the first statement after the DO statement to the specified statement number that marks the end of the DO loop as follows:

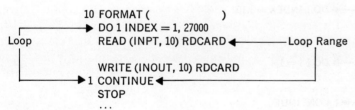

The range of the DO loop is quite distinct from the loop itself. In writing a DO statement as shown above:

1. n is a statement number.
2. INDEX is a nonsubscripted INTEGER variable name.
3. M1, M2, M3 are either nonsubscripted INTEGER variable names or (unsigned, nonzero) INTEGER constants.

When control passes to a DO statement from any point in the program except the last or end statement of the DO loop:

1. The value of the index variable name — i.e., INDEX, above — is preset to the *value of M1*.
2. Control now rests with the DO statement.

When the control goes back from the end statement of the DO loop to the DO statement:

1. The value of the index variable name — i.e., INDEX — is incremented by the given amount.
2. The amount of the increment is either the value specified by M3, or is 1 if M3 is not specified.
3. The value of the index variable name is tested against the test value — i.e., M2 — to determine whether the loop is satisfied or not.

If the loop is not satisfied — i.e., if INDEX is less than or equal to M2 — the range of the loop is executed again. If the loop is satisfied — i.e., if INDEX is greater than M2 — control moves to the statement following the last statement of the *range*.

The last statement of a DO loop must be executable but must *not* be a CONTROL statement:

a) any GO TO statement (unconditional, computed, or assigned),
b) any IF statement,
c) another DO statement,
d) a STOP statement, or
e) a RETURN statement (discussed below).

It is often desired to have one of these prohibited statements as the last statement in a DO loop. However, since this is prohibited, the CONTINUE statement is used as the last statement, and the prohibited statement follows the CONTINUE statement.

In using DO loops, it is never permissible to change the values of INDEX, M1, M2, M3 by any statements inside the *range* of the loop.

When establishing a loop, it is permissible to have a second loop inside the first; and it is also permissible to branch out of a loop before it is satisfied. If a branch is made out of a loop, the value of INDEX is reserved for later use.

A. Nested or DO statements: *Proper*

```
     ┌──► DO 1 INDEX = 1,100
     │      ...
     │      ...
     │      ...
     │  ┌─► DO 1 I = 1,4
     │  │    ...
     │  │    ...
     └──┴─► 1 CONTINUE
```

B. Nested DO Loops: *Proper*

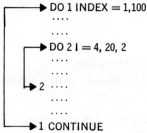

```
     ┌──► DO 1 INDEX = 1,100
     │      ....
     │      ....
     │  ┌─► DO 2 I = 4, 20, 2
     │  │    ....
     │  │    ....
     │  └─► 2 ....
     │      ....
     │      ....
     └────► 1 CONTINUE
```

C. Nested DO Loops: *Incorrect*

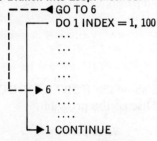

```
        ┌──► DO 1 INDEX = 1, 100
        │    ....
        │    ....
        │    ....
        │    ....
        │  ┌──► DO 2 J = 1, 60
        │  │  ....
        └──┼► 1 CONTINUE
           │  ....
           │  ....
           │  ....
           └─► 2 ....
```

D. Branch Into Loop: *Incorrect*

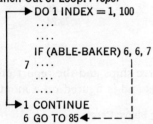

```
   ┌ ─ ─ ─◄ GO TO 6
   │   ┌── DO 1 INDEX = 1, 100
   │   │   ...
   │   │   ...
   │   │   ...
   │   │   ...
   └─►│ 6 ....
       │   ....
       │   ....
       └─►1 CONTINUE
```

E. Branch Out of Loop: *Proper*

```
   ┌──► DO 1 INDEX = 1, 100
   │    ....
   │    ....
   │    IF (ABLE-BAKER) 6, 6, 7 ┐
 7 │ ....                       │
   │    ....                    │
   │    ....                    │
   └──►1 CONTINUE               │
     6 GO TO 85◄ ─ ─ ─ ─ ─ ─ ─ ─┘
```

QUESTIONS
FOR DISCUSSION

1. Some of the following DO statements (loops) are wrong. Which are wrong and why?

   a. IF (I .EQ. 1) GO TO 2
       DO 2 I = 2, 10
     2 S = S + A (I)

   b. DO 3, J = 5, N
     3 READ (5, 2) A (J)

   c. DO 4 I = 1, 10
     4 WRITE (6, 6) A(M)

   d. DO 5 L = 1, N(J)
     5 S = S

   e. DO 6 M = 1, N − 1
     6 X(M) = M

   f. DO 7 I, J = 1, N
     7 C (I, J) = A(I, J) + B(I, J)

g. DO 8 I = 1, N
  7 I = 1
  S = S + A (I)
  I = I + 1
  IF (I .LE. N) GO TO 7
  8 CONTINUE

2. What is wrong with the following program segment? Why is it wrong?

   GO TO 10
   DO 9, J = 1, 30
   10 X = Y + ABLE
   9 A = Z**3

3. Are each of the following DO statements comparable — that is, will each count up to 37? Explain why or why not.

   DO 3 I = 3, 40, 1
   DO 3 I = 2, 74, 2
   DO 3 I = 317, 353, 1

4. Assume the following inventory situation and show the FORTRAN DO program to calculate the value of the inventory. Discuss the program.

Number	Quantity	Value per Unit
1	340	$ 7.53
2	4210	.49
3	27	39.24
. . .	. . .	. . .
25	743	4.56

5. Assume that the Puritan Company has three ships and the report on the total cargo carried is submitted each six months and is figured on a monthly basis.

Month	Sailing Ships: Cargo		
	1	2	3
1	4300 tons	1214 tons	7416 tons
2	7200	3916	9416
3	2400	3844	8421
4	8600	3641	9163
5	9431	1824	8614
6	1826	1601	7921

Write a program with a DO loop in it to calculate and print total tonnage hauled for each month, tonnage for six months, total tons by ship, and average monthly tonnage hauled by ship.

(*Hint:* A variable with 2 subscripts [rows and columns] is called a matrix. The dimensioned variable would be TONS (6,3). The first subscript shows the number of months. The second shows the number of ships. To start the problem, let TOTAL 1, TOTAL 2, and TOTAL 3 equal the total tons for each of the three ships. The total tonnage for the first ship would be:

   TOTAL1 = 0.
   DO 10 I = 1, 6
   10 TOTAL1 = TOTAL1 + TONS (I, 1)

Following this example, work out the rest of the problem.

6. Using the New York ships study in Chapter 3, refer to the A-Card (which you have designed). Write a program with a DO statement in it to READ the

A-Cards (14,000), and calculate the average tonnage of each of the following types of vessels:

SHIP	PINK
SLOOP	GALLEY
BRIGN	SNOW
SCHNR	BRIG

7. A variation on the DO statement is the implied DO, as shown below. Discuss this to be sure that you understand how it works. What data (type and form) will be transmitted from the computer by the following WRITE statements?

```
1. DIMENSION ABLE (100, 33)
   DO 1 J = 1, 33
1 WRITE (6,3) (ABLE (I,J), I = 1, 100)
3 FORMAT (- - -)
```

Why does the WRITE statement contain an implied DO?

A6

Subprograms

INTRODUCTION

In the preceding chapters we discussed the components of a FORTRAN program — the "initializing" part, the input section, the main body, the output section, and the termination. Normally, since the input and output sections of the program are separate routines, they are referred to as the input/output part of the program or the I/O section.

The initializing segment of the program specifies variable names, arrays, and explicit type statements. The main body of the program contains the statements that comprise the actual calculation to be done. The input/output routines, or segments, provide for getting data into the computer and for printing out or otherwise outputting the results. The termination of the program comprises the STOP and END statements.

The FORTRAN program is executed sequentially, statement by statement, beginning with the first FORTRAN source program statement and ending with the last one. Whenever the normal execution of the program is interrupted by an IF test or a GO TO statement, the program control branches to the designated statement, and then continues to execute statements sequentially beginning with the statement to which control branched.

The final conceptual element of a FORTRAN program involves a *branch out of the main program* to a designated subprogram. A subprogram is an independent program that operates within the framework established by the main program. A subprogram is always at least one FORTRAN statement in length. As far as we are concerned, it always represents a program branch out of the main program to a subprogram. The subprogram is a complete program that carries out an operation or a series of operations and then provides certain answers or calculated values back to the main program. The values provided by the subprogram are then used in further calculation by the main program.

Figure A6-1 illustrates the basic idea of a subprogram. The main program simply illustrates a series of steps in which data are read into the computer, certain tests are made, certain calculations are performed, and the answers are printed out. The program executes each statement in the FORTRAN source program, step by step, sequentially. In the event of a test, the program control branches according to the noted arrow.

252

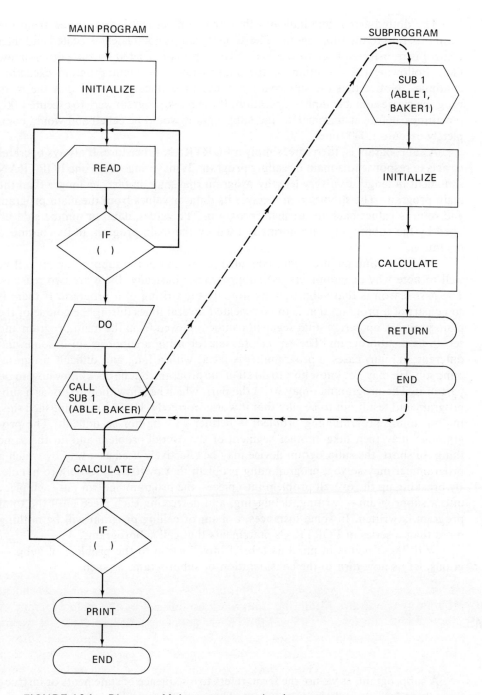

FIGURE A6-1. Diagram: Main program and subprogram.

Just over half-way down the flowchart (which represents the program) there is a box labeled CALL SUBI. This represents a control statement to the compiler that program control is to leave the main program and to begin executing he subprogram. Information in the main program may be transferred to the subprogram if desired. Information in or developed by the subprogram may be transferred back to the main program (also known as the calling program).

The dotted-arrow line indicates that program control is transferred from the main program to the subprogram. The subprogram is completely executed and then control is transferred back to the main program (as indicated by the dotted-arrow line). Following the execution of the subprogram, the main program execution continues. Notice that the subprogram is executed once *each time* that the main program carries out a complete operation. If the main program were to execute 1,000 repetitions before it terminated, the subprogram would be called and would completely execute 1,000 times.

A subprogram is, therefore, simply a FORTRAN procedure. It always operates or acts in response to a main or calling program. It may range from one FORTRAN statement in length to a very lengthy program that may, in fact, be longer than the main program. The subprogram receives its data or values from the main program and returns values back to the main program. The values, data, or numbers developed by the subprogram are normally used by the main program in its continued operation.

Before continuing into a more detailed discussion of the subprogram, it will be well to note why programmers use subprograms. Basically, there are two reasons. The *first* reason is that subprograms simplify the writing of a program. If there is some part of a program that is to be repeated several times during the course of the main program operation, that segment can be removed from the main program and set up as a subprogram. The *second* reason for using a subprogram is somewhat different; in many cases, a programmer is faced with a long and difficult programming job. He may not know how to do all of the program, but he does know how to do part of it. The programmer may write the part, which he knows how to do, as a subprogram and test it out to be sure that it works correctly. Having accomplished this, the remaining programming problem is neither so long nor so difficult. The programmer may then take another segment of the overall problem and do the same thing. In short, the subprogram device may be effectively used as a way by which a programmer may solve a programming problem that by itself is too big to handle. By breaking up the overall problem into pieces, the programmer can put each piece into a subprogram — writing, debugging, and correcting each piece until the total program is written. In some instances, a main or calling program will be nothing more than a series of FORTRAN statements that call subprograms.

With these points in mind as a brief introduction to the problem of subprograms, let us now turn to the consideration of subprograms as such.

TYPES OF SUBPROGRAMS

A subprogram, as we use the term, refers to a sequence of statements or instructions that carry out a desired procedure. The result of the subprogram operation is incorporated into a main or calling program.

Most FORTRAN compilers recognize one or more of the following categories of subprograms:

1. Statement functions provided in program.
2. Intrinsic functions compiled in line — FORTRAN IV.
3. External functions supplementary to FORTRAN IV compiler.
4. External subroutines provided as separate program.

We might distinguish between functions and subroutines as follows:

A. A function is a procedure or method of calculating a *single* specified value needed in a FORTRAN program. A function call must appear within an expression; it may not appear by itself in a program.

B. A subroutine may return many values to the main program. It may appear by itself in a program.

The basic difference between a function and subroutine is that a function may develop a *single* value which can be used in the main program, while a subroutine may return *any number* of values. These points should be kept in mind, as they will be considered below.

Statement function

A programmer, in the course of developing his program, will often find it necessary to carry out a relatively simple calculation several times in the program. In many instances, this needed calculation will not be supplied by the FORTRAN system. In this situation the programmer has two choices. He can simply write out the desired calculation each time that it is needed, or he can write what is known as a statement function.

The first step in developing and using a statement function is to designate a *name* for the function. The name follows the normal naming conventions of variables in FORTRAN. Following the name, the argument appears in parentheses. The argument refers to the number or value that is to be used in the calculation. We noted above that a programmer will often find it necessary to carry out or perform some calculation. The result of the calculation may be referred to as the value. An example may be helpful.

Let us say that a businessman is trying to estimate the sales of his product. The man sells his product in 180 cities. The man notices that each time the average income of the city increases by any amount, his product sales will go up by:

$$E = -6Y^2 + 60Y + 80.$$

In the formula, E refers to the magnitude of expenditures on the product, Y refers to the *change in income.*

Thus, in programming to determine how his sales will vary in each city, the businessman notes that if he applies the formula to the Department of Commerce estimated personal income by cities, he can forecast reasonably accurately his changes in sales by city. The businessman also realizes that the formula is pragmatic rather than ideally theoretical.

Thus, in setting up his computer program he knows that he must calculate E for each city in order to make up his own production schedule: E is then the value of the expression.

$$E \text{ (Value)} = -6Y^2 + 60Y + 80. \text{ (Expression)}$$

Since the businessman "knows" the change in income for each city, he knows what Y is. In this example, Y is the argument, E is the value of the expression. When the expression is calculated, it has a value represented by E.

We can assume now that the name of the statement function is SALE, and that it would appear in a main program as follows:

Name of Statement Function

```
...
SALES = SALE(Y)
...
```
Argument

The statement function itself causes a particular operation to be carried out and a single value returned to the main or calling program. In short, in order to use that statement function in a FORTRAN source program it is necessary to have: 1) a statement function, 2) a call for the statement function. The point is that the value of "Y" is the key in estimating product sales. The variable name Y is the *argument* of the calling statement in the main program. The value of Y has been determined elsewhere in the main program or is given. The *name* of the statement function is SALE.

The statement function describes a given relationship that must be worked out. The statement function is in the following form:

$$SALE(X) = (-6.*X**2) + 60.*X + 80.$$
$$\quad\; 1 \quad\; 2 \qquad\qquad 3$$

The statement function itself is divided into three separate parts as numbered above:

1. The name (label) of the statement function.
2. The dummy argument name. (They are called dummy arguments because they take their values from the statement call. The argument [Y] in the statement call replaces the dummy argument [X] in the statement function.)
3. The arithmetic expression which is evaluated. (This expression is calculated to determine the value [estimate of sales] using the argument [Y or income]. The *value* is then returned to the main program as the replacement for SALE [Y]. This value is then used in the main program.)

The statement function must be written once in any calling program; it may be used any number of times in a program by inserting the function name and argument(s) in an expression.

The example above uses only a single argument in the statement call (Y), and a single dummy argument in the statement function. The general forms of the *statement call* and the *statement function* are as shown below:

Statement Call: NAME (A,D)
Statement Function: NAME (c, f) = EXPRESSION

Subprogram functions

In some cases it is necessary to have a subprogram function perform an operation that requires more than one statement. In this instance, FORTRAN users are provided with two types of functions: Intrinsic functions and External functions. A function is simply a statement of a relationship among values, some of which are variables. In the statement function discussed above, the estimate value of sales (E) was related to (dependent upon) the expression:

$$E \text{ (Value)} = -6Y^2 + 60Y + 80 \text{ (Expression)}$$

In the expression, Y is a variable, 6, 60, and 80 are constants. The value of the expression (E) depends upon (is related to) the value of Y. This relationship of one value (E) to other values is a (functional) relationship. In any event, the function is a procedure for ascertaining a particular relationship or for carrying out a particular operation.

Intrinsic functions

In many instances, certain subprograms will be required by nearly everyone using the computer, whether the problem involved is statistical, mathematical, engineering, or other. For instance, one type of operation that almost every programmer will have to do at one time or another is to convert an INTEGER value to a REAL value, and the reverse.

An alternative to writing all the steps in a FORTRAN source program form is to write a generalized subprogram that becomes a part of the FORTRAN compiler. This kind of subprogram is *external* to any program but is *internal* to a particular computer-compiler system. This kind of subprogram that is internal to a computer-compiler system is called an *intrinsic function*.

Intrinsic functions carry out a single operation; for instance, the use of the word FLOAT in a FORTRAN source program causes a constant to be converted from INTEGER to REAL mode. The standard intrinsic functions available to most FORTRAN IV systems are shown in Table A6-1.

External functions

External functions are subprograms that are external to a given program and external to a given compiler-computer system. These external functions are often called *library functions* in that they are *written* and stored (on cards or tape) to be used as desired. The library function is external to the compiler-computer system and must be made available to the compiler system usually together with the main FORTRAN source program. The general form used to call an external function is:

$$\text{NAME}^1 \quad (\text{A}_1, \text{A}_2)$$

Part 1   Part 2

Part 1 of the call is the source program label for the function called. Part 2 consists of the arguments. The arguments are the variables used to compute the value of the function.

The external function call SQRT (16) would instruct the subprogram execution to calculate the square root of 16 (the argument). The resultant value will then be returned to the main program for use. For instance, in the program segment:

```
    ...
    A = SQRT (16.)
    C = A + 3
```

The square root of the argument (16.) is calculated by the subprogram function and is assigned to A. A is then used in ascertaining the value of C. A second example is:

```
    ...
    A = SQRT (ABLE/4.) + BAKER
    ...
```

---

[1]Some FORTRAN compilers require the designation: NAMEF (arguments). For instance, in calling the external function to calculate square roots, one uses either **SQRT** (arguments) or **SQRTF** (arguments), depending on the given compiler.

TABLE A6-1.   Instrinsic functions*

INTRINSIC FUNCTION	DEFINITION	NUMBER OF ARGUMENTS	SYMBOLIC NAME	TYPE OF	
				ARGUMENT	FUNCTION
Absolute Value	$|a|$	1	ABS	Real	Real
			IABS	Integer	Integer
			DABS	Double	Double (Precision)
Truncation	sign of a times largest integer $\leqq |a|$	1	AINT	Real	Real
			INT	Real	Integer
			IDINT	Double	Integer
Remaindering	$a_1 \pmod{a_2}$	2	AMOD	Real	Real
			MOD	Integer	Integer
Choosing Largest Value	Max $(a_1, a_2, ..)$	$\geqq 2$	AMAX0	Integer	Real
			AMAX1	Real	Real
			MAX0	Integer	Integer
			MAX1	Real	Integer
			DMAX1	Double	Double
Choosing Smallest Value	Min $(a_1, a_2, ...)$	$\geqq 2$	AMIN0	Integer	Real
			AMIN1	Real	Real
			MIN0	Integer	Integer
			MIN1	Real	Integer
			DMIN1	Double	Double
Float	conversion from integer to real	1	FLOAT	Integer	Real
Fix	conversion from real to integer	1	IFIX	Real	Integer
Transfer of Sign	sign of a_2 times $|a_1|$	2	SIGN	Real	Real
			ISIGN	Integer	Integer
			DSIGN	Double	Double
Positive Difference	$a_1 -$ Min (a_1, a_2)	2	DIM	Real	Real
			IDIM	Integer	Integer
Obtain Most Significant Part of Double Precision Argument		1	SNGL	Double	Real
Obtain Real Part of Complex Argument		1	REAL	Complex	Real
Obtain Imaginary Part of Complex Argument		1	AIMAG	Complex	Real
Express Single Precision Argument in Double-Precision Form		1	DBLE	Real	Double
Express Two Real Arguments in Complex Form	$a_1 + a_2 \sqrt{-1}$	2	COMPLX	Real	Complex
Obtain Conjugate of a Complex Argument		1	CONJG	Complex	Complex

*"FORTRAN vs. Basic FORTRAN", *Communications of the ACM*, Vol. 7, No. 10 (Oct., 1964), p. 616, reprinted by Permission.

In this instance, the value of ABLE is divided by 4 and the square root is calculated by the subprogram. The square root is returned to the main program replacing (essentially) the call:

$$\ldots \text{SQRT (ABLE/4.)} \ldots$$

The calculated square root value is added to BAKER. The sum is then assigned to A.

The subprogram operation calculates the value and returns the calculated value to the main program.

```
       DIMENSION LIST
                 "
                 "
                 "
  ****   SIGMA5 = SQRT (SQD5*(SQSUD5/CN) )/(CN-1.)
                 "
                 "
                 "
       PRINT 999, X LIST
         ...
       END
```

The point is that at the stage in the program indicated by the asterisks (*) series, it is necessary to obtain the *square root* divided by (CN−1.) of an expression and to assign that *square root* to the variable name SIGMA5. (SQD5*(SQSUD5/CN)) is evaluated to obtain a single numeric value according to the rules of evaluation of FORTRAN expressions.

Starting with the innermost set of parentheses — i.e., (SQSUD5/CN) — the value of SQSUD5 is divided by the value of CN. This value is then multiplied times SQD5 to obtain a value. Use of the external function[2] SQRT causes the *square root* of the numeric value of the expression to be obtained.

This square root is a number that we shall identify as n. The expression now looks like:

$$\text{SIGMA} = n/(CN-1)$$

In the example above, the value of the function is divided by (CN−1). This result is then assigned to SIGMA.

This square root is returned to the main program replacing the value of the original expression. The original number(s) to be evaluated by the function are called the ARGUMENT(S) of the function. The value returned to the main program is referred to simply as the square root.

There are ten basic external functions that will operate with most FORTRAN IV systems, as illustrated on Table A6-2.

As seen above, the FORTRAN IV functions are primarily oriented to mathematical or statistical uses. As with other topics discussed in the book, it is necessary to turn to your computer manual to determine exactly which types of intrinsic and external functions are available to your computer system.

Subroutine subprograms[3]

Subroutine subprograms differ from functions in three ways. *First*, there is no value associated with subroutine name. All outputs are defined in terms of the

[2]Function is external to the main program but internal to the FORTRAN IV library routines.

[3]For explanation of a function subprogram, see the computer manual for your FORTRAN system.

TABLE A6-2. Basic external functions*

EXTERNAL FUNCTION	FORTRAN SOURCES PROGRAM FORM	NUMBER OF ARGUMENTS	USED WITH DATA TYPES
EXPONENTIAL	EXP (Argument)	1	Real
	DEXP (Argument)	1	Double Precision
	CEX (Argument)	1	Complex
NATURAL LOGARITHM	ALOG (Argument)	1	Real
	DLOG (Argument)	1	Double Precision
	CLOG (Argument)	1	Complex
COMMON LOGARITHM	ALOG 10 (Argument)	1	Real
	DLOG 10 (Argument)	1	Double Precision
TRIGONOMETRIC SINE	SIN (Argument)	1	Real
	DSIN (Argument)	1	Double Precision
	CSIN (Argument)	1	Complex
TRIGONOMETRIC COSINE	COS (Argument)	1	Real
	DCOS (Argument)	1	Double Precision
	CCOS (Argument)	1	Complex
HYPERBOLIC TANGENT	TANH (Argument)	1	Real
SQUARE ROOT	SQRT (Argument)	1	Real
	DSQRT (Argument)	1	Double Precision
	CSQRT (Argument)	1	Complex
AVC TANGENT	ATAN (Argument)	1	Real
	DTAN (Argument)	1	Double Precision
	ATAN2 (Argument 1, Argument 2)	2	Real
REMAINDERING	DMOD (Argument 1, Argument 2)	2	Double Precision
MODULUS	CABS (Argument)	1	Complex

*"FORTRAN vs. Basic FORTRAN," *Communications of the ACM*, Vol. 7, No. 10 (Oct., 1964), p. 617, reprinted by permission.

arguments, and there may be any number of outputs. *Second,* a subroutine is not called into action or referenced by writing its name — a CALL statement is necessary to specify the *arguments* (data input) and *results* (data output). *Third,* subroutines permit the use of various types of storage areas that allow getting data into a subroutine from a main program, and the reverse.

The general idea is that a subroutine is a complete series of steps that completes one or more calculations for the main program. The general form of the subroutine CALL is:

CALL NAME (A₁, A₂, A₃, . . . Aₙ)

The word CALL simply alerts the compiler that the *next* executed instruction will be the first executable instruction in the named subroutine. NAME, as used here, is simply the label of a given subroutine. The first executable instruction in a subroutine is the one immediately following the *NAME* statement of the subroutine. The diagram in Figure A6-2 shows schematically the way in which a main program and subprogram subroutine are set up.

As shown by the arrows, the development of the program begins with the main program. The main-program execution proceeds (as indicated by the arrows) until a subroutine CALL is encountered. The CALL indicates the name of the subroutine

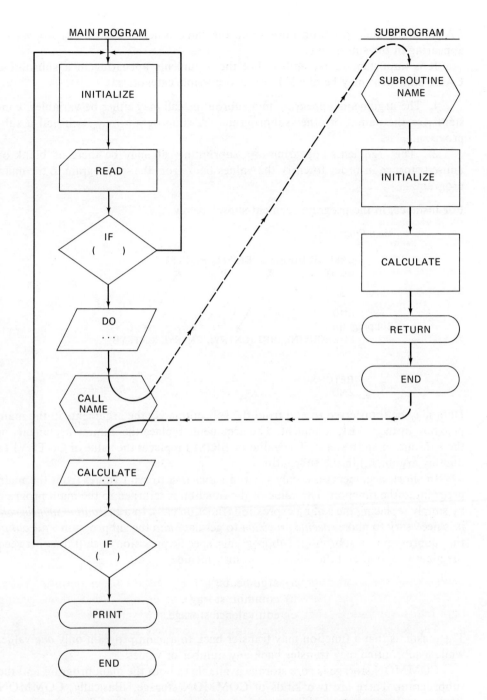

FIGURE A6-2.   Flowchart: Generalized main program—subprogram.

i.e., NAME — and the names of the three arguments (A_1, A_2, A_3). In the operation of the subroutine, A_1 replaces X_8, A_2 replaces X_2, and A_3 replaces B_{13}. The subroutine is executed until the statement RETURN is encountered. The control then returns to the main program. Execution of the main program continues with the first statement *following* the subroutine CALL. A subroutine is written in general terms using *dummy arguments*. The arguments actually transferred to the subroutine contain the values actually used. The second point is that arguments presented in the

CALL in the main program must be in the same order as the *dummy arguments* appearing in the subroutine.

It is important to remember that the arguments appearing in a subroutine CALL statement may be divided into two possible categories:

1. The arguments appearing in a subroutine call may either be variables, constants, or the names of other subprograms. A subprogram may itself call a subprogram.

2. The arguments appearing in a subroutine call may be there as blank or unused storage in order to carry the values back from the subprogram to the main program.

For instance, in the program segment shown below:

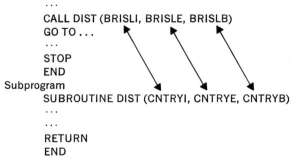

```
Main Program
        ...
        CALL DIST (BRISLI, BRISLE, BRISLB)
        GO TO ...
        ...
        STOP
        END
Subprogram
        SUBROUTINE DIST (CNTRYI, CNTRYE, CNTRYB)
        ...
        ...
        RETURN
        END
```

Data may be transferred to and from the subroutine via the arguments in the main program in the CALL statement. The arguments replace the dummy arguments of the subroutine and reverse. The value of BRISLI replaces the value of CNTRYI (a dummy argument) in the subroutine.

In short, arguments are only used in a *function* to send values from the main program to the function. The value of the function is returned to the main program by simply replacing the calling expression (function call). In a *subroutine subprogram* it is necessary to make *specific provision* to get data *into* the subprogram and *out of* the subprogram. In subroutine subprograms, specific provision to shift data between the main program and the subprogram may include,

   a) arguments,
   b) common storage,
   c) equivalence storage.

The reason is that a function may transfer back to a main program only *one* value, while a subroutine may transfer back any number of values.

COMMON storage is core storage available to both the main program and the subprogram. There are two kinds of COMMON storage.[4] Basically, COMMON storage assigns two variable names — or arrays, etc. — in different programs (main program and subprogram) *to the same core storage location(s)*.

The first and most usual kind of COMMON is unlabeled or blank COMMON. The general form of the COMMON statement is:

   COMMON NAME1, NAME2, NAME3, . . . NAMEi

---

[4]Unlabeled COMMON is usually available to most or all FORTRAN systems, FORTRAN II and FORTRAN IV. Labeled COMMON is not available to all systems and has rather specialized uses. In using COMMON, it is urged that the reader consult the computer manual for the computer-compiler available.

The labels NAME1, etc., indicate the variable names or array names that are allocated to COMMON storage. All the rules for handling arrays hold for arrays in COMMON. The COMMON statement must appear in both of the programs (program and subprograms) using the COMMON statement.

Main Program	Subprogram
...	...
COMMON ABLE (100), BAKER (15)	COMMON BLACK (100), TABLE (15)
...	...

The variable or array names that appear in the COMMON statements in the two routines are identified not by the label (NAME) but by their *location* in the series of names following the word COMMON.

In the example above, the array ABLE in the main program and the array BLOCK in the subprogram are assigned to the same defined core storage. There are certain differences allowed here, but it is a good rule to have the dimensioned variables for arrays and tables in COMMON storage specified to the same length.

Labeled COMMON is defined as named or identified COMMON. The general form of labeled COMMON is:

COMMON/LABEL/NAME1, NAME2, ... NAMEi

When using COMMON storage, it is necessary to take great care in lining up the elements. This can become a real problem when dealing with double precision or complex data. The value of labeled COMMON is that it insures that the array or table elements are precisely aligned in the COMMON storage by the use of subscripts.

Unlabeled COMMON will be more often used in normal social science programming. The programmer should be careful to consult the manual for his particular FORTRAN system before attempting to use labeled or unlabeled COMMON.

In the subroutine illustrated above, the use of COMMON storage would cause the noted changes:

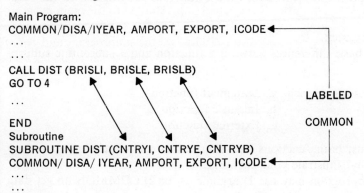

```
Main Program:
COMMON/DISA/IYEAR, AMPORT, EXPORT, ICODE
...
...
CALL DIST (BRISLI, BRISLE, BRISLB)
GO TO 4
...                                          LABELED

END                                          COMMON
Subroutine
SUBROUTINE DIST (CNTRYI, CNTRYE, CNTRYB)
COMMON/ DISA/ IYEAR, AMPORT, EXPORT, ICODE
...
...
RETURN
END
```

The arguments shown above are transferred into the subroutine from the main program. Any data in the COMMON block DISA is available to both the main program and to the subroutine. Data in COMMON may be *used* or *modified* in or by both the subroutine and the main program.

EQUIVALENCE is also a means of altering the normal procedure of the FORTRAN compiler. An EQUIVALENCE statement is defined as a statement that assigns two different variable or array names to the same core locations in the same program or subprogram.

The general form of this statement is:

$$\text{EQUIVALENCE (NAME1, NAME2, ..., ABLE, BAKER, ...)}$$

Each pair of parentheses indicates the variable or array names that are to occupy the same storage location. The user should consult his computer FORTRAN manual before using the EQUIVALENCE statement.

QUESTIONS FOR DISCUSSION

1. Define: a. Argument
   b. Dummy argument
   c. Common
   d. Blank common
   e. Labeled common
   f. Equivalence

2. Give three reasons for using subprograms. Discuss the reasons with others in the class.

3. Can FORTRAN programs be written without bothering with subprograms? If so, why use them?

4. Can the name of a subroutine subprogram be used in a FORTRAN expression?

5. Is a subprogram a complete program by itself? Is this true even if the subprogram is only one statement long?

6. In most subprograms, a *branch* occurs out of the main program to the subprogram. Is this also true of the statement function?

7. a. In function subprograms, how is information transmitted from the main program to the subprogram?
   b. How is information returned from the function subprogram to the main program?

8. Define a subprogram.

9. What are the basic differences between a function and a subroutine subprogram?

10. Contrast and illustrate each: a. Statement function
    b. Intrinsic function
    c. External function

11. In subprograms, both functions and subroutines are written using dummy arguments. Why? Illustrate your answers.

12. Subroutine subprogram may use 1) arguments, or 2) COMMON to get data into and out of the subprogram. Explain each of these methods and why each would be used.

13. The nature of a function is that the value calculated is automatically returned to the main program.
    a. How is this done?
    b. How many values may be returned?

14. A subroutine must provide its own way of getting data back to the main program.
    a. How is this done?
    b. How many values may be returned?

15. To document a program so that anyone may use the program, the following steps are involved:

    1. Statement of the problem.
    2. List of data names and mnemonics.
    3. Input and output formats.
    4. Sample I/O listings.
    5. Instructions for use of program.
    6. Description of program.
    7. Numerical, arithmetic, statistical or other analysis.
    8. Report on program reliability.
    9. Flowchart and list or program.
   10. Error and warning messages.

Discuss the use of program documentation. What types of information should be included in each of the ten points above? What is the most effective way of keying the points noted to the program?

GLOSSARY

ADDRESS — The label of the core-storage location by which that location is identified (an identifier).

ALGORITHM — A procedure to be used in solving a problem (a recipe).

ALPHABETIC DATA — Data consisting of the letters of the alphabet.

ALPHAMERIC CHARACTER — Refers to any one of the 46 characters, digits, and special characters that comprise the standard FORTRAN alphabet.

ALPHANUMERIC CHARACTER — Any letter, number, or special character (comma, etc.) recognized by FORTRAN. A component part of the FORTRAN language.

ANALYSIS — The process of breaking an issue into its component parts.

ARITHMETIC "IF" TEST — A test with subsequent transfer of control based on the value of an expression being a number that is:

> EQUAL TO ZERO
> LESS THAN ZERO
> GREATER THAN ZERO.

ARITHMETIC/LOGICAL UNIT — (Computer functional unit). Performs the basic arithmetic operations (addition, subtraction, multiplication, and division). Performs the logical operations.

ARITHMETIC OPERATORS — Special Characters:

Defined Symbol	Process Performed
+	Addition
−	Subtraction
*	Multiplication
/	Division
**	Exponentiation

ARGUMENT — (Function). The variable name representing the variables (data) transferred from the main program to the subprogram.

ARGUMENT — (Subroutine). The variable names representing the variables (data) transferred from the main program to the subprogram *and the reverse*.

ARRAY — A variable named structure in computer storage that is subscripted (see DIMENSION STATEMENT).

BEGINNING — (of DO loop). The first FORTRAN source program statement after the DO statement.

BRANCH — A synonym for "transfer of control."

CANNED PROGRAM — (Standardized program). A program written by another programmer to perform a standard statistical or mathematical operation or routine that is available to any programmer.

CHARACTER — Any letter of the FORTRAN alphabet, number, digit, or special character — e.g., period, comma.

CLOSED-FORMAT PROGRAM — A canned program that has the capacity to use only that format layout which is supplied by the program.

CODE — To change data from one form to another — e.g., from English to Morse code, English to Hollerith code; sometimes used to mean changing an algorithm into a program.

COMMENT CARD — Indicated by a C in Column 1 of the program Hollerith card, this card contains a comment for the programmer and is ignored by the compiler.

COMPLEX CONSTANT — See CONSTANT.

COMMON STATEMENT — A FORTRAN statement that assigns variable or array names in two separate programs (subprograms) to the same storage location.

COMPUTER — A machine consisting of five functional units or parts:

1. Input unit (transfers data into core storage).
2. Output unit (transfers data out of core storage).
3. Storage unit (computer memory or core).
4. Arithmetic/logical unit (performs arithmetic operations and logical operations).
5. Control unit (serves as supervisor of program operation and data flow).

COMPUTER SYSTEM — Synonym for computer and the associated control programs (software).

CONDITIONAL TRANSFER OF CONTROL — Transfer of control occurs when a specified condition is met. See DEFAULT CONDITION OF COMPILER.

CONSTANT — A fixed and unvarying quantity, of which there are six types of constants:

1. Integer constant (a whole number written *without* a decimal point).
2. Real constant (a number written *with* a decimal point; it may include the letter "E" followed by an Integer Constant).
3. Logical constant (there are only two logical constants — .TRUE. and .FALSE.).
4. Complex constant (a pair of real constants separated by a comma and enclosed in parentheses).
5. Double-precision Constant (assumes several forms [see your own computer manual], a real constant with a "D" instead of an "E"), see page 202.
6. Hollerith constant. See your FORTRAN manual or Chapter A-2, p. 218.

CONTINUATION CARD — Used in writing a FORTRAN source program when one FORTRAN *statement* requires more than *one* Hollerith card.

CONTROL UNIT — (Computer functional unit). This unit controls the movement of information among the various computer functional units. It also interprets and performs the sequences of operations provided by the program in solving the problem.

DATA — Data are observations.

DATA DENSITY — Measured by the number of characters that can be stored in a given unit of a storage medium:

1. Hollerith cards (low density — 80 characters per card).
2. Magnetic tape (high density — 800 characters per inch).

DATA MATRIX — A two-dimensional array for storing data (see DIMENSION STATEMENT).

DEFAULT CONDITION OF COMPILER — The procedure or action of the compiler in absence of a specific contrary instruction. Among the default conditions of FORTRAN compilers: each program will be executed sequentially from the first statement to the last; a variable name beginning with I, J, K, L, M, N is assumed to be an INTEGER variable name.

DIGIT — 0, 1, 2, 3, 4, 5, 6, 7, 8, or 9

DIGITAL COMPUTER — Computer that deals with numbers as discrete units — e.g., numeric digits.

DIMENSION STATEMENT — Defines a variable name to include more than one core location. The statement, DIMENSION NAME (50), defines the label NAME to contain 50 consecutive core locations. This refers to a single column of data (numbers) that is often called a (column) *vector*. DIMENSION NAME (50,50) defines the label NAME to contain a table with 50 columns and 50 rows in each column. This is often called a data matrix.

DOMAIN — (of algorithm). The acceptable input quantities to be used in the algorithm.

DOUBLE-PRECISION CONSTANT — See CONSTANT

DUMMY ARGUMENT — The variable names used in writing the subprogram. Argument values replace the dummy argument values when the subprogram is executed.

ENTER (or input) — To physically present data into a computer for processing by the computer.

EQUIVALANCE STATEMENT — A FORTRAN statement that assigns different variable or array names to the same storage location *in the same program*.

EXPLICIT-TYPE STATEMENT — A FORTRAN source program statement that overrides the default condition of the compiler. These include:

1. Dimension statement (to define a variable name to include more than one core location).
2. Integer, real, double-precision, complex, logical type statements (to define any variable name to assume the form and character indicated).

EXPRESSION — One or more terms connected by operations signs or operators.

FIELD — A series of characters comprising a discrete, unique or complete unit.

FILE — All of the records on some defined topic (a collection of records).

FLOWCHART — A geometric picture of the method of solving a problem — a symbolic algorithm.

FORMAT — The layout of data — e.g., in fields located somewhere on Hollerith cards or other input and output device records.

FORTRAN — A language allowing instructions to be written for directing computer operations.

FORTRAN COMPILER — A program that translates FORTRAN language to machine language for a given computer (see COMPUTER SYSTEM).

FORTRAN CONSTANT — A quantity or value that represents itself (see CONSTANT).

FORTRAN PROGRAM — A series of statements written according to the rules of FORTRAN using the FORTRAN alphabet.

FORTRAN STATEMENT — An instruction written in FORTRAN. There are four types of FORTRAN statements: input/output, arithmetic/logical, control, specification (definition). The FORTRAN statement is written on Columns 1–72 of a Hollerith card.

FORTRAN VARIABLE — (Name). The label given to a specific location in computer core storage.

FUNCTION — A subprogram that may return one value to the main program. It is at least one statement in length.

INCREMENT — (of a DO statement). Indicates by what quantity the DO counter is to be incremented each time the loop is performed. The increment always appears as an INTEGER number or variable name, immediately following the second comma in a DO statement. When not present, the increment of a DO statement is assumed (default condition of compiler) to be 1.

INDEX — (Variable). An (INTEGER) variable name that is the counter of a loop — e.g., DO loop.

INFORMATION PROCESSING — The total manipulation of data, whether by computer or manually.

INPUT (or entering) — Physically presenting information to the computer or machine.

INPUT UNITS — (Computer functional unit). Any device by which information or data may be transferred into the computer — e.g., card reader, magnetic-tape unit, etc.

INTEGER ARITHMETIC — Arithmetic operations involving only whole numbers. Any fractional values are truncated or dropped.

INTEGER NUMBER DATA — Any fact or observation expressed as a whole number.

INTRINSIC FUNCTION — A procedure (more than one statement long) compiled in line. It returns *one* value to the main program.

KEYPUNCH — To transform data from the normal language form — e.g., from English, French, etc. — to Hollerith-punched cards.

LABEL — A name, designation or identification.

LIMIT — (of DO statement). The maximum number of times that a DO loop may be performed. The limit of the DO loop is indicated by the value of the integer variable name or constant that appears immediately following the first comma in a DO statement.

LOOP — Any series of instructions that will be executed more than once.

MACHINE LANGUAGE — The computer language for a given computer. The language used by a given computer in carrying out specific instructions.

MEMORY — Labeled storage locations that are directly available to the computer.

NUMBER — A concept familiar in mathematics meaning any mark or symbol defined to have an arithmetic value.

OBJECT PROGRAM — A program that has been translated by the compiler into machine language. Also called "Object Code" or "Target Code."

OBJECT TIME — Execution (time) of the program.

OBJECT TIME FORMATTING — An operation by which the object program (at execution) is supplied with the formats to handle data.

ONE-COLUMN CODING — A field on a Hollerith card that is one-column in width. All necessary values are contained in the single-card column.

OPEN-FORMAT PROGRAM — See VARIABLE FORMAT PROGRAM.

OPERATOR — (FORTRAN). A symbol that indicates that some kind of process is to be carried out. There are 14 defined FORTRAN operators: 5 arithmetic, 6 relational, 3 logical. All operators are binary, meaning that each operator must connect two objects.

OUTPUT UNIT — (Computer functional unit). Any device or unit by which information is transferred out of the computer (storage) — e.g., printer, magnetic-tape unit, etc.

PARAMETER STATEMENT — A nonstandard FORTRAN statement that is used in some FORTRAN IV compilers to establish numeric values used in FORTRAN controls — e.g., as in controlling dimension limits, or in controlling the DO loop limit.

POINTER — A technique used in FORTRAN programming by which the value of one variable name or array is the location in an array or matrix of a desired value.

PROCEDURE — A course of action, a series of steps to accomplish a given end.

PROGRAM — A series of instructions that cause the computer to carry out certain (defined) operations as specified in the instruction.

PROGRAM-CONTROL CARDS — The indicated control cards that direct the operation of a canned program, contrasted with computer system control cards that direct the compilation and execution of any program on a specific computer system.

RANDOM ACCESS — Storage where any location may be addressed, regardless of the location of the last or previously accessed location.

RANGE — (of algorithm). The acceptable output values of the program — all possible results.

RANGE — (of DO loop). The FORTRAN statements between the beginning of a DO loop and the end of a DO loop.

SAMPLE — Part, but not all, of the data on any given subject.

SEQUENCE NUMBER — (FORTRAN program). A number often used by programmers to visually identify the location of a FORTRAN statement in the FORTRAN source program. It appears in the last 8 columns of the FORTRAN program card (Columns 73–80). It is ignored by the compiler completely.

SERIAL ACCESS — A storage where only the next sequential location or record may be referenced.

SOURCE PROGRAM — A program written in a nonmachine language — e.g., FORTRAN.

SPECIAL CHARACTER — The term used to refer to one of the symbols acceptable to FORTRAN — e.g., comma, period, etc.

STANDARDIZED PROGRAM OR SUBPROGRAM — (Canned program). A program written by another programmer to perform a standardized statistical or mathematical routine that is available to any programmer.

STATEMENT FUNCTION — A subprogram (procedure) that is only one statement long that is provided in the main program. It returns *one* value to the main program.

STATEMENT NUMBER — A *label* in numeric form appearing in Columns 1–5 of a Hollerith card. Statement numbers identify FORTRAN statements.

SUBPROGRAM — An independent operating program or procedure that exists within the framework of the main program.

SUBROUTINE — A subprogram that may return many values to the main program.

TRANSACTION — A particular event, occurrence, or happening.

TRANSFER OF CONTROL — A specific and defined instruction that causes the default condition of the compiler to be violated in that the next instruction executed is not the next sequential instruction. Any FORTRAN statement causing a transfer of control will normally specify which statement is to be executed next by specifying the statement number or label of the next executed statement.

TRANSFER RATE — (also ENTER or INPUT RATE). The number of characters per second that a computer may read from an input device (into memory).

TRUNCATE — To drop the fractional value of a number. Many computers will truncate fractional values under certain conditions rather than follow conventional rules of rounding. All fractional values in integer division are always truncated.

UNCONDITIONAL TRANSFER OF CONTROL — A FORTRAN statement causing *other than* the next sequential statement to be executed *each time* the statement is encountered.

VALUE — The (arithmetic) number or quantity represented by a symbol or name.

VARIABLE FORMAT PROGRAM — (open format). A program capable of handling input data according to any designated layout. The indicated format is given to the program as data, which then controls the input data.

VARIABLE NAME — A variable name is a label that refers to some designated core location in computer storage. It normally may not be more than six characters in length, must start with a letter, and may not contain special characters. One of the default conditions of the FORTRAN compiler: when a variable name begins with I, J, K, L, M, or N, the variable name refers to an INTEGER value. When it begins with any other letter, it refers to a REAL value.

INDEX